The Normative Basis of Culture

The Normative Basis of Culture
A Philosophical Inquiry

Henry McDonald

Louisiana State University Press
Baton Rouge and London

For Kirsten

Designer: Christopher Wilcox
Typeface: Granjon
Typesetter: G & S Typesetters
Printer: Thomson-Shore, Inc.
Binder: John Dekker and Sons, Inc.

Library of Congress Cataloging-in-Publication Data

McDonald, Henry, 1947–
   The normative basis of culture.

   Includes index.
   1. Ethnology—Philosophy. 2. Ethnology—Methodology. 3. Cultural relativism. 4. Wittgenstein, Ludwig, 1889–1951. 5. Semantics (Philosophy)
6. Social ethics. 7. Meaning (Philosophy) 8. Religions. I. Title.
GN345.M43   1986   306   85-23795
ISBN 0-8071-1280-1

Publication of this book has been assisted by a grant from the Andrew W. Mellon
Foundation.

I delight in a palpable imaginable *visitable* past—in the nearer distances and the clearer mysteries, the marks and signs of a world we may reach over to as by making a long arm we grasp an object at the other end of our own table. The table is the one, the common expanse, and where we lean, so stretching, we find it firm and continuous. That, to my imagination, is the past fragrant of all, or of almost all, the poetry of the thing outlived and lost and gone, and yet in which the precious element of closeness, telling so of connexions but tasting so of differences, remains appreciable. With more moves back the element of the appreciable shrinks—just as the charm of looking over a garden-wall into another garden breaks down when successions of walls appear. The other gardens, those still beyond, may be there, but even by use of our longest ladder we are baffled and bewildered—the view is mainly a view of barriers. The one partition makes the place we have wondered about *other*, both richly and recogniseably so; but who shall pretend to impute an effect of composition to the twenty? We are divided of course between liking to feel the past strange and liking to feel it familiar; the difficulty is, for intensity, to catch it at the moment when the scales of the balance hang with the right evenness.

Henry James
The Art of the Novel

Contents

Abbreviations   xi

Introduction: The Normative Concept of Culture   1
I   Language and Culture   10
II   Wittgenstein and the Normative Basis of Belief   35
III   Nature and Culture: The Individual and Society   74
IV   Meaning and Morality   112
V   The Causal Fallacy: Cultural Anthropology and
       Comparative Religion   156
VI   The Subjectivistic Fallacy: History of Religions   189
VII   Culture and History   209

Index   235

Abbreviations

A	Allen, Douglas. *Structure and Creativity in Religion*. The Hague, 1978.
B-AML	Boas, Franz. *Anthropology and Modern Life*. London, 1929.
B-ANA	———. *Anthropology in North America*. New York, 1915.
B-JAF	———. "The Mind of Primitive Man." *Journal of American Folk-Lore*, XIV (January–March, 1901), 1–29.
B-MPM	———. *The Mind of Primitive Man*. New York, 1938.
B-RLC	———. *Race, Language, and Culture*. New York, 1940.
BI	Bidney, David. *Theoretical Anthropology*. New York, 1967.
BL-R	Bleeker, C. J. *The Rainbow*. Leiden, 1975.
BL-S	———. *The Sacred Bridge*. Leiden, 1963.
E-H	Eliade, Mircea. *From the Stone Age to the Eleusinian Mysteries*. Chicago, 1978. Vol. I of Eliade, *A History of Religious Ideas*. 3 vols. projected.
E-K	———, and Joseph M. Kitagawa, eds. *The History of Religions: Essays in Methodology*. Chicago, 1959.
E-M	———. *Myths, Dreams, and Mysteries*. New York, 1960.
E-P	———. *Patterns in Comparative Religion*. New York, 1958.
E-Q	———. *The Quest*. Chicago, 1969.
E-S	———. *Shamanism: Archaic Techniques of Ecstasy*. Translated by Willard R. Trask. Princeton, 1964.
E-SP	———. *The Sacred and the Profane*. New York, 1959.
EP-S	Evans-Pritchard, E. E. *Social Anthropology and Other Essays*. Glencoe, 1962.
EP-T	———. *Theories of Primitive Religion*. Oxford, 1965.

H-ATHN   Hume, David. *An Abstract of a Treatise of Human Nature*. 2nd ed. Revised by P. H. Nidditch. Edited by L. A. Selby-Bigge and P. H. Nidditch. Oxford, 1978.

H-EHU   ———. *Enquiry Concerning Human Understanding*. 3rd ed. Revised by P. H. Nidditch. Edited by L. A. Selby-Bigge. Oxford, 1975.

H-EPM   ———. *Enquiry Concerning the Principles of Morals*. 3rd ed. Revised by P. H. Nidditch. Edited by L. A. Selby-Bigge. Oxford, 1975.

H-THN   ———. *A Treatise of Human Nature*. 2nd ed. Revised by P. H. Nidditch. Edited by L. A. Selby-Bigge. Oxford, 1978.

HA   Hatch, Elvin. *Theories of Man and Culture*. New York, 1973.

HO   Hoebel, Adamson E., and Everett L. Frost. *Cultural and Social Anthropology*. New York, 1976.

HR-I   Bleeker, C. J., and Geo. Widengren, eds. *Religions of the Past*. Leiden, 1969. Vol. I of Bleeker and Widengren, eds. *Historia Religionum: Handbook for the History of Religions*. 2 vols.

HR-II   ———. *Religions of the Present*. Vol. II of *Historia Religionum: Handbook for the History of Religions*. 2 vols.

K-CI   Kant, Immanuel. *Critique of Pure Reason*. Unabridged ed. Translated by Norman Kemp Smith. New York, 1929.

K-CII   ———. *Critique of Practical Reason*. Translated by Lewis White Beck. Indianapolis, 1956.

K-G   ———. *Foundations of the Metaphysics of Morals*. Edited by Robert Paul Wolff. Translated by Lewis White Beck. Indianapolis, 1969.

K-P   ———. *Prolegomena to Any Future Metaphysics*. Translated by Peter G. Lucas. Indianapolis, 1950.

SA   Saliba, John A. *Homo Religiosus in Mircea Eliade: An Anthropological Evaluation*. Leiden, 1976.

SH   Sharpe, Eric J. *Comparative Religion: A History*. London, 1975.

W-BB   Wittgenstein, Ludwig. *The Blue and Brown Books*. Oxford, 1958.

W-BUF   ———. "Bemerkungen über Frazers 'The Golden Bough.'" *Synthese*, XVII (1967), 233–53. (An English translation appeared in the May, 1971, issue of *Human World*.)

W-E   ———. *Letters from Ludwig Wittgenstein*. With a memoir by Paul Engelmann. Edited by B. F. McGuinness. Translated by L. Furtmüller. Oxford, 1967.

W-LC   ———. *Lectures and Conversations on Aesthetics, Psychology and Religious Belief*. Edited by C. Barrett. Oxford, 1966.

W-LE   ———. "A Lecture on Ethics." *Philosophical Review*, LXXIV (1965), 3–12.

W-LF   ———. "Some Remarks on Logical Form." *Proceedings of the Aristotelian Society*, CXCII (1929), 162–71.

W-N   ———. *Notebooks, 1914–1916*. Edited by G. E. M. Anscombe and G. H. von Wright. Translated by G. E. M. Anscombe. Oxford, 1961.

W-NLPE   ———. "Notes for Lectures on 'Private Experience' and 'Sense Data.'" *Philosophical Review*, LXXVII (1968), 271–320.

W-OC   ———. *On Certainty*. Edited by G. E. M. Anscombe and G. H. von Wright. Translated by Denis Paul and G. E. M. Anscombe. Oxford, 1969.

W-PB   ———. *Philosophische Bemerkungen*. Edited by Rush Rhees. Oxford, 1965.

W-PG   ———. *Philosophische Grammatik*. Edited by Rush Rhees. Oxford, 1969.

W-PI   ———. *Philosophical Investigations*. Translated by G. E. M. Anscombe. New York, 1953.

W-PP   Moore, G. E. "Wittgenstein's Lectures in 1930–33." In Moore, *Philosophical Papers*. London, 1959.

W-RC   Wittgenstein, Ludwig. *Remarks on Colour*. Edited by G. E. M. Anscombe. Translated by Linda L. McAlister and Margarete Schättle. Berkeley, 1978.

W-RFM   ———. *Remarks on the Foundations of Mathematics*.
             Edited by G. H. von Wright, Rush Rhees, and
             G. E. M. Anscombe. Oxford, 1956.

W-RPI   ———. *Remarks on the Philosophy of Psychology*.
             Translated by C. G. Luckhardt and A. E. Aue. Vol.
             I of 2 vols. Chicago, 1980.

W-RPII   ———. *Remarks on the Philosophy of Psychology*.
             Translated by C. G. Luckhardt and A. E. Aue. Vol.
             II of 2 vols. Chicago, 1980.

W-RR   Rhees, Rush, *Discussions of Wittgenstein*. London,
             1970.

W-T   ———. *Tractatus Logico-Philosophicus*. Translated by
             D. Pears and B. McGuinness. London, 1961.

W-VB   ———. *Culture and Value*. Translated by Peter
             Winch. Chicago, 1980. (Previously published as
             Vermischte Bemerkungen.)

W-WA   Waismann, Friedrich. *Wittgenstein und der Wiener
             Kreis*. Frankfurt am Main, 1967.

W-WCI   Lee, Desmond, ed. *Wittgenstein's Lectures, Cambridge,
             1930–1932*. Totowa, N.J., 1980

W-WCII   Ambrose, Alice, ed. *Wittgenstein's Lectures, Cam-
             bridge, 1932–1935*. Totowa, N.J., 1980.

W-Z   Wittgenstein, Ludwig. *Zettel*. Edited by G. E. M.
             Anscombe and G. H. von Wright. Translated by
             G. E. M. Anscombe. Oxford, 1967.

The Normative Basis of Culture

Introduction
The Normative Concept of Culture

The study of culture is in many respects comparable to the study of foreign language. In both cases, the student uses his own culture or language as a tool to understand the foreign culture or language. Just as the English speaker learns the meanings of foreign words by being told what they mean in English, so too the student of culture learns the meanings of foreign beliefs and practices by comparing them, at least implicitly, with his own more familiar ones. Although the student of culture or language may eventually learn to "think" in the new language he has learned, thereby dispensing with all translation, such a goal will be achieved, if at all, gradually. Initially, what is foreign will need to be hoisted into view with the lever of what is familiar.

This analogy between the study of culture and the study of foreign language points up one of the main contentions of this work: that the social scientist's task of assessing the meaning of cultural phenomena is necessarily a normative one.[1] By *normative* or *norm*, I do not refer to an ideal or even fixed standard or rule, but rather to the moving reference point by which we give sense and meaning to our practices and beliefs. The study of culture is thus normative in a manner analogous to the way the study of foreign language is normative; it proceeds on the basis of certain rules, standards, and values built into, and evolving with, the cultural beliefs and practices of the researcher.

Now, such a contention may not, on the face of it, be considered a very interesting one, for certainly most social scientists would agree that the researcher brings a certain amount of bias into his studies. It is for just this reason that he must adhere to a methodology that eliminates, as far as is possible, such bias and gives him a clear and objective view of the culture being studied.

1. *Normative* means to be "based upon or prescribing" a norm or standard. My use of the term draws more on the former connotation ("based upon") than the latter ("prescribing").

But in claiming that the task of the social scientist is a normative one, I am not talking about bias in this sense. The norms I refer to are not the personal inclinations and preferences of the researcher—all of which may or may not be minimized or even eliminated—but rather those norms that the researcher possesses as a member of a particular culture and society and that he could not dispense with, no matter what his personal inclinations and preferences were. He could not dispense with them, not because he couldn't imagine violating them, but because he couldn't imagine what life would be like under conditions in which such norms were neither violated nor adopted, but were simply inapplicable. As a given language contains a limited number of possibilities of expression, so too a given culture contains a limited number of possibilities of belief and practice. We do not know, for example, what it would be like to believe, as some African peoples are said to believe, that the chameleon is responsible for man's mortality; we do not even know what it would be like *not* to believe that the chameleon is responsible for man's mortality (though this is not due to the fact that such a belief lacks empirical grounds, for we do know what it is like to believe or disbelieve in, for example, eternal life). This belief of certain African peoples is so foreign to us that we could very well ask whether such peoples really mean what we do by *man's mortality*.

The claim that the task of the social scientist is normative is thus significant, not because it raises questions about the proper state of mind or attitude of the researcher in his studies, but because it raises questions about the object of those studies—about the kind of reality it is and the appropriate methods of describing this reality. My argument is not that the task of the social scientist *should* be normative for a given set of reasons. Rather, it is that our understanding of other cultures *does* necessarily proceed on a normative basis; therefore, it behooves us to explicitly recognize our task *as* normative and to cultivate a critical consciousness of such norms. Clearly, the crucial part of this argument is the first part, that our understanding of other cultures necessarily proceeds on a normative basis. The truth or falsity of this contention will depend not on how committed, involved, or empathetic the researcher feels. It will depend, rather, on the validity of the concept of culture entailed by it.

What, then, is the concept of culture argued for in this work? Its

general features are that the meaning of cultural phenomena is
grounded neither in external natural processes nor in the internal
mental processes of individuals, but in the rules, norms, and values
governing (but not rigidly dictating) practice and belief. The sources
of such norms are nonsubjective and nonempirical. They cannot be
known *prior* to empirical investigation, but neither can they be
defined in empirical terms. Rather, such norms exhibit a certain
(though often blurred and continuously shifting) range of possibility
of belief and practice; they are the logical space—built up over time
and possessed of historical depth—in which a community of people
think and see.[2]

Such a normative concept of culture stands in opposition to the
view of culture held by the majority of social scientists today, a view
that is at once empirical and theoretic. It is empirical in that the content of culture is thought to consist in what has been factually observed and recorded with regard to people's beliefs and practices. It is
theoretic in that the central task of the researcher is seen as explanation and interpretation, requiring him to advance hypotheses and
theories that account for such psychological and physical data.

The normative concept of culture, by contrast, is nonempirical
and nontheoretic. It is nonempirical in its effort to throw into question methods of explaining the meaning of cultural phenomena,
methods that objectify such meaning by treating it as either an external, natural condition or an inner, subjective state of mind. It maintains that culture be thought of not on the model of objects and facts
(whether internal or external), but on the model of the norms, rules,
and values that govern people's ways of acting and thinking.

The normative concept of culture is also nontheoretic in its view
that norms and values are not something a culture *has*, but something it *is*. (We judge *according to* norms; only within limits do we
judge the norms themselves.) There is, strictly speaking, no "thing"
about culture that needs to be explained or interpreted; there is only
a conceptual terrain, a range of presuppositions partially revealed,
that needs to be *described*. Debate and discussion, of course, still have

2. Wittgenstein uses this phrase in W-T.2.11, 2.202, and 4.463. In W-PP, he also says
that "the meaning of a word is its 'place' in a 'grammatical system.'" The relationship
between these concepts and my own uses of the term *logical space* will become clearer in
later chapters.

a central role in such description. They should, however, focus more on bringing to light what we already know, rather than discovering or assembling empirical evidence to prove what we do not know. Argument-by-hypothesis must give way to persuasion-through-example.

The normative concept of culture is thus not a theory posed in opposition to other theories of culture; it is, rather, a philosophical attack on the conceptual foundations that underlie any and all such theories. It seeks to redirect the study of culture away from its currently empirical and theoretic preoccupations toward concerns moral and aesthetic.

What are the scholarly sources of such a nonempirical, nontheoretic account of culture? Its principal source is the later works of the philosopher Ludwig Wittgenstein (1889–1951). In those works, Wittgenstein sets forth a model of, or way of thinking about, language that is similar to the one I am suggesting we adopt for culture. He views the meanings of words as grounded not in the empirical objects (psychological or physical) to which they refer, but in the norms and rules governing their use within a social and cultural context. What I have tried to do, in other words, is apply and extend what Wittgenstein says about the meanings of words to the meanings of cultural phenomena.

It is important to understand that Wittgenstein's notion of meaning as use was not intended to cover *all* uses of language; it applied in very different ways, and more or less fully, to particular uses. In some cases, Wittgenstein allowed, it might not apply at all. The notion of meaning as use was not a definition, but rather a means of making propaganda for a certain way of thinking, as well as a handy way of getting people to *stop* thinking about words in terms of their empirical correlates.

My use of the term *meaning* has a similar purpose. When I say that the meaning of cultural phenomena is grounded in the norms and values that govern people's ways of thinking and acting, I am not claiming that such an assertion covers all ways of thinking and acting. Nor am I offering a definition of culture. Rather, I am emphasizing the conceptual, as opposed to the empirical, features of culture. I am saying that our concept of culture *presupposes* ways of acting and thinking that in a large number of cases can be described by means of norms, rules, and values. To use the word *meaning* in relation to cultural phenomena is to force one's attention *away* from the model of culture as a collection of objects and facts.

A different, though related, point needs to be made about my use of the other scholarly sources of this study. The principal opposing concept of culture with which this study is concerned is what I call the subjectivistic concept of culture, adopted by many modern social scientists, including American cultural anthropologists in the tradition of Franz Boas and historians of religions or practitioners of *Religionswissenschaft* (both of which may be classified under the rubric "comparative religionists").[3] The subjectivistic concept of culture is one example of the empiricist, theoretic, nonnormative view of culture mentioned above.

My purpose in focusing this study on American cultural anthropologists and historians of religions is to provide an anchor for what is predominately a philosophical argument.[4] Indeed, the choice of these groups—one empiricist (American cultural anthropologists), the other phenomenological (historians of religions)—was dictated by philosophical considerations. The opposing, yet fundamentally similar, positions of these two groups provide me with a good tool for bringing out the philosophical points I want to make. They provide a good tool, in particular, because Boas and American cultural anthropologists have much in common, philosophically, with David Hume (1711–1776); because historians of religions have much in common, philosophically, with Immanuel Kant (1724–1804); and because both the Humean–anthropological position and the Kantian– historian of religions position can be contrasted to the perspective of Wittgenstein.[5]

3. As virtually everyone would agree, there is no general agreement concerning the meaning of the term *comparative religion*. For discussions of the issues involved, see A, 4–5, 120; E-K, 15; E-Q, 8; SH, xiii, 31, 45, 136, 240; Guilford Dudley, *Religion on Trial: Mircea Eliade and His Critics* (Philadelphia, 1977), 5–6; Michael Pye, *Comparative Religion: An Introduction Through Source Materials* (New York, 1972), 8. I also use the term *comparative religionists* to refer to nineteenth-century evolutionists; see Chapter I, section 3.

4. My treatment of "American cultural anthropology" focuses on Boas and touches only slightly on the large number of anthropologists who have been influenced by him.

5. From a historical point of view, of course, Boasians tended to associate themselves with neo-Kantians such as Dilthey.

Such a tool, however, should not be mistaken for its purpose. These two groups were chosen to be representative philosophically, not anthropologically or sociologically. I object to the subjectivistic concept of culture not because I think it leads to false conclusions, but because it gives those conclusions (whether true or false) an improper, nonnormative status. For example, I do not attack Franz Boas' theory of the soul as the product of memory images because I think it is wrong. I attack it because I think it makes uncritical use of a certain culturally imposed and normatively grounded concept of the soul. It may be that when the normative functions of a theory are unmasked, so too will be the lack of evidence for it. But that is not the main point. The divergent views and conclusions of social scientists, past and present, that have developed *within the conceptual confines* of an empiricist, theoretic, nonnormative account of culture are *not* what is at issue in this study.

The question, however, still remains, How does the normative concept of culture serve as the basis for the contention that the task of the social scientist is a normative one? To say that the meaning of cultural phenomena is normatively grounded is to say that there can be no meaning apart from norms of practice and belief. But the only norms of practice and belief that the researcher is possessed of come from his own culture and that culture's history. Neither by means of intuition nor by means of empirical evidence can he have an immediate and direct access to the norms of other cultures. In the same way that the student of a foreign language can learn the meanings of foreign words only by bringing them into relation with his own, the social scientist can gain an understanding of the norms of distant cultures only by bringing them into relation with his own. His only grounds for understanding are those that he does in fact stand on.

Of course, one may want to object to this: "But why can't the social scientist 'learn' the norms of a culture without mixing them up with his own? Even if we grant that the meaning of cultural phenomena consists in a description of the norms or rules governing practice and belief, why can't the process by which this meaning is understood be nonnormative?" But that is like asking why an Englishman cannot learn German just as though he were not an Englishman when in fact an Englishman's knowledge of English is not something he can use or withdraw at will. Rather, it is a capacity that has become a part of him and that he does not have the power to lose. It is by means of such capacities that we understand other cultures—and we do this even when the peoples being studied have very different concepts than ours. We "see" on the basis of our own concepts, because they are the logical space in which we move and without which we would see nothing at all.

It is for similar reasons that efforts to "convert" one language (for example, Hebrew) into another (for example, English) cannot succeed. We tend to reason: "The signs used to convey the meanings of words are incidental to such meanings; hence, different conventions or systems of signs can be adopted without change in meaning." It is true that it is not the mere marks on a piece of paper that are essential to what a word means. Such marks can be replaced by others (for example, שָׁלוֹם can be converted to *peace*), and there will still be a word, and this word will have meaning. But the *same* meaning? In fact, as anyone acquainted with the Hebrew language knows, שָׁלוֹם does not mean the same as *peace*. The connotations and associations that the former has acquired distinguish it sharply from the latter.[6] What we need is a third language, a system of signs into which both *peace* and שָׁלוֹם can be converted. This third language cannot have a history, for then it would have acquired particular connotations and associations. It cannot even be used, for then it would acquire a history. It must be a language of the gods—or rather, a language of *invented* gods.

When I say, therefore, that the task of the social scientist is a normative one, I am not recommending that the researcher go about prescribing norms or values to his own culture or to other cultures. Rather, I am pointing up the need of the student of culture to cultivate a consciousness of the finiteness of his perspective, that is, to become aware of the extent to which that perspective is derived from or based on norms by which he, as a member of a particular culture or society, lives, acts, and *thinks*. Only by cultivating such a consciousness will the researcher stop investing his own social and cultural presuppositions with a universal and absolute status, and thereby stop allowing such presuppositions to obscure his view of other cul-

---

6. For example, the traditional greeting "How are you?" in Hebrew uses the word *shalom* and means literally, "What is your peace?" or "What is your welfare?"

tures. Moreover, by cultivating such a consciousness, the researcher will gain greater control of his own normative concerns and in this way increase his ability to use such concerns as a tool in understanding other cultures. Of course, he must not think that such control of his presuppositions could ever be complete, for in order for this to be the case, he would have to control that which grounds all his efforts *to* control. He would have to step outside that which encompasses him. Nonetheless, although his perspective will never be more than partial, this very partiality will be the grounds of his understanding. Indeed, the researcher's *awareness* of his own cultural presuppositions, on one hand, and his *understanding* of foreign cultures, on the other, are reciprocal and interdependent. A normative concept of culture entails the adoption of a normative stance on the part of the researcher.

In sum, since the meaning of cultural phenomena consists in a certain range of possibilities of belief and practice, it is the task of the student of culture "to read" such possibilities out of the data he is presented with, letting the text "speak," as much as possible, for itself. But no one can understand a foreign tongue without first translating it, and no translation can be made without reliance on, and critical use of, the meanings that have become embedded, over the course of history, in one's own tongue. To point up the limitations inherent in any cultural perspective is thus not to make the relativistic claim that objective understanding is impossible or that the limits of one's understanding might not be widened with time and study. It is simply to claim that one gains understanding by making use of the norms of one's own culture, not by trying to eliminate them. Objectivity can never be guaranteed or assumed to be complete, but it can be approached by a continuous series of critical appraisals and reappraisals. Objectivity, it might be said, can be earned.

In Chapter I, I return to the analogy between the study of culture and the study of a foreign language. Pursuing this analogy provides a convenient way of outlining the subjectivistic concept of culture adopted by American cultural anthropologists and historians of religion. Chapter II then lays a philosophical foundation for this subjectivistic concept of culture in the work of Hume and Kant, juxtaposing their perspectives with that of Wittgenstein. Chapter III advances some of the basic features of the normative concept of culture, criticizing the dichotomies of nature and culture and of society and the individual as they are presented by comparative religionists and social scientists in general. Chapter IV discusses the roles value and morality play in culture. Chapters V and VI present a series of examples in which some of the assumptions and methods of study characteristic of comparative religionists are criticized. Chapter VII discusses the interdependence of our concepts of history and culture and the relevance of such interdependence to the problem of cultural relativism.

I   Language and Culture

Many people, if asked to describe the process by which a person goes about learning a foreign language, would answer, I think, roughly according to the following conception: At the beginning the student associates certain unfamiliar sounds (sounds representing the words of the language he is learning) with the familiar sounds representing the words of his own language. The English speaker is told, for example, that the French word *chaise* is the same as the English word *chair*. Since he already knows the meaning of the word *chair*—that is, the kind of object to which it refers—the meaning of the word *chaise* will also be clear to him. In this way, the student "translates" a strange sound into its meaning—the external object to which both the French and English words have reference. The word *chair* thus functions as a kind of stand-in for ostensive definition; in place of using it, the teacher of French might simply have uttered the word *chaise* while pointing to a chair.

The question, however, now arises, How do we learn the meanings of words that cannot be ostensively defined? Among the many kinds of words that do not allow for such a definition are those describing moral qualities (as *good* and *bad* often do), those pointing to a reality of a religious nature (*soul, spirit*), and any number of others belonging to a multitude of categories (*concept, beautiful, economy*). Clearly, there is an issue here that did not arise—or that did not *seem* to arise—in the case of words like *chair*. How do we really know that the meanings signified by *bon* and *mal* are the same as those signified by *good* and *bad*, since these words do not have the sort of external reference that words like *chair* have? In the case of French, of course, we simply believe what people who know both French and English—of which there are a considerable number—tell us. In the case of languages at greater cultural and conceptual remove, however, the question points up a practical difficulty that has been felt by many philosophers and students of culture. G. B. Kerford, for example, wrote that "it is difficult for a modern philosopher not to either misconstrue or wholly condemn Aristotle's ethical thought."[1] One of the reasons for this is that Aristotle uses words (e.g., *eudaimonia*) describing moral qualities that have no exact counterpart in modern languages. A similar sort of difficulty can be seen in the controversies concerning the proper translation of Jesus' words: "The kingdom of God is within you" (Luke 17:21). What kind of reference does the phrase "kingdom of God" have, and should not "within you" (*entos hymon*) be translated "among you" or "within your grasp" or "will be among you" or even "inside you and outside you," as has been variously suggested? Even such a seemingly straightforward sentence as the first line of Genesis ("In the beginning God created . . .") raises problems, for although Hebrew has a perfectly good way of saying "the beginning," the article is in fact left out in the Hebrew text. So what kind of beginning was the author of Genesis talking about? Surely not *a* beginning? And how much greater these problems become when considered in relation to the meanings of words used by, for example, Australian aborigines and translated as "soul" or "spirit." Such "souls" are capable of getting hungry, growing tired, being wounded, and dying—all qualities that do not seem to belong to our modern concept of soul.

The apparent difficulty in all these cases is that moral, religious, and other terms have no external object of reference and therefore cannot be learned in the same way that *chaise* can. If presented, for example, with a photograph (and no accompanying explanation) of one person holding a knife to another person's throat, we would be unable to say in most cases whether the action pictured was good or bad, because the same photograph could easily portray both an act of murder (to be judged bad) and an act of heroism (to be judged good). What makes the statement "That action is good" true or false is nothing *in* the action as such (it is not something we can tell, in all cases, about the action just by observing it); whereas what makes the statement "That object is a chair" true or false is precisely something we can tell about the object just by looking at it.

At this point, a seemingly obvious solution suggests itself, one that implies that there is, in a sense, something that one can "point to" as the meaning of *good*. Granting that for *good* (as opposed to *chair*)

---

1. *Encyclopedia of Philosophy* (henceforth *EP*), I, 161.

there is no object in the external world to which it corresponds, may it not correspond to an object in the internal world of the mind or consciousness? Of course, such an internal object of the mind is neither so public nor so tangible as a chair; it might be conceived rather as a feeling or a mental act or an atmosphere accompanying the utterance of a word—all "objects" that are hidden from view and accessible only to the subject or self in which they reside. Moreover, such internal objects are essentially dependent; they do not stand alone the way external objects do, but rather go before, after, or along with external events and actions. They serve to give such events and actions life and meaning. Thus, a photograph, as a bare representation of an event, is "dead," or neutral; only when it is interpreted—when it has added to it human feelings and sensations and states—does it "come alive." In this way, a mere photograph of one person holding a knife to another's throat becomes, in the view of the subject, a picture of either an act of heroism or an act of murder.

The function, then, of such internal objects of the mind is similar to that of external objects; they give the meanings of words a reference and a ground, assuring us that the words mean *something* and are not just empty sounds. The difference is that the meanings of words like *chair* are objective, grounded in external, public events; whereas the meanings of words like *good* are subjective, grounded in mental and other private processes of the self or subject.[2] The fact that these processes are private provides, in addition, a plausible explanation of why words like *good* have a far more indefinite and wide-ranging sense than words like *chair*. The meaning of *chair* can

2. To say that the meaning of a word (or a belief or practice) is "subjective" is to say that it has its *source* or *origin* in the self or subject, notwithstanding claims made later about its ultimately "objective" status (claims that in the philosophies of Hume and Kant are made on the basis of the idea or belief corresponding to empirical data in the external world). It should be noted that this use of the term *subjective* is distinctively modern. Harold Alderman says: "In its original sense 'subject' bore no special relation to the term subject meaning man, the ego, the I. Man as subject is only one possible *hupokeimenon*. In Plato the *hupokeimenon* is the *eidos*; in Aristotle it is actuality. When man becomes the *hupokeimenon* in the thought of Descartes, the foundation of science and technology has been laid—and that foundation is human subjectivity" (Harold Alderman, "Heidegger's Critique of Science and Technology," in Michael Murray [ed.], *Heidegger and Modern Philosophy* [New Haven, Conn., 1978], 36–37.) See also W. Hale White's preface to the *Ethic of Benedict De Spinoza* (Oxford, 1978), vii–viii.

be known directly (it can be shown publicly by ostensive definition); but the meaning of *good* can be known by others only indirectly (an individual can "display" such a private object to himself, but can only describe it to others).

This account solves the problem of how an English speaker can learn the meaning of *bon*. He does it in a way similar to that in which he learns the meaning of *chaise*—by connecting an unfamiliar sound to an object. The difference is that, in the case of *chaise*, making such a connection is straightforward. One knows exactly what does or does not constitute a mistake, for one always has the opportunity to check with other people. In the case of *bon* (or, more clearly, in the case of moral and religious terms of very distant and alien cultures), the connection must be made with an internal object—a feeling or atmosphere or sensation that accompanies the word—and what that object is can only be inferred. Of course, such inferences will become easier to make as the student acclimates himself to the language he is learning. But the degree of certainty with which we know *chaise* means the same as *chair* can only be approached—never reached— in the case of words like *bon* and *good*. Words in different languages with a subjective, internal reference—unlike words with an objective, external reference—do not *necessarily* have anything in common. The first step the student must take, therefore, in learning a foreign language, is to learn the meanings of a number of words like *chaise*. Only then will he be in a position to understand the meanings of words like *bon*. (For example, one could not judge whether the above-mentioned picture depicted an action as good or bad unless one knew what a knife was and that it could be used to harm people.) What makes learning a foreign language possible is that the native language of the student has something in common with the language he is studying; there exists an extramental, extralinguistic bedrock of meaning to which at least some of the terms of the two languages refer.

2

How can this account of the study of foreign language be applied to the study of culture? The answer, very simply and generally, is, by treating the meanings of cultural beliefs and practices as analogous to the meanings of words with subjective reference, words such as *good*. In this way, culture can be contrasted with natural processes and conditions in the external environment in a manner similar to that in which words like *good* can be contrasted with words like *chair*. The reference of what is natural will be events and processes in the external world, whereas the reference of what is cultural will be internal processes in the minds of the individuals who make up that culture. Moreover, just as the meaning of *bon* can be learned only by first learning the meanings of a number of words like *chaise* that are common to all languages, so too the meanings of cultural beliefs and practices can be learned or understood only by the researcher adopting an extracultural (normatively neutral and value-free) standpoint that takes as its grounds the natural conditions and forces that all cultures are subject to.

Such a subjectivistic concept of culture is implicit in many of the formulations given by twentieth-century social scientists (I use the term *subjectivistic* to emphasize that comparative religionists view culture *as* subjective; they do not view culture subjectively). Such formulations have their origin in certain uses of the word that became widespread in the nineteenth century and that convey the idea of a social state or condition very much akin to what is connoted by the word *civilization*.[3]

They differ from the older, more metaphorical uses of the term, which are derived from the act of cultivating the soil (Latin, *cultura*) and express the idea of an active process rather than an achieved state.[4] A classic rendering of the more modern meaning is given by Alfred Kroeber and Clyde Kluckhohn, who define *culture* as a "set of attributes and products of human societies, and therefore of mankind, which are extrasomatic and transmissible by mechanisms other than biological heredity."[5] Elsewhere, Kroeber refers to culture as "a body or stream of products of mental exercise."[6]

The capacity for culture, according to this conception, is a fixed

3. The first modern use of the word *culture* is generally attributed to Edward Burnett Tylor in his book *Primitive Culture* (New York, 1871).

4. See Raymond Williams, "Culture and Civilization," in *EP*, II, 273–75.

5. Quoted in Marvin Harris, *The Rise of Anthropological Theory* (New York, 1968), 9.

6. Alfred Kroeber, *The Nature of Culture* (Chicago, 1952), 40.

state or condition possessed by man and not by animals. It is by means of such a capacity that man can act not only purposefully and rationally but also morally. Animals, on the other hand, cannot act in these ways, because their behavior is dictated by material causes; they lack that "interior room" of the soul that Edith Wharton spoke of. For although animals may be capable of understanding what a chair is in the sense that they may be able to form a mental image of it, they cannot go beyond the confines of the sensory data they are presented with to form, for example, images of nonexistent chairs or, much less, the notions of God or good. That is why animals, as opposed to man, are incapable of belief. They may be able to passively receive sensory data—and thus form images—but they cannot form "images" that are independent of any sensory data, that is, concepts or ideas, much less assert or maintain or believe such concepts or ideas.

Moreover, this capacity that man possesses and animals do not is a feature of man as an individual, not as a social being. Whether or not man always expresses such a capacity socially, the capacity itself is not grounded in society or in any forms of social organization. Rather, man is able to form societies and "make" cultures because he is, in the first place, a reasoning, moral being; his social and cultural activities are a manifestation, an effect of this capacity. Our cultural beliefs and practices, in sum, have their basis in the internal states and processes of individuals; their sources are subjective.

Many twentieth-century social scientists thus adopt a subjectivistic concept of culture. It is important, nonetheless, to draw a sharp distinction between the *kinds* of subjectivistic concepts adopted by different groups of social scientists. There is perhaps no better illustration of the extremity of such differences than that presented by the two groups in this study, Boasian anthropologists and historians of religions. The difference may be broadly characterized by saying that the concept of culture adopted by Boasian anthropologists is subjectivistic and nonrational, whereas the concept of culture adopted by historians of religions is subjectivistic and rational. For an understanding of what I mean here, some background on comparative religion is necessary. Since both Boasian cultural anthropology and the history of religions had their genesis, in part, as a reaction against the naturalistic perspective of nineteenth-century comparative religionists, it is useful to start with a brief description of the latter.

3

Modern comparative religion is largely the creation of a small but extremely energetic group of nineteenth-century thinkers, including James Frazer, Edward Tylor, and Herbert Spencer.[7] These men, imbued with a spirit of naturalism and positivism fostered by Darwin and Comte, and using a now defunct model of cultural evolution as their principal interpretive apparatus, gathered an immense amount of anthropological and historical data on religious beliefs and practices throughout the world and synthesized these data into a more or less coherent form. I say "more or less coherent form" because, from the modern perspective, it was very much less. Although nineteenth-century comparative religionists succeeded in explaining a great deal about religion, they succeeded in explaining an even greater amount *away*, neglecting what is often today regarded as the most fundamental and definitive aspect of the religious experience—its irreducible, sui generis character. The result was that they tended to treat religious belief as derivative and even imaginary—"a system of hallucinations," in the words of French sociologist Emile Durkheim.[8]

Durkheim was criticizing here the naturalistic tendencies of nineteenth-century comparative religionists—their propensity not just to subordinate the moral and religious aspects of culture to its material aspects, but also to equate the former with the latter. For men such as Spencer, Frazer, and Tylor, the religious and moral aspects of culture could be understood only if they were seen as ultimately prompted by certain basic needs and wants of man. For example, Spencer likened human society to a biological organism, noting that both were "aggregations"—one of "individuals," the other of "cells." Just as an organ will increase in bulk in proportion to

7. Max Müller, often called the Father of Comparative Religion, is omitted from this brief account because of the relative complexity of his views. Although he was a naturalist in his theory of naturism, he was a follower of Kant and not terribly enthusiastic about the theory of evolution. See SH.

8. Emile Durkheim, *The Elementary Forms of Religious Life*, trans. Joseph Ward Swain (New York, 1915), 99.

"the duties" that the organism requires of it, so too "a class of laborers" will increase in size and importance according to the duties that society requires of it.[9]

In a similar fashion, Tylor and Frazer tried to explain the origin of religion—and therefore also (or so it followed from a nineteenth-century point of view) the nature of religion—on the basis of naturalistic considerations alone. According to Tylor, the most primitive form of religion was animism, or the belief in souls. The origin of such a belief could be understood as primitive man's solution—his mistaken solution—to two essentially scientific problems: "What the doctrine of the soul is among the lower races, may be explained in stating the present theory of its development. It seems as though thinking men, as yet at a low level of culture, were deeply impressed by two groups of biological problems. In the first place, what is it that makes the difference between a living body and a dead one; what causes waking, sleep, trance, disease, death? In the second place, what are those human shapes which appear in dreams and visions?"[10]

According to Tylor, the "savage thinker," reflecting on these two problems (the difference between life and death, on the one hand, and the nature of dreaming, on the other), made a number of inferences and came to the conclusion that they could best be solved by positing certain nonphysical, or at least insubstantial, entities or souls. In this way was born what Tylor regarded as the defining feature of religion: the "belief in Spiritual Beings."[11]

Tylor's account of the origin and nature of religion is thus psychological—but not subjectivistic in the sense that I have been using the term. For the belief in spiritual beings was not regarded by him as the manifestation of a special, nonnatural mental capacity on the part of man; it was rather the product of certain naturalistic, albeit psychological events that happened to occur in men's minds—events that were linked to and could be explained in terms of processes in the external world. Religion was not given a subjective reality of its own; it was reduced to or equated with naturalistic events. It is due

9. Lucy Mair, *An Introduction to Social Anthropology* (Oxford, 1972), 33.
10. Tylor, *Primitive Culture*, 33.
11. *Ibid.*, 424.

to such reductionism—a reductionism that has the effect of denying the integrity and distinctive character of religion—that modern scholars have harshly criticized Tylor's acccount of the origin of religion. Thus, Eric Sharpe noted acidly that Tylor viewed religion less as the belief in spiritual beings than as "the mistaken belief in nonexistent Spiritual Beings" (SH, 56).

Such a condescending attitude toward primitive man, sustained by a naturalistically psychological interpretation of his beliefs and behavior, is also reflected in the work of Frazer. Thus, Frazer treated magic—a phenomenon he regarded as prior historically to religion—as essentially a false science prompted by certain innate and universal tendencies of man's psyche: "Recent researches into the early history of man have revealed the essential similarity with which under many superficial differences, the human mind has elaborated its first crude philosophy of life" (SH, 56).

Frazer spells out the psychological principles on which magic is based:

> If we analyze the principles of thought on which magic is based, they will probably be found to resolve themselves into two: first, that like produces like, or that an effect resembles its cause; and, second, that things which have once been in contact with each other continue to act on each other at a distance after the physical contact has been severed. The former principle may be called the Law of Similarity, the latter the Law of Contact or Contagion. From the first of these principles, namely the Law of Similarity, the magician infers that he can produce any effect he desires merely by imitating it: from the second he infers that whatever he does to a material object will affect equally the person with whom the object was once in contact, whether it formed part of his body or not.[12]

As an example of homeopathic magic, Frazer cites the practice of the Dyaks of Borneo, in which "wizards," in order to facilitate the delivery of babies when mothers are in labor, stand outside the room and pretend to go through the process of giving birth themselves.[13] As an example of contagious magic, Frazer cites the belief of tribes in New South Wales that a tooth extracted from a boy will, when

12. James G. Frazer, *The Golden Bough: A Study in Magic and Religion* (Abr. ed., New York, 1958), 12.
13. *Ibid.*, 16.

placed under the bark of a tree near a river, reveal the boy's fate.[14] Frazer's point throughout is that such beliefs and practices are misapplications of certain empirical principles and laws of causality common to modern science. For Frazer, as for many other naturalists, there was no need to posit an independent, subjective basis for the meaning of cultural practices and beliefs—even when such practices and beliefs were moral and religious in nature. Rather, it was adequate to view the moral and religious aspects of culture as derived from, and closely dependent on, its material aspects. As Frazer said: "To live and to cause to live, to eat food and to beget children, these were the primary wants of man in the past, and they will be the primary wants of man in the future so long as the world lasts" (HR-I, 24).

It is thus within the context of their tendency to reduce the moral and religious aspects of culture to its material aspects that the perspective of nineteenth-century evolutionists must be understood. For it was precisely the assumption that what is true of man as a material being must also be true of man as a religious and moral being that formed the basis for the use of Darwin's ideas in the province of culture.[15] Since *homo naturalis* is the product of evolutionary processes, *homo religiosus* must be the product of evolutionary processes as well. Moreover, it was such evolutionism that allowed these nineteenth-century scholars to be so chauvinistic. There seemed to be as little reason to doubt that modern, scientific man was superior to primitive man as there was to doubt that man as a species was superior to animals.[16] As Spencer said, "The conduct to which we apply the name good is the relatively more evolved conduct and . . . bad is the name we apply to conduct which is relatively less evolved."[17] Primitive man was to be regarded, in Tylor's words, as "forgetful of yester-

14. *Ibid.*, 43–44.

15. On nineteenth-century evolutionism, see Edward B. Tylor, *Anthropology: An Introduction to the Study of Man and Civilization* (Abr. ed.; Ann Arbor, 1960), 18–19; Frazer, *Golden Bough*, 824–25; SH, 142; E-H, 5. It is interesting to note Darwin's response to Tylor's 1871 *Primitive Culture*, quoted in Godfrey Lienhardt, *Social Anthropology* (Oxford, 1966), 8. See also Herbert Spencer's "reply" in his book (first published in 1879) *The Data of Ethics* (3rd ed.; New York, 1905), 27.

16. See HA, 32; EP-S, 159, 161; SH, 192.

17. Spencer, *Data of Ethics*, 26–27.

day and careless of tomorrow, lolling in his hammock when his wants are satisfied."[18]

In terms of the analogy with foreign languages, it could be said that nineteenth-century comparative religionists regarded words like *good* as not essentially different from words like *chair*. It was possible to tell just by looking at a picture that the action depicted in it was good or bad; there was no need to posit a subjective process or state by which it could be interpreted. Hand in hand with this naturalism—this failure to separate the facts from our judgments and interpretations of them—went the good conscience to commit what we would at any rate regard today as value judgments. For the nineteenth-century comparative religionist, such judgments were not the product of subjective bias imposed on the researcher, but rather were scientific conclusions based on the evidence. Spencer even went so far as to claim that his methods were purely inductive.[19]

4

Starting in the early decades of this century, such a naturalistic view of culture, and the cultural chauvinism associated with it, began rapidly to lose favor. Of the two major groups considered in this work, Boasian anthropologists and historians of religions, who might be considered lineal descendants of nineteenth-century comparative religionists, both have been at pains to create as wide a gap between themselves and their forebears as they possibly could. It is not just that modern comparative religionists have repudiated the theory of cultural evolution embraced by most nineteenth-century scholars; it is also that they have found the general esprit of the nineteenth-century comparative religionists—their condescension and sense of moral superiority—distasteful and contrary to any serious effort to understand the religious beliefs and practices of other peoples. During the early nineteenth century, anthropologists had acquired the reputation of gloating over the "dirty rites of dirty savages," as Andrew Lang, himself a nineteenth-century comparative religionist, put it (SH, 48). It is not surprising that as the "science of religion"

18. Edward B. Tylor, *Anthropology: An Introduction to the Study of Man and Civilization* (New York, 1881), 407.
19. Jack Kaminsky, "Herbert Spencer," in *EP*, VII, 527.

began to gain maturity in the twentieth century, its proponents would want to expunge references and viewpoints from the past they regarded as unworthy. Malinowski shows this desire when, in a book published in 1926, he speaks of the evolutionists' "lengthy litanies of threaded statement, which make us anthropologists feel silly and the savage look ridiculous" (EP-T, 9). So too does the modern anthropologist Marvin Harris when he titles, in bold capitals, a section of one of his books EDWARD BURNETT TYLOR, RACIST.[20]

Yet, if Boasian cultural anthropologists and historians of religions have reacted against the naturalism of nineteenth-century comparative religionists, they have done so in very different ways. American cultural anthropology in its present form was shaped in the early decades of this century by German-born Franz Boas. Boas, who was trained as a physicist, is generally credited with bringing a new, critically scientific attitude to anthropology. As Alexander Goldenweiser, one of Boas' students, said, Boas "bestowed upon American anthropology that clarification of issues and stiffening of scientific fiber which it stood so sorely in need of."[21]

The fiber that Boas managed to stiffen was, of course, that of the nineteenth-century evolutionists. They were condemned by Boas, "an anti-evolutionist even in the heyday of evolutionism" (SH, 187), principally for two faults: their a priori theorizing and their failure to pay attention to the social and historical context in which cultural and religious phenomena occur. Boas' point, in making such criticism, was *not*, however, that anthropology should try to constitute itself as a purely scientific discipline. On the contrary, it was the illusion that anthropologists could attain the scientific rigor present in the natural sciences that had led the nineteenth-century evolutionists astray. For Boas, the rigorously scientific methods of study by anthropologists should have been balanced by a recognition that there were some features of culture *not* subject to scientific methods of study: "In my opinion a system of social anthropology and 'laws' of cultural development as rigid as those of physics are supposed to be are unattainable in the present stage of our knowledge, and more important than this: on account of the uniqueness of cultural phe-

20. Harris, *Anthropological Theory*, 140.
21. *Ibid.*, 253. See also B-RLC, 285, 625, 676; B-ANA, 323; B-AML, 292.

nomena and their complexity nothing will ever be found that deserves the name of a law excepting those psychological, biologically determined characteristics which are common to all cultures and which appear in a multitude of forms according to the particular culture in which they manifest themselves." [22]

For Boas, in contrast to the naturalists, what makes our beliefs and practices distinctively cultural cannot be equated with the

22. B-RLC, 311. The terms *social anthropology* and *cultural anthropology* have very different connotations today than they did in Boas' time. As a result of the divergence in conceptual orientation that has occurred between British and American anthropologists, the meanings of the two terms are today quite different, though in just what way depends on whether it is an American, British, or French anthropologist explaining it. Boas, however, did not make the distinction. Although he often spoke of "social anthropology," his orientation was at the conceptual pole opposite that of Durkheim, Radcliffe-Brown, and Levi-Strauss. From a modern point of view, he was a cultural anthropologist.

It is important to note, however, that the terms *culture* and *society* have very different meanings for the two groups. Cultural anthropologists separate (at least theoretically) *culture* from *society* but, because of their focus on individuals and their mental states, see the former, not the latter, as what is most distinctively human. Alfred Kroeber said: "Culture can exist only when a society exists; and conversely every human society is accompanied by a culture. This converse, to be sure, is not complete; it applies only to *human* societies. In principle, however, the limitation is extremely important. The existence of cultureless or essentially cultureless subhuman societies, especially the highly elaborate ones of the social insects, serves as an irrefutable touchstone for the significant discrimination of the concepts of the social and the cultural; they *can* exist separately" (Kroeber, *Nature of Culture*, 118–19).

Social anthropologists such as Radcliffe-Brown and Evans-Pritchard also separate the social from the cultural, but do so in a manner very different from that in which Kroeber does. Influenced by Durkheim's concept of society as an entity sui generis that is more than the sum of its parts (*i.e.*, more than just a collection of individuals), social anthropologists posit the social as what is most distinctively human and view the cultural, ethnological phenomena that American anthropologists focused their attention on as functions of social structure. In the words of David Bidney: "For the anthropologists, culture was the ultimate reality *sui generis* and society but the vehicle of culture, a necessary but not sufficient condition of culture. For the sociologists, on the contrary, society was the ultimate reality which rendered intelligible the nature of man and the social institutions by which he is governed" (BI, 96).

My own perspective on these issues inclines toward the Durkheimian. I would stress in addition, however, the interdependence of our concepts of culture and society; there can be no culture without society, and no recognizably human society without culture.

merely natural or material; it must be something "other" that is contributed independently by the subject and is added onto the natural. This subjective factor, moreover, is not accessible to scientific study. Though culture is shaped, in a general way, by certain universal conditions that underlie all cultures,[23] the factors that make any culture what it is are nonrational and emotional and can no more be determined scientifically than can the subjective states of an individual.[24] Our cultural beliefs and practices, though *subject* to natural laws, conditions, and needs, are not *determined* by them.[25] On the contrary, beliefs and practices that are distinctively cultural (for example, those of a religious nature) will be most unpredictable and nonrational. Practices that are amenable to rational understanding, on the other hand, will be precisely those that are least cultural in a strict sense. Boas' formulation of culture as subjective and nonrational thus explains why American anthropologists in his wake have, on the one hand, concentrated so heavily on the analysis of the more organic and material aspects of culture (those that can be traced to a base common to all cultures), neglecting, on the other hand, as anthropologists themselves concede (SA, 24), those aspects of culture that are presumed to be emotionally and psychologically grounded (such as religion) and that cannot be easily traced to a base common to all cultures.[26]

23. See B-MPM, 159–60; B-RLC, 261–62.

24. See HA, 55, 80; B-RLC, 259, 305, 596–97, 621, 624; B-JAF, 11; B-MPM, 209, 232–34, 237, 239, 249–50; B-ANA, 348.

25. See B-MPM, 191–93, 195, 255, 271; B-AML, 231; B-RLC, 234–45, 266–67.

26. How similar is Boas' concept of culture to that held by the more modern anthropologists following in his wake? Is there a basis for generalizing Boas' views to those of American cultural anthropologists as a whole? Space does not permit an answer to these questions. However, for an indication of the partly affirmative answer that might be given to them, see the following: Kroeber, *Nature of Culture*, 22, 152–66; P. J. Pelto, *The Nature of Anthropology* (New York, 1966), 3; HO, 511; SA, 11, 73, 83; Harry Hoijer, "Language and Writing," in Harry L. Shapiro (ed.), *Man, Culture, and Society* (Oxford, 1956), 196, 201; Ralph Linton, *The Tree of Culture* (New York, 1958), 8; Edmund Leach, "Sermons by a Man on a Ladder," *New York Review of Books*, October 20, 1966, p. 31; Mair, *Introduction to Social Anthropology*, 35; HA, 96; Robert Redfield, *The Primitive World and its Transformation* (Ithaca, N.Y., 1953), 45; A. R. Radcliffe-Brown, *Structure and Function in Primitive Society* (New York, 1965), 178; Talcott Parsons, "The Integration of Social Systems," in Kurt H. Wolff (ed.), *Essays on Sociology and Philosophy* (New

In terms of the analogy with the study of foreign languages, Boasian cultural anthropologists would not make the meanings of cultural phenomena analogous to the meanings of words like *chair*, which have objective reference in the external world. Nor would they make them strictly analogous to the meanings of words like *good*, which are so subjective as to lack cross-cultural grounding altogether (a lack that makes them unsuitable for systematic study). Rather, Boasian anthropologists would make the meanings of cultural phenomena analogous to the meanings of a type of word in between those of *chair* and *good*—what I will call the secondary subjective meanings of *chair*. By these I refer to connotations of the word *chair* that are distinct from any basic definition of *chair* and are contributed largely by the subject on hearing the word *chair* pronounced. They include everything from the images of a stool and armchair to those of a kind of chair never before made but only imagined. Such secondary subjective meanings of *chair* bear the same ostensive relationship to the chair as the different systems of food production of different societies bear to the noncultural, biological need of man to provide himself with adequate nutrition (this need, grounded in man's physiological makeup, is independent of culture in the same way that the object, chair, is independent of any connotations of the word). In sum, what is cultural about man's systems of food production are not those factors that are common to them, but those that are unique or intrinsically different—that is, those factors in the particular histories of different cultures that cannot be traced to external circumstances. The economic organization of a society, regarded as a distinctively cultural phenomenon, is constituted not by biological needs or even environmental conditions—however much such needs and conditions may impose limits on the forms of economic organization—but rather by subjective factors that are particular to that culture or society itself. The reference of cultural beliefs and practices is ultimately to the elements of the consciousness of the people who make up that culture.

York, 1964), 125; for pertinent comments by Claude Levi-Strauss, Clyde Kluckhohn, Edmund Leach, Bronislaw Malinowski, Clifford Geertz, and Talcott Parsons, see William A. Lessa and Evon Z. Vogt (eds.), *Reader in Comparative Religion: An Anthropological Approach* (New York, 1958), 112, 131, 152, 210, 574, 576; Peter Berger, *The Sacred Canopy* (New York, 1969), 22–23.

5

This subjectivistic understanding of culture can be sharply contrasted to the subjectivistic understanding of culture adopted by historians of religions. Like Boasian anthropology, the discipline of the history of religions (or *Religionswissenschaft*, as it is called in Europe) arose on a conceptual basis fundamentally opposed in spirit to nineteenth-century comparative religion. This conceptual basis—shaped largely in the early decades of this century by the three Protestant theologians Nathan Söderblom, Rudolf Otto, and Gerardus van der Leeuw, as well as by a host of other scholars—revolves largely around the notion that religious experience is a phenomenon sui generis and cannot be reduced to economic, sociological, psychological, or any other nonreligious terms (E-Q, 51, 70; E-SP, 16).

Men like Mircea Eliade (perhaps the leading exponent of the history of religions today) do not contest the view of anthropologists that all cultures have a material basis and that therefore an empirical method of study is essential to comparative religion (SH, 160). Nor do they contest the view of anthropologists that the characteristic features of culture are subjective and therefore not fully accessible to such empirical methods. What they do contest is that the subjective nature of culture is something nonrational and emotional in character—that it may be looked on as the residuum left over when all the objective, rational features have been accounted for. Rather, for historians of religions, culture as a subjective entity is something *in itself*—a substance in its own right and therefore of a rational, even fixed, nature.

Two points in particular will help to bring out the contrast between the subjectivistic notions of culture adopted by historians of religions and Boasian anthropologists. First, the method of study practiced by historians of religions is not primarily empirical, as it is for Boasian anthropologists, but phenomenological. For our purposes here, suffice it to say that the main intent of the phenomenological method of the study of religion is to allow the historian of religions to penetrate the meaning, or essence, of the religious experience[27]—

27. See SH, 224; Maurice Merleau-Ponty, "What Is Phenomenology?" in Joseph Dabney Bettis (ed.), *Phenomenology of Religion* (New York, 1969), 14–15; E-P, xiii; Joachim Wach, *Sociology of Religion* (Chicago, 1944), 5.

an experience that lies beyond not only natural processes but also, in contrast to Boasian anthropology, any *particular* religious belief or practice. This universal experience is not to be described in naturalistic terms, but it is nonetheless, according to historians of religions, quite as real as any naturalistic phenomenon; its reality is of a different nature than that toward which the natural sciences direct themselves.

The second point is that, whereas Boasian anthropologists have directed little attention to religious beliefs and practices as such, the latter have been one of the major preoccupations of historians of religions, as can be seen by their efforts to give a general definition of religion. The most common definition advanced by historians of religions is that all religious experience involves a dichotomy of the sacred and the profane. By such a concept, historians of religions hope to account at least somewhat specifically for the great diversity of religious beliefs and practices in cultures. The notion of the sacred and the profane is seen as a kind of structure, or framework, behind the religions of all cultures. It points to what is universal in religions. Moreover, the notion itself reflects the radically nonnaturalistic understanding that most historians of religions (and Eliade in particular) have of religion.[28] What historians of religions mean to do by their use of the term *sacred* is to give the religious experience an independent, autonomous foundation. The sacred is obviously not to be adequately assessed in naturalistic terms. On the contrary, the sacred is the negation of those naturalistic conditions that man is subject to; it is the negation of the profane.

In terms of the analogy with the study of foreign languages, then, historians of religions would agree with Boasian cultural anthropologists that the meanings of cultural phenomena are not analogous to the meanings of words like *chair*. However, in contrast to anthropologists, they would claim that they *are* analogous to the meanings of words like *good*, so long as such words are seen to be elements of a moral consciousness intrinsic to and universal in man. Historians of religions, in other words, not only give culture a subjective basis but also regard such a basis as imposing a consistent, rational, and explicable structure on man's beliefs and practices.

28. See E-SP, 11, 151, 165, 187; E-P, 268, 461; E-Q, 5; HRI, 3; A, 83; SA, 165.

Consider, for example, what is referred to as "man's consciousness of death," an attribute that is often cited by social scientists and historians of religions in particular as one of man's defining characteristics—one that not only distinguishes him from animals but also forms the basis of many of his higher cultural beliefs and activities, from his conceptions of the afterlife to many of his artistic endeavors. To what can such a consciousness of death be traced? Surely not simply to the fact that all men must die, for if that were the case, animals would be conscious of death quite as much as man. Man's consciousness of death is, of course, ultimately dependent on the fact that there *is* such a thing as death (in the same way that man's judgments of good are dependent on the fact that there are things to be so judged). The sources of such consciousness of death, however, lie not in the external, natural world, but in the nature, or structure, of man's mental capacities, which have—as one might put it—an added dimension, by comparison with the mental capacities of animals. Thus, for example, man's various conceptions of the afterlife all have their ground in, and ultimately gain their meaning from, the special nature of man's consciousness. They are not defined—secondarily or otherwise—with reference to external, material conditions or needs. Rather, their reference is to innate mental capacities, in the same way that different individuals' or different cultures' conceptions of good may be thought to have their ground in man's moral consciousness.

For both anthropologists and historians of religions, then, culture is an entity subjective in character. The difference between the two disciplines—which are generally hostile to each other and which "have not been in dialogue for several decades" (SA, 24)—is that anthropologists read this condition as a limitation on how well and how systematically they can study certain types of cultural phenomena. Historians of religions, on the other hand, are quite content to regard culture as subjective in nature, for it allows them with good conscience to throw off the straitjacket of what they feel is a narrow methodology used in the natural sciences and uncritically applied to phenomena of a very different character in the social sciences. For the anthropologist, culture tends to be subjective in the sense of a quasi-fictional entity, as when one says, "Such and such is a cultural belief; the reality is . . . ." Whereas for the historian of religions, it is subjective in a more autonomous sense, as when one says, "Such and such a belief can neither be proven nor disproven; it has a reality of its own." For the anthropologist, culture is an entity subjective and nonrational; for the historian of religions, it is an entity subjective and rational.

Although the subjectivistic concepts of cultures adopted by Boasian anthropologists and historians of religions are quite different, there is one important similarity between the two that should not be missed: both strongly advocate that the researcher refrain from all value judgments and that his stance be extracultural and normatively neutral.[29] To see how such a view is imposed by their subjectivistic concepts of cultures, let us consider once again the analogy with the study of foreign language.

In learning a foreign language, the first task, as we saw, is to learn the meanings of a number of object-terms. Only with this fixed, objective basis established will we be in a position to infer the meanings of subjective terms like *good* or the secondary subjective meanings of object-terms like *chair*. Similarly, in the study of a foreign culture, we must first acquaint ourselves with the extracultural and purely natural conditions and forces which that culture—as well as our own—is subject to. Only after we have gained an understanding of such extracultural forces and conditions, which stand at the basis of and are common to the economic activities of all cultures and societies, will we be in a position to judge the nature and character of the economic organization of a particular culture or society. Similarly, only by keeping in mind the universal conditions of man's mortality will we be able to appreciate the sense in which it is true that

29. On anthropologists, see B-AML, 201–204; HA, 53; Lessa and Vogt (eds.), *Reader*, 4; SA, 146–47; EP-S, 155–71. The manner in which Robert Redfield is an "exception" only proves the rule. See Redfield, *Primitive World*, 153–55, 165. On historians of religions, see A, 116; E-K, 19, 88; BL-S, 21; BL-R, 6, 28; W. Brede Kristensen, *The Meaning of Religion* (The Hague, 1960), 12–13; SH, 220, 237, 277; Ninian Smart, *The Science of Religion and the Sociology of Knowledge* (Princeton, 1973), 21; SA, 31, 34; Philip H. Ashby, "The History of Religions," in Paul Ramsey (ed.), *Religion* (Englewood Cliffs, N.J., 1965), 27–28. It should be noted that many interpreters of Mircea Eliade (including those highly sympathetic) have charged that his work is not value-free (A, 222; Dudley, *Religion on Trial*, 36), despite the fact that he, along with many other prominent historians of religions, signed a statement in 1960 that seems to require that it be so (see SH, 278).

all men are conscious of death and hence the particular attitudes toward death or conceptions of the afterlife seen in particular cultures or societies. In the latter case, of course, our basis of understanding will necessarily be subjective (*i.e.*, grounded in man's consciousness of death). But it will be subjective only to the extent that such subjectivity is made universal to all men, and *that* universal basis will be inexplicable except in relation to the extracultural and purely natural condition of man's mortality. In no case can we make the basis of our understanding of a foreign belief or practice that which is particular to our own culture. For any such judgment could have only a subjective (and nonuniversal) basis and therefore would carry with it a bias that might very well distort the meaning of the foreign belief or practice being studied. Our standpoint must in all cases be extracultural and normatively neutral. A subjective concept of culture— in either of the two related senses of the word *subjective*—carries with it the dictate that the methodological stance of the social scientist be neutral.

6

The subjectivistic concepts of culture adopted by comparative religionists are inspired by a well-intentioned effort to give culture autonomy; by conceiving of culture as subjective in nature, comparative religionists wish to sharply separate culture from the empirical conditions that culture is subject to. The problem, however, is that all such a conception succeeds in doing is to transform culture into a special (ethereal or quasi-mental) *object*. The separation effected is at once too much and too little. It is too much in the sense that although man's natural activities (eating, sleeping, running, laughing) are surely different from his cultural activities (hoping, praying, calculating, willing), such differences are too complex and too manifold to be adequately depicted by a simple division. What we call man's natural activities and cultural activities are in fact deeply embedded in one another. Thus, in terms of the analogy with language, it is simplistic to say that the difference between *chair* and *good* is that the former refers to an external object, the latter to an inner object. For in the case of *chair*, it is not the object, *as* object—for example, the properties of the wood or the way the seat is attached to the legs— that defines its meaning, but rather the way the word is used in a social context (which may, however, include as one of its components the properties of the wood or the way the seat is attached to the legs). Contrary to the account above, it is not ostensive definition alone that gives us the meaning of the word *chair*, for such ostensive definition presupposes a use of and familiarity with chairs. A Martian, that is, might not be able to understand what a chair is through ostensive definition; seeing the object would tell him nothing, for he might not know what the object was for. The difference between *chair* and *good*, therefore, is not as one-dimensional as the subjectivistic accounts indicated.

On the other hand, the separation between nature and culture effected by comparative religionists is too little in the sense that it fails to grasp the immense difference that exists between the way man as a cultural being lives and the way animals do. It is extremely misleading to say that the nature of this difference consists in the fact that man undergoes various mental processes (or he has the capacity to undergo them), whereas animals do not. For this makes it sound as though the difference between man and animals were not directly observable, but only indirectly so, constituted by inner activities and processes that are of the same logical type as outer activities and processes, except that they take place where no one can see them. If this were true, then it would be possible for such characteristically human concepts and practices as, for example, hoping and doing mathematical calculations to be shared by animals. It would be possible for the following reason. If hoping and doing mathematical calculations are conceived of as mental processes that take place in the head, then there will always be a possibility that any living creature with a head could have them. That is, if a concept is defined in terms of an individual, private experience or mental process, then by definition the individual will have final authority for deciding whether or not a given experience falls under a given concept, for only he knows what that experience was. Animals, however, are "individuals" and have brain processes, too. If they are unable to effectively report a given experience, that doesn't prove that they don't have it. Or, in terms of the analogy with language, if *good* refers to an inner, private object, then we can never prove that animals do not have this concept, too.

Thus, the effort to ground man's capacity for culture in inner processes or private mental states leads to an absurd conclusion, the conclusion that animals may, *possibly*, pray or do mathematical calculations. The proper response to the question "Do animals pray or do mathematical calculations?" is indeed not to answer it positively or negatively, but to reject the question as nonsensical—in the same way we would reject the question "Are squares yellow or red?" as nonsensical. All we can say is that it belongs to the concept of man that he can pray and do mathematical calculations—and does not so belong to the concept of animals. The difference between man and animals is not empirically grounded, but logical or conceptual— where these terms are meant to refer not to an abstract category of thought but to the life forms and everyday practices from which our concepts arise. Analogously, the difference between the meanings of *chair* and *good* is not that they refer to different kinds of objects, but that they are used in different ways and for different purposes.

Comparative religionists, however, do not seem to fully recognize this point. They are continually seeking an empirical foundation or even a cause for what is a conceptual or logical, meaning-filled distinction. (It is important to understand that the distinction between *empirical* and *logical* does not coincide with the distinction between *material* and *mental*. There are empirical and logical elements in material phenomena, and there are empirical and logical elements in mental phenomena.) Comparative religionists do not think, perhaps, that their accounts of culture are empiricist, because the empirical processes they refer to are hidden and ethereal, grounded in man's subjectivity and consciousness. But one does not objectify culture any less by seeing it as an internal, mental process than by seeing it as an external, material one. In both cases, one is investing with logical force what can only be contingent and factual.

Consider, for example, the assertion that culture is founded on or caused by man's ability to reason, to will, and to intend. This assertion is the product of a failure to distinguish between the sense in which reasoning, willing, and intending are conceptual categories and the sense (if any) in which they are mental processes. If, on the one hand, reasoning, willing, and intending are taken as conceptual categories, then they cannot be what "causes" culture or what it is grounded on; rather they are what, in part, constitutes it. The above assertion then becomes tautological, or empty of all content (compare: "My idea of red is founded on the fact it is a color"). If, on the other hand, reasoning, willing, and intending are taken as mental processes, then their status is empirical, and however valid it may be to say that they cause certain forms of cultural behavior (the validity of such assertions will be a function of the adequacy of the empirical methods adopted), they cannot be said to define the meaning of such behavior. A mental process, as an empirical phenomenon, does not and cannot carry its meaning in itself. Even if a psychologist or neurologist were to establish a given mental or neurological process as the cause of a given type of behavior, it must be remembered that the original "home," or context, in which such behavior gains its significance (that is, whether it is called rational or irrational, happy or sad) is not a laboratory or experimental situation, but the culture in which such experimentation takes place. (For similar reasons, efforts to explain man's cultural capacities in terms of biological evolution—as, for example, the product of some quite remarkable development of the brain—are futile; the explanation never makes contact with what it is trying to explain.)

In either sense we wish to take them, then—as mental processes or conceptual categories—it is wrong to say that man's capacity for culture derives from his ability to reason, to will, and to intend. We are accustomed to making such assertions only because we fail to distinguish the diffferent ways in which they are significant. Our minds, as it were, flit back and forth between two distinct senses of a term and through this process make plausible a third and wholly illegitimate sense—one that is an amalgam of fact and concept. This failure to *distinguish* between the empirical and conceptual features of phenomena, however—and this is the crucial point—would not occur had not an illegitimate *separation* between material and mental processes established itself. Our tendency to objectify our concepts—to equate them with activities or processes of one sort or another—hangs together with a tendency to divide such activities or processes into two essentially different kinds, that is, mental and material, for it is only by such a separation or division that our concepts, once objectified, seem to gain meaning. But the "facts" (physical or psychological) do *not* speak for themselves. Meaningful differences between phenomena exist not on the basis of the phenomena themselves (not on the basis of a division or separation between phenomena *as* phenomena), but on the basis of differences between the concepts under which phenomena fall.

Consider, for example, the concepts of throwing and intending. They are obviously very different concepts, each of which has very different sorts of phenomena falling under them (which is to say that there are very different sorts of criteria that we make count for what constitutes throwing and what constitutes intending). When we are faced with the sentence "He intended to throw the ball," however, the nature of these differences easily becomes obscured; we oppose intending to throwing as though one were a mental act and the other a physical act, forgetting that the difference between throwing and intending is conceptual, not empirical. "Intending to throw the ball" then becomes a sort of "throwing the ball" in the mind—the shadow of an external action to be performed. The concept of intention becomes obscured (*i.e.*, it is equated with a private ethereal act of the mind), and in its place an illusory division of mental and material processes is erected.

Thus, comparative religionists' separation of the material and subjective phenomena of culture is closely linked to their failure to distinguish between the empirical and logical (meaning-filled) features of any given cultural phenomenon. The concept of culture (which has a logical status grounded in the way man lives) is confused with certain subjective mental processes that man undergoes (and that have an empirical status). According to the notion of culture I am suggesting, on the other hand, the significance of cultural phenomena is radically distinct from any empirical processes, material or mental, that could be observed or reported on. What culture is runs through all of man's activities; it does not have its basis in any division or separation between such processes. If one wishes, for example, to understand the concepts of laughing and hoping (both of which are fundamental to man as a cultural being and are not characteristic of animals), one should proceed by essentially the same methods, asking what constitutes laughing (how do we tell when someone is laughing)? and what constitutes hoping (how do we tell when someone is hoping)? Just as the answer to the first question is not to be found by examining the physiology of the facial muscles, the answer to the second will not be found by postulating a special mental capacity (acquired through the evolutionary development of the brain). The *concept* of hoping is no more a private, internal process than the *concept* of laughing is a physical, external one. In the sense that the logic of a way of life can be understood (not, of course, in the sense that observable behavior can be interpreted), both are equally open to view.

The normative concept of culture I am suggesting thus draws a radical distinction between the empirical features and the logical features of cultural phenomena but does not separate the phenomena, *as* phenomena, into two different kinds, mental and material. It defines culture nonempirically, without conceiving of it as a special (subjective or mental) object. This is what I mean by saying that the norms or rules (which express the meaning of cultural phenomena) cannot be known prior to empirical investigation, nor can they be defined in empirical terms. Rather, they exhibit a certain range of possibility of belief and practice, allowing meaning to *show*.

II Wittgenstein and the Normative Basis of Belief

The philosophical sources of the normative concept of culture briefly discussed in the last chapter can be found in the works of Ludwig Wittgenstein (1889–1951)—especially those dating from about 1932 (the year *Philosophische Grammatik* was begun) and represented, above all, by *Philosophical Investigations* (though Wittgenstein's early works, such as the *Tractatus Logico-Philosophicus* and the *Notebooks, 1914–16*, are vital as well). Wittgenstein conceived of language in a manner analogous to the way I am suggesting we conceive of culture. For Wittgenstein, the meanings of words are grounded neither in the external objects to which they refer nor in the internal objects, sensations, images, or feelings accompanying them.[1] Rather, the meanings of words are given by the rules or norms governing (but not rigidly dictating) their use.[2] *Use* here means necessarily public use and refers not just to a conceptual, linguistic sphere, but also to the life forms in which our concepts are grounded.[3] *Rule* or *norm*, on the other hand, means not so much that which tells a person unambiguously what he must do (for a rule can always be interpreted differently); rather, it is that which, once an action is performed or a practice carried out, can be said to display (not constitute) the sense or meaning of that action or practice. Wittgenstein's notion of meaning is thus accurately characterized as normative when norm or rule is thought of according to the model

1. See W-Z, sec. 19; W-WCI, 43, 44, 62, 85; W-BB, 34, 64; W-LC, 29; W-WCII, 44–45, 64, 85, 151; W-PP, 261; W-PI, sec. 288, pp. 185, 193–94, 199, 200, 212; W-OC, secs. 105, 110, 559; W-RC, secs. 14, 158; W-RFM, bk. I, sec. 8, pp. 159–60; W-RPII, secs. 253, 325, 392.

2. See W-PI, secs. 141, 241, pp. 147, 227; W-PP, 276–77, 257; W-WCI, 59, 62, 64, 85, 112; W-WCII, 21; W-OC, sec. 62; W-Z, sec. 320; W-RFM, bk. I, secs. 9, 74, 131; W-RFM, bk. II, secs. 28, 34; W-RFM, appendix I, sec. 4; W-RPII, secs. 352, 392; W-PG, 17, 108, 171, 180, 165–66, 173–75.

3. See W-PI, secs. 9, 20, 30, p. 209; W-OC, secs. 61, 351; W-Z, sec. 173; W-WCI, 36, 112; W-WCII, 29, 48; W-RC, sec. 123; W-PG, 30, 54, 58, 55, 65, 122, 182.

of a person learning the rules of a game by watching it being played (or by actually playing it), not according to the model of a person who knows in advance, just by having the rules recited to him, exactly how the game *will* be played.[4] By such an understanding of rule or norm, Wittgenstein could advance a notion of meaning that was at once concrete, grounded in the patterns of familiar uses or "channels of meaning" in which our concepts have their home, and nonempirical, given by standards or norms that are readily distinguishable from any empirical conclusions drawn on the basis of them. He could, in other words, draw radical distinctions between the empirical features and the logical features of any given phenomenon without separating phenomena, as phenomena, into two essentially different kinds.

As an example of where Wittgenstein accomplishes this distinction, not separation, the following may be cited: "There are what can be called phenomena of seeing and phenomena of imaging; and there is the concept of seeing and the concept of imaging. Within both pairs one can speak of 'differences'" (W-RPI, sec. 130). Wittgenstein's use of the term *differences* (*Unterschieden*) here corresponds to my use of the term *distinctions*. He is asking us to distinguish between the empirical phenomena of seeing and the concept of seeing. At the same time, we must not separate the language games of seeing and imaging (*Vorstellens*) in such a way as to see one as an inner, the other as an outer activity: "Nothing could be more mistaken than to say seeing and forming an image are different activities" (W-RPI, sec. 138). The difference between seeing and forming an image is not empirical, but conceptual: "With the sentence, 'Images are voluntary, sensations are not,' one differentiates not betweeen sensations and images, but rather between the language games in which we deal with these concepts" (W-RPI, sec. 129). The differentiation is *stipulated* in the different norms and rules that govern the different languages games. Wittgenstein's sharp distinction between the empirical and logical features of a given phenomenon hangs together with his recognition that there is nothing *in* the phenomena them-

4. On Wittgenstein's concept of rule or norm as presupposed in, but not prescribing, use, see W-PI, secs. 31, 131, 188, 437, p. 210; W-PP, 258; W-Z, sec. 302; W-WCI, 44, 84; W-WCII, 4, 16, 86, 153–55; W-RC, sec. 303; W-LC, 5; W-RFM, bk. I, sec. 20.

selves that allows them to be separated into two essentially different kinds. Rather, the difference is conceptual.

2

Before discussing Wittgenstein's normative account of meaning further, however, I would like to set the philosophical context for this account by providing some remarks on the philosophies of Hume and Kant. Both Hume's and Kant's accounts of meaning were (in radically different ways) subjectivistic and empiricist and entailed what I have been calling "a separation but not a distinction" between the empirical and the logical aspects of meaning. A clarification of the nature and extent of their failures in these regards will prepare the way for a better appreciation of Wittgenstein's successes.

Hume defines what he calls "relations of ideas" as intuitively or demonstrably certain propositions that are true, independent of experience or testimony of the senses; they are of a logical character.[5] The examples that Hume gives are mostly mathematical, such as three times five is equal to half of thirty: "Propositions of this kind are discoverable by the mere operations of thought, without dependence on what is anywhere existent in the universe" (H-EHU, 25).

The truth or falsity of propositions expressing what he calls "matters of fact," however, is very much dependent on what is "existent in the universe." Matters of fact are contingent and can be justified only with reference to experience or empirical evidence—which means ultimately, for Hume, to be traced back to some corresponding sense-datum or impression that appears "clearly and distinctly" before the mind's eye. If an idea or concept contained in a proposition expressing a matter of fact cannot be so traced—and this is more often the case than not—then Hume is inclined to conclude "We have no idea of it" or "We cannot conceive of it" or "The idea lacks meaning."[6] Propositions containing matters of fact include every-

---

5. When discussing Hume's views, I will use—as Hume did himself—the term *proposition*. Elsewhere, however, I will follow Wittgenstein and make no distinction between *proposition* and *statement*, using the two interchangeably.

6. Hume's concept of meaning rests, to a large extent, on his use of two key terms: *impressions* and *ideas*. For an account of *impressions*, see H-THN, 456; H-EHU, 22, 65, 74, 78; H-ATHN, 657; Barry Stroud, *Hume* (London, 1977), 18–33; Norman Kemp

thing from scientific to metaphysical propositions. Examples are: "The temperature of this room is 60 degrees F."; "God exists"; and "The sun will rise tomorrow." In all these cases (according to Hume), it is perfectly possible to conceive of their being false, though such a possibility is extremely unlikely, Hume would agree, in the third case. Propositions expressing relations of ideas, however, are "conceivable" and have meaning only to the extent that they are true.[7] They are necessarily and universally true—if they are true at all. "Every proposition [expressing a relation of ideas] which is not true is there confused and unintelligible. That the cube root of 64 is equal to the half of 10 is a false proposition and can never be distinctly conceived" (H-EHU, 164).

Hume's distinction between matters of fact and relations of ideas shows that he takes the term *meaning* in at least two different senses. On the one hand, an idea (occurring in a statement of matter of fact) has meaning only when it can be traced back, via empirical examination, to some prior, corresponding impression. On the other hand, a statement expressing a relation of ideas has meaning and is true logically; there is nothing in experience that could ever contradict it. Two and two equals four is true by virtue of the way these symbols are defined; to say that two and two does not equal four would be simply to contradict oneself (to violate the law of noncontradiction).[8] If tomorrow the universe were destroyed, the statement "The sun will rise tomorrow" would be untrue. But not so the statement "Two and two equals four"; its truth is guaranteed—one feels tempted to say—in *any* universe.

What does this distinction between matters of fact and relations of

---

Smith, *The Philosophy of David Hume: A Critical Study of its Origins and Central Doctrines* (New York, 1941), 105–106; A. J. Ayer, *Hume* (Oxford, 1980), 40. For an account of *ideas*, see H-EHU, 55, 62, 69, 77, 82, 153; H-THN, 3, 67–68, 74–75, 183, 190, 193, 209, 251–52, 254, 283.

7. Norman Kemp Smith points out in a note: "'Conception' Hume uses in a quite general, non-technical sense as covering all perceptions that are cognitive in character" (Smith, *Philosophy of David Hume*, 107).

8. According to Antony Flew, the test of noncontradiction is for Hume the sole criterion for determining the truth of statements about relations of ideas. See Antony Flew, "Hume," in D. J. O'Connor (ed.), *A Critical History of Western Philosophy* (New York, 1964), 258.

ideas amount to? The first point to take note of is that it is an abstract, a priori distinction that derives from purported properties of the two different kinds or types of propositions. For Hume, there is something intrinsic in the proposition "Two and two equals four" that makes it logical—that is, universal and necessary. Similarly, there is something intrinsic in the proposition "The sun will rise tomorrow" that makes it empirical—that is, contingently true or false. Moreover, the meaning of neither of these propositions is in any sense normative. The meaning of a proposition expressing relations of ideas is not normative, because it is somehow extrahuman; "Two and two equals four" is true in any universe and has no reference to the way people live or even, for that matter, to the nature of reality. The meaning of a proposition expressing matters of fact is not normative by virtue of its empirical character. Hume's adherence to the theory of ideas dictated that he view meaning as a mental content held before the mind's eye—a sort of observation—not as a judgment made by an individual or, much less, as a value posited by a culture.

What this shows is that Hume's two notions of meaning as given in his formulations of relations of ideas and matters of fact are not separate but interdependent. When Hume maintains that an idea could be determined to have meaning only by being shown to have its origin in some impression that could be made to appear before the mind, he is essentially defining meaning as that which appears "clearly and distinctly" to the individual consciousness. Indeed, in at least a few passages, Hume uses this same phrase, a phrase that is heavily laden with the conceptual baggage of seventeenth-century rationalism (H-EHU, 157, 164). In other places, he says "distinct and compleat" (H-THN, 23) or "clear and precise" or "clear and evident" (H-ATHN, 648). Such terminology accords well with his formulation of the difference between ideas and impressions as consisting in "the degrees of force and liveliness with which they strike upon the mind." This formulation is, in turn, dictated by the "theory of ideas"; if meaning is something one can hold up before one's mind to observe and contemplate, then it makes sense to say further that it can be observed and contemplated in some cases clearly and distinctly—and in other cases, not so clearly and distinctly. But now, it must be demanded, when Hume talks about statements expressing relations of ideas being universally and necessarily true, what *other* criteria, besides that of their obviousness or clarity and distinctness, has he given? What indeed is the difference between saying that a concept is clear and distinct and saying that it is logically necessary? With matters of fact, we have a potential impression that appears before the mind; either the consciousness grasps it or it does not. In the case of relations of ideas we have a proposition presented for inspection by the mind; either the consciousness *conceives* of it or it does not. In both cases, thus, there is (1) a disembodied self or consciousness that is able to consider, in a detached way, whether the proposition is conceivable and (2) an empirical criterion of meaning that consists in determining whether a certain "act" of consciousness has or has not occurred.

Of course, one may object that Hume stipulates that the negation of an empirical proposition is conceivable or possible, whereas negation of a logical one is not. But that is just the question: What constitutes being conceivable? An appeal to the nature of logic or even to the law of noncontradiction is not legitimate here, for it is precisely the concepts of logic and contradiction that are in question. Like the rationalists, Hume thinks that, as Barry Stroud puts it, "he can start from the 'evident' distinctness of two ideas, but he never says how he can recognize that distinctness."[9] Hume's answer in fact does little more than report the results of a mental experience, and presupposes throughout that there exists a self or consciousness (or bundle of mental processes) capable of reliably assuring itself of what it can and cannot conceive. By formulating the difference between logical and empirical statements in such an a priori, abstract way, Hume actually does not distinguish between them at all. There is a revealing passage in the *Enquiry Concerning Human Understanding* where in the process of explaining the difference between matters of fact and relations of ideas, he gives the same criteria for determining their meaning—that is, clarity and distinctness, intelligibility, conceivability, and "implying no contradiction" (H-EHU, 164). In *A Treatise of Human Nature*, he explicitly likens the necessity of statements expressing matters of fact and those expressing relations of ideas. "Thus as the necessity, which makes two times two equal to four, or three

9. Stroud, *Hume*, 48.

angles of a triangle equal to two right ones, lies only in the act of understanding, by which we consider and compare the ideas; in like manner the necessity or power, which unites causes and effects, lies in the determination of the mind to pass from the one to the other" (H-THN, 166).

If the necessity of propositions expressing relations of ideas, like that of propositions expressing matters of fact, consists only in an act of understanding, one may wonder—as Kant was in fact to do— why mathematics should not be open to the same sort of skeptical scrutiny as science. Hume's answer to this, though wholly inadequate, is at least clear: the propositions of arithmetic, *as* arithmetical, are inherently indubitable. Which is to say, Hume does not really distinguish between the empirical and logical features of a given phenomenon; rather, he marks a separation between different *kinds* of propositions and processes. This he does, first, by simply pointing to what everyone in philosophical circles agrees are very different sorts of propositions—scientific and mathematical—and, second, by associating the former with external, material processes and the latter with internal, mental ones, with what he calls the "mere operation of thought" (H-EHU, 25). Of course, this latter association is not clear-cut; logical propositions are linked to mental processes only insofar as they are invested with necessity ("We *can*not conceive that three added to three does not equal six"). But precisely because that inner god or consciousness that is the ultimate arbiter of what is conceivable is never acknowledged, it is extremely easy to invest mental processes—which are intangible—with logical force. To put this another way, when Hume says "We cannot but conceive that . . ." or "It is contradictory to say that . . ." he continually flits back and forth between two senses of *conceive*—one empirical and associated with a mental experience, the other logical and necessary. Once the domain of the logical is determined by the reference point of intangible mental processes, the domain of the empirical or contingent is quite easily determined by the reference point of tangible, material processes where anything can happen. In the case of logical propositions, what makes them conceivable is implicitly understood as an internal mental process that, as it were, presses itself on us and compels assent. In the case of empirical propositions, what makes them contingent is that they are associated with external, material processes.

My point is that this is a *separation* in the sense in which one would separate apples and oranges—not a *distinction*, in which one would differentiate between the logical categories of color and shape and any *particular* apple or orange. In a distinction the identity of the apple or orange is determined on the basis of such categories and the two features, though distinct, can't be separated (as, for example, when we assume the different logical categories of shape and color, and then say, "As regards color, an apple is this, an orange that"). In order that the difference between the logical categories of shape and color and the empirical phenomena themselves be a true logical distinction, the former must be explicitly acknowledged. This entails recognizing that the distinction does not have an empirical (material or mental) basis; it derives from the norms or rules of use built into our practices and activities. But these cannot be justified empirically or by ostensive definition (by pointing to things that have shape and color), because any category we can be made to see by such pointing is itself presupposed in the pointing.

The crucial issue, then, comes to this. Hume, through his distinction between relations of ideas and matters of fact, wishes us to believe that there is a sense in which the statement "The sun will not rise tomorrow" is not contradictory and the statement "Two and two equals five" is contradictory. When it is asked, "On what grounds, by what criteria, is this true?" Hume's only answer is that the former contention involves an idea clear and distinct, and the latter an idea that is not clear and distinct. This sort of answer only confirms what we may have suspected to begin with: that Hume has simply adopted a certain criterion of truth based on a particular activity or practice (that of doing mathematics), treated this as somehow intrinsic to the nature of human reason itself, and then used it as a standard for judging the status of statements of a very different sort than those found in mathematics. What I object to about this is not that there isn't a very great difference between mathematical statements and so-called empirical ones, but that there is no single, common standard of reason by which they can both be judged. Any standard we use carries the marks of such use and therefore cannot be common or equally applicable to all uses. There is, in other words, no absolute standard of reason that *we* will not use in particular ways for particular purposes, that we will not invest with *normative* components.

That is why Hume's definitions of matters of fact and relations of ideas are interdependent; they are used to indicate the different "domains" of reality to which they apply. His empirical criterion of meaning is the counterpart of his uncritical account of logical truth, just as his critique of the rationality of our common ideas and beliefs presupposes an absolute standard of reason.

3

The work of Kant presents a much more critical account of meaning than anything that can be discovered in Hume. Indeed, an understanding of the presuppositional method that Kant introduced into philosophy—seen, for example, in his notion of the distinct but inseparable functions of the sensibility and the understanding—is vital to an appreciation of what Wittgenstein was trying to do not just in the *Tractatus*, but in his later works as well. Nonetheless, however valuable certain elements within Kant's philosophical system, the system is open in a very general way to the same sort of criticism made in the case of Hume.

The crucial notion that holds up the massive philosophical architecture of Kant's first and second *Critiques* is his distinction between epistemological (a priori and a posteriori) and logical (analytic and synthetic) propositions. The first category deals with propositions insofar as they can be related to experience: the truth of an a posteriori proposition can be seen only after experience, whereas the truth of an a priori proposition can be seen before experience. The second category deals with propositions insofar as they are unrelated to experience and are purely logical: the truth of an analytic proposition is guaranteed just by the meaning of its terms, whereas the truth of a synthetic proposition can never be so guaranteed (it must be synthesized or put together from mutually independent terms). An analytic proposition is thus comparable (though not, of course, equivalent) to what Hume means by a proposition expressing a relation of ideas, with the important additional qualification that Hume includes mathematical propositions in this category, but Kant exempts them.[10] An example of an analytic proposition is "All unmarried

10. For Hume, relations of ideas are opposed to matters of fact, the latter being defined as empirical. For Kant, analytical judgments are opposed to synthetic judgments,

women are single." This proposition satisfies the two main criteria Kant variously gives for determining analytic propositions. The first is that it not violate the law of noncontradiction; the second, that the concept of the predicate be contained in the concept of the subject (K-P, 14; K-CI, 49, B12). An analytic proposition is absolutely and under all conditions true; it defines the range of what is conceivable or possible.

Kant's distinction between analytic (as well as synthetic) and a priori (as well as a posteriori) propositions is thus *very* roughly analogous to Hume's distinction between relations of ideas and matters of fact. But Kant actually uses this distinction to make an assertion that Hume denied: that there exists a form of nonlogical necessity that guarantees the truth or provides a rational foundation for science, mathematics, and morals. This nonlogical necessity Kant calls "synthetic a priori"—for which there is no counterpart in Hume's system. By synthetic a priori propositions, Kant refers to propositions that are neither empirical (and therefore of only probable truth) nor analytic. As an example, Kant gives this: "Everything which happens has its cause" (K-CI, 50, A9, B13). This proposition is not empirical because, according to Kant, it is a priori true; within the limits of human experience, it is impossible to conceive of an event that is not caused. At the same time, it is not analytic, for beyond the limits of mere human experience, there may exist a realm (which Kant called "noumenal," in contrast to the phenomenal world of experience) not subject to the laws of causality. More precisely, the proposition "Everything which happens has its cause" violates both of the criteria Kant gives for defining an analytic proposition; its negation is possible. Synthetic a priori propositions thus have a status in between those of empirical and analytic propositions. They are universal and necessary (within the limits of human experience), and there-

---

but the latter are *not* defined as empirical. On the contrary, a synthetic judgment may be known "prior to all experience." Conversely, an analytical judgment may involve "empirical concepts" (a condition that tended not to be true of Hume's relations of ideas). See K-P, 14–15. For Kant, whether a statement is analytical or synthetic has nothing to do with experience. It is, in this sense, a wholly logical distinction to be contrasted with Hume's distinction between relations of ideas and matters of fact.

fore not a mere generalization *from* experience. At the same time, they are applicable only *to* experience.[11]

Kant's views thus represent an enormous advance over Hume's insofar as they critically examine what is presupposed *in* our experience and deny that the status of this experience is adequately described as merely contingent. But Kant was considerably less critical in his view of *logical* necessity. Just as Hume based his notion of logical necessity on an ideal set within mathematics, Kant let traditional, Aristotelian logic[12] (or rather, his conception of traditional, Aristotelian logic) set the standard for what was conceivable (*i.e.*, logically necessary). Kant believed that traditional logic (as opposed to what he called "transcendental logic," or the logic of the synthetic a priori proposition) "abstracted from all content of experience"; the criteria he used to define analytic propositions were indeed taken directly from the logic of the Aristotelian syllogism.[13] Kant, in other words, established (and fixed) the domain of nonlogical necessity by accepting uncritically the boundary he thought Aristotle had determined for *logical* necessity. This can be seen clearly, for example, in that part of the first *Critique* referred to as the "metaphysical deduction" (K-CI, 104–19). There is the empirical, phenomenal world (wherein the logic of the synthetic a priori laws of science and mathematics

11. Kant's distinction between a priori and a posteriori was by no means a revolutionary one, but was widely employed by philosophers, especially those in the rationalistic tradition in which Kant was trained, prior to his time. Nonetheless, although Kant did not introduce this distinction, it certainly underwent a transformation in his hands. As Lewis White Beck has said, Kant provided "a radically new theory about the *a priori*" (Lewis White Beck, *Studies in the Philosophy of Kant* [New York, 1965], 93). See also K-CI, 65 (A 19), 438 (A 489, B 517) 41 (A 19), 257–75; K-P, 36; P. F. Strawson, *The Bounds of Sense* (London, 1966), 16; A. E. Taylor, *Aristotle* (New York, 1955), 82.

12. Kant called this "general logic"; for the difference between *general logic* and *transcendental logic*, see K-CI, 111 (A76–77).

13. K-CI, 95–96 (B 80, A 56), 262–63 (A 244, B 302–303), 305 (B 363), 487–88 (A 572, B 600), 511–12 (A 610, B 638); Norman Kemp Smith, *A Commentary on Kant's "Critique of Pure Reason"* (New York, 1962), 184; Thoams Kaehao Swing, *Kant's Transcendental Logic* (New Haven, Conn., 1969), 357–58; Bella K. Milmed, *Kant and Current Philosophical Issues* (New York, 1961), 45; Lewis White Beck, "Kant's Theory of Definition," in Moltke S. Gram (ed.), *Kant: Disputed Questions* (New York, 1967), 219, 224; Friedrich Ueberweg, *System of Logic and History of Logical Doctrines* (London, 1871), 5, 32.

reign supreme); and there is also the nonempirical, noumenal world (wherein the laws of traditional logic, of what is conceivable or possible, hold sway). When one asks what exactly is the criterion for distinguishing between these two domains (or, in logical terms, between analytic and synthetic a priori propositions), Kant, like Hume, has no real answer. Kant would say, of course, that one applies to experience, the other does not; that one derives from the laws of logic, the other does not. But how do we know that Newtonian physics and Euclidean geometry, for example, are "right"? Why should we accept Kant's version of Aristotelian logic as abstracting from all content of experience? To cite the laws of noncontradiction, excluded middle, and identity or to say that in an analytic proposition the concept of the predicate is contained in the concept of the subject is to say nothing, for we want to know what the laws of logic mean (*i.e.*, what their application is) and how we are to recognize or know that in a given case the concept of the predicate is contained in the concept of the subject. Just as Hume did not distinguish, but only separated, propositions expressing relations of ideas and matters of fact, so too Kant does not distinguish but only separates analytic and synthetic a priori propositions. He gives us examples of different kinds of propositions and, claiming the authority of traditional logic rather than that of mathematics, as with Hume, says, *This* type is fundamental to our thought processes (*i.e.*, they *have* to be true), but *that* type must be grounded in external reality (*i.e.*, they are presupposed by experience).

There is, however, another important difference between Hume's and Kant's views. In the case of Hume, the autonomous self, or "inner god," who is capable of selecting which of our propositions are empirical and which are logical is wholly implicit. The question "What is the nature of this 'self' that has the power to examine the grounds of its own possibility?" is never asked. In the case of Kant, however, the self is explicitly identified with such a ground of possibility; its home is the realm of noumena. What was only implicit in Hume becomes explicit in Kant—that is, it becomes clear that the empirical criterion of meaning adopted by both philosophers (and used in both cases to justify the propositions of science and undermine those of metaphysics) has as its basis a subjective understanding of possibility. But although Kant explicitly identifies the self with the possibility of experience, his attitude toward what determines the bounds of such possibility—what constitutes the nature of this self which is the "original synthetic unity of apperception," in Kant's technical vocabulary—is still uncritical. He assumes that there is some one range of possibility (defined by Aristotelian logic)[14] against which some one range of contingency (defined by Newtonian physics and Euclidean geometry) can be posited. He assumes, in other words, that reality can be compartmentalized into two domains, the phenomenal and the noumenal. It does not occur to him to ask what justifies drawing the line where he has drawn it (*i.e.*, what justifies Aristotelian logic and Newtonian physics). Like Hume, he gives no real grounds for distinguishing between the empirical and logical features of phenomena other than the inherent power of the self to recognize or see the distinction. In the end Kant, like Hume, masks the normative basis of meaning with an account both empirical and subjective.

4

In the early work of Wittgenstein, represented above all by the *Tractatus Logico-Philosophicus* (published in 1921), many of the fallacies implicit in Hume's and Kant's views are overcome. Wittgenstein's main accomplishment in this work is to bring a fresh perspective, and heightened critical awareness, to the issue of what constitutes logic. This awareness can be seen already in the first line of Wittgenstein's 1914 Notebook: "Logic must take care of itself" (W-N, 2; W-T.5.473). Whatever might be the limits or range of the laws of logic, they cannot be expostulated or circumscribed conceptually by us because we are ourselves subject to them. What is logical must therefore show itself through us (through our language, actions, and thoughts); it cannot be defined abstractly by us.[15]

Wittgenstein's revolutionary ideas about logic in the *Tractatus*

14. That Kant's transcendental logic was constructed in the shadow of general or formal logic is shown by those sections of the "Transcendental Analytic" that deal with the metaphysical and transcendental deductions of the categories of the pure understanding. See K-CI, 57 (B 23), 487–89, 162 (B 147), 220 (B 236, A 191), 181 (B 178, A 139); Milmed, *Kant*, 73, 117; Smith, *Commentary*, 177.

15. See W-T.3.031, 4.0312, 5.4731, 5.5563, 5.61, 6.123, 6.124, 6.111, 6.13; W-N, 2, 4, 9, 99; G. E. M. Anscombe, *An Introduction to Wittgenstein's "Tractatus"* (London, 1959),

were, in part, an attack on what he referred to as the "traditional logic" (*alte Logik*) (W-T.4.126; W-N, 89, 108) or the "old conception of logic" (W-T.6.125), which included, it is generally agreed, not just Aristotelian logic but the logic of Frege and Russell.[16] This old logic was flawed because, according to Wittgenstein, it treated logic as a system of laws that could be clearly stated and then applied to our reasoning processes (as, for example, the rules of basketball might be stated and then applied to the playing of the game).[17] But for Wittgenstein what was logical was presupposed in our thought and language and could not be formulated by them; to do this would require another, extrahuman form of thought and language. Language, he proposed, is really a "logical picture" of reality; it mirrors the world (W-N, 5; W-T.4.01). But language mirrors the world not, of course, by duplicating it but by symbolically representing it (W-T.5.511). Between language and the world there exists an identical structure such that the elements that make up language (propositions and names) are arranged in a configuration identical to that in which the elements of the world (facts and objects) are arranged. It is this identical structure that Wittgenstein referred to when he called language a logical picture of the world. Propositions are determinate arrangements of names; what determines their arrangement is the way objects are arranged in facts.

What allows language to represent reality, therefore, is that it has a form or structure in common with reality. This form or structure, by virtue of the fact that it is the basis of our languages, cannot be represented in language ("A picture cannot . . . depict its pictorial form; it displays it") (T.2.172, 2.174). Logic can thus be shown by a correct logical notation, but this notation cannot, in turn, describe itself: "My fundamental idea is . . . that there can be no representatives of the logic of facts."[18]

165; James C. Morrison, *Meaning and Truth in Wittgenstein's "Tractatus"* (The Hague, 1968), 71–72, 76, 86.

16. Rush Rhees, "Questions on Logical Inference," in Godfrey Vesey (ed.), *Understanding Wittgenstein* (New York, 1974), 44; Brian McGuinness, "The Grundgedanke of the Tractatus," in Godfrey Vesey (ed.), *Understanding Wittgenstein* (New York, 1974), 50; Max Black, *A Companion to Wittgenstein's "Tractatus"* (Ithaca, N.Y., 1964), 198, 337.

17. See W-T.5.132, 4.01; N, 5.

18. W-T.4.0312. This is why there can be no logical objects and why the logical con-

Wittgenstein recognized, of course, that not all the elements of our languages picture reality; language is possessed of many arbitrary or conventional signs replaceable by other signs. His point, however, was that what is not arbitrary in any language or logical notation is that which is common to all signs that can be replaced by one another—and such a common element or elements will derive not from the signs themselves, but from the properties of the world that make the languages possible.[19]

But what are the properties of the world that make any language possible? Wittgenstein's answer in the *Tractatus* is a difficult one. However, a rough idea of what he had in mind is this: Our languages possess names that "go proxy," or stand for, nonmaterial objects in the world (W-T.2.023). The notion of objects is Wittgenstein's basic ontological principle: "Objects make up the substance of the world" (W-T.2.021). It is the ability of names to stand for objects that enables language to be connected to reality—that makes for what Wittgenstein calls the "possibility of propositions" (W-T.4.0312). These names, or simples, however, never appear in isolation but only in combination in the form of propositions (W-T.2.0122, 2.0121); they represent not so much objects in the ordinary sense as possibilities of the combination of objects—which is to say, possibilities of facts.[20] To say that language and reality possess a common structural form is therefore to say that the form of names in propositions mirrors the form of objects in facts.

Wittgenstein's conception of logic differs from that of either Hume or Kant in two striking ways. First, logic does not constitute a separate sphere apart from the empirical world but is built into it. "Logic pervades the world: the limits of the world are also its limits" (W-T.5.61). Second, precisely because logic forms the structural basis of the empirical world and can't be separated from it, logic is not in

stants are operations. See W-T.5.46; N, 40; Morrison, *Meaning and Truth*, 55; McGuinness, "The Grundgedanke of the Tractatus," in Vesey, *Understanding Wittgenstein*, 52.

19. See W-T.3.341, 3.3411, 3.344, 5.47, 5.512, 6.022; N, 15, 60, 90, 113; Anscombe, *Introduction "Tractatus,"* 61–62.

20. W-T.2.0121; N, 60; Anscombe, *Introduction "Tractatus,"* 110–11; Morrison, *Meaning and Truth*, 21–22; P.M.S. Hacker, *Insight and Illusion* (Oxford, 1972), 42–43; Garth Hallett, *Wittgenstein's Definition of Meaning as Use* (New York, 1967), 28. For the later Wittgenstein's criticism of his earlier notions, see W-PI, secs. 47, 55, 58.

any sense an empirical (material or mental) element *of* this world, but rather must be radically distinguished from it. Logic cannot be accounted for empirically, because it is itself the basis of all empirical accounts.

These features of Wittgenstein's notions about logic can be illustrated by his solution to the age-old problem of what it is to make a false assertion. The problem might be put compactly as follows: If a true statement consists in a correspondence between fact and belief, then in the case of a false statement there will be no fact corresponding to the belief. So how can there be a belief in the first place? How can it make sense to say something falsely? Wittgenstein's answer is implicit in his picture theory of language. A statement has sense or meaning (that is, meaning as *Sinn*, not *Bedeutung*)[21] when it has a logical structure or form in common with reality, which means that it consists in some possible arrangement of names (these possibilities being given by the objects for which the names stand). Whether any given possible arrangement does or does not in fact turn out to be the case—whether the proposition is true or false—must be empirically determined. Whether or not the proposition has sense, however, depends only on whether it is a *possible* arrangement. The meaning of a proposition, therefore, consists in the possibility of its being true or false, but this possibility is independent of the *fact* that the proposition is true—or the *fact* that the proposition is false. In this way, the empirical and logical aspects of phenomena are distinguished, not separated; the possibility that a proposition be true or false is not something that can be separated from the fact that it is true or that it is false (*i.e.*, one cannot talk about such a possibility without also giving the form in which the proposition would in fact be called true or false). At the same time, this possibility is clearly distinguishable from either of these two facts (*i.e.*, we say that a proposition *could* be true or false).[22]

By empirical and logical, then, we have—in contrast to Hume and Kant—not two different spheres of reality grounded in two different types of processes (one material, the other mental), but rather two different aspects or ways of viewing the same reality. There is

21. The early Wittgenstein used the term *Bedeutung* to connote "reference."
22. W-T.4.023, 4.061; Morrison, *Meaning and Truth*, 110–127.

that which can be "said"; this refers to all those propositions that can be verified as true or false and that are grounded in empirical reality. And there is that which can only be "shown." The latter kinds of propositions cannot be verified as true or false, because they form the logical basis of all possible verification; they lend sense or meaning to empirically true or false propositions (more precisely, that such propositions can be verified as true or false *shows* their meaning).

Wittgenstein, in comparison with Hume and Kant, thus brings a more critical understanding to logical necessity, to that which determines the range of what is possible or conceivable. For Wittgenstein, such necessity applies as much to thought and language as to world and reality; it cannot, therefore, be given in language or thought. That is, what is possible cannot be stated in the form of the laws of logic and then applied to our thoughts and statements to determine what has sense and what is nonsense. Rather, the laws of logic can only be grasped from within thought and language. Whatever is thought or said already obeys these laws:

> We cannot say in logic, "The world has this in it, and this, but not that." For that would appear to presuppose that we were excluding certain possibilities, and this cannot be the case, since it would require that logic should go beyond the limits of the world; for only in that way could it view those limits from the other side as well. (W-T.5.61)
>
> Thought can never be of anything illogical, since, if it were, we should have to think illogically. (W-T.3.03)
>
> Logic is not a field in which *we* express what we wish with the help of signs, but rather one in which the nature of the natural and inevitable signs speaks for itself (W-T.6.124).

5

Notwithstanding its achievements in certain respects, Wittgenstein's philosophy in the *Tractatus* bears more than a passing resemblance to the Kantian architectonic of the first two *Critique* volumes; the transition from the early to the late philosophy is a long and difficult one. As a means of understanding why Wittgenstein's later philosophy was not marked by any sort of plunge into relativism or conventionalism—a point that is extremely important in grasping the nature of his later work as a whole—let us now briefly examine this transitional period.

Kant's inquiry centered upon the question "How is it possible that we have knowledge?" This question was actually sufficient only when applied to the natural sciences, for in the areas of metaphysics and morals, it was necessary to ask not only *how* knowledge is possible, but *is* it possible? Kant, in other words, took it for granted that the sciences gave us knowledge; it was only a question of explaining how it did so. But in metaphysics and morals, the situation was very different, for it wasn't obvious that there were objects to which our beliefs in these areas could correspond. Kant ended by maintaining that knowledge in metaphysics was *not* possible—and that moral knowledge has a subjective basis in the self.

Wittgenstein's approach to these problems in the *Tractatus* is generally similar to that of Kant's, except that he gives a larger role to logic and language and a smaller one to metaphysics and morals than did Kant. Like Kant, Wittgenstein makes a sharp distinction between the empirical and conceptual orders of reality. On the conceptual side, there is language, which is made up of propositions, which are in turn made up of elementary propositions, which are in turn made up of names. On the empirical side, there is the world, which is made up of facts, which are in turn made up of atomic facts, which are in turn made up of objects. Between each of these components of the conceptual and empirical realms, there exists a correspondence: names refer to objects, propositions to facts, and language to world.

Wittgenstein connects these two orders of reality through his picture theory of language, which is ultimately founded on the ability of names to go proxy for objects. But despite the all important role given to objects in Wittgenstein's theory, he does not give a single example of an object. The reason for this is that from Wittgenstein's point of view, it was not necessary to give such examples; his investigation into the nature of language was a priori and not concerned with matters of fact or any existing states of affairs in the world. Just as Kant asked how it is possible for us to have scientific knowledge of the world—all the while assuming we did have such knowledge and limiting his investigations to the conditions necessary in our consciousness and thinking for such knowledge to exist—so too Wittgenstein asked how it is possible for us to make statements about the world, statements which may be true or false and not merely senseless—all the while assuming that our statements do refer to the world and that they therefore possess a structure or form that enables them to do so. Wittgenstein wanted to know only what conditions are necessary for our language to work, what characteristics it must possess in order for it to refer to reality (assuming that it does make such reference). Finding examples of those objects that are in fact dictated by the nature of language is an empirical matter independent of the logical investigation Wittgenstein carried out. (Wittgenstein did, of course, later ridicule this view; see W-PI, sec. 97.)

Since language, for Wittgenstein, is a "picture" of reality, there must exist elements that allow for the possibility of its being an accurate picture of the world. It follows that whatever the differences between various languages, or whatever the conventional or arbitrary elements of any given language, the existence of these elements guarantees that such languages have the capability of representing reality. These elements are fixed and unalterable; they are what all sign languages capable of representing reality have in *common* with one another.

Wittgenstein's philosophy in the *Tractatus* is thus comparable to the Kantian architectonic of the first two *Critiques*. Although he, more than Kant, brings a critical understanding to logic, grounding it in reality, this does not prevent him from positing, like Kant, an otherworldly sphere set in opposition to the empirical one. This otherworldly sphere, unlike Kant's, is a nonlogical one. Its boundaries are not given by an uncritical conception of what constitutes logical necessity; rather, the *Tractatus* otherworld is preeminently the world of what can only be shown, not said. To *try* to say something about it would be to talk "nonsense," for it would be an attempt to say in language what all languages presuppose (it would be an attempt to define the substance of the world).

Wittgenstein believed that this is what the propositions of metaphysics, ethics, and aesthetics try to do; they speak of a realm "outside the world," the realm of what he calls the "metaphysical self." He therefore relegates them to the domain of his otherworld and calls them "nonsensical." But Wittgenstein means by the use of this pejorative term not that such propositions are unimportant, but that they are supraimportant, beyond logic. It is only the presumption that one can express in words what these propositions wish to express that is to be condemned; that what these propositions express is real—or rather, is the basis of reality—Wittgenstein never doubts. His perspective is thus quite similar to that of Kant's, who, in relegating the propositions of metaphysics to a nonempirical domain of mere possibility (the noumenal sphere), wished to place them beyond the reach of any scientific skepticism. Indeed, Wittgenstein's metaphysical self is a rough counterpart of Kant's transcendental self, except that the domain of the metaphysical self is, unlike that of Kant's, an extralogical one. It cannot be defined even in terms of possibility (nothing, strictly speaking, can be said about it). If Kant's noumenal sphere was an "empty space" of mere possibility, Wittgenstein's otherworld might be regarded as an empty noumenon. (Kant's conception of the functions of the sensibility, understanding, and Reason might be compared with Wittgenstein's conception of sense, senselessness, and nonsense.)

Thus, it can be said that although Wittgenstein brought a critical understanding to the nature of logic, the *Tractatus* system as a whole compartmentalizes reality in a way similar to that in which Kant did. In both cases, an otherworld or domain of the metaphysical self is set against an empirical world defined by science. The difference between these two domains is, moreover, fixed; there is one reality (or at least one system of possible worlds) and therefore one correct way of characterizing the nature of this reality. What grounds a proposition is not (as in Wittgenstein's later works) the actual ways in which it is used, but rather that it is made up of a configuration of objects. Its meaning is the possibility of its truth or falsity, and it has this possibility only by being composed of simple signs. From this it follows that the rules of use of language are built into it by virtue of the signs of which it is composed; how a proposition is used will at best help us see this meaning that is already there. The use will in no sense constitute the meaning. Rather, words carry their meaning along with them.

How did Wittgenstein advance from this narrow, nonnormative position to his later open-ended and normative one? The key step was his abandonment of the theory of simples, along with its presumption that there exists some one structure of reality or substance of the world that can be read a priori out of language. It is important, however, not to misunderstand the nature of the change in Wittgenstein's views that took place when he abandoned his theory of simples. The function of this theory was, as noted, to anchor language to reality. In abandoning the theory, then, did Wittgenstein come to the conclusion that language was a kind of autonomous entity that floated freely over the terrain of reality guided only by convention? Some accounts of Wittgenstein's transitional period have actually come close to representing it this way. Although Wittgenstein certainly went through a time of intense philosophical confusion and disorientation, nothing in his writings starting in the early 1930s suggests that he viewed language as autonomous in *that* sense. For the later, quite as much as for the early, Wittgenstein, language was embedded in reality; what the later Wittgenstein rejected was the presumption that it is embedded in reality in any *one* way. Wittgenstein rejected, not the *answer* that the *Tractatus* gave to his question "What is the connection between thought and reality, language and world?" but the *question*. This comes out clearly in a remark he made to Waismann: "Unklar war mir die logische Analyse und die hinsweisende Erklärung. Ich dachte damals, dass es deine 'Verbindung der Sprache mit der Wirklichkeit' gibt." (When I wrote the *Tractatus* I was unclear about logical analysis and ostensive definition. I then thought that there was a "linking up of language and reality") (W-WA, 56).

We do not have to posit some a priori basis by which language is connected to reality; we need merely to accept that they *are* so and then look to see *in what way*, that is, to see in any particular case what kind of language game is being played. It is therefore wrong to say that for the later Wittgenstein the world is "inside language," a view similar to Emile Durkheim's view in *The Elementary Forms of Religious Belief* that the world is "inside society." For the later as much as the early Wittgenstein, language and reality are on an equal footing; they are bound together by one logical structure. Only now this one logical structure is not the *only* one. Rather, there exists a multiplicity of languages and worlds, of "language games" and their accompanying "forms of life," each of which may have various features in common with one another (and therefore be related like members of a family) but no single feature common to all. Within any given language game, the logical or conceptual features may be sharply distinguished from the empirical features (as a standard of measurement may be distinguished from the particular results of measurement, or as a paradigm or model may be distinguished from the judgments made on the basis of the paradigm or model). That is why Wittgenstein throughout his later writings spends so much time and energy providing detailed examinations of concepts and the ways they are expressed in language. What he is doing in all cases is unraveling the logical or grammatical features of our uses of words from their empirical ones; he is trying to show the conceptual features of our language that are presupposed by its use. Of course, it is often difficult to make such distinctions between the empirical and logical features of phenomena, precisely because they always appear in our language and its systems of uses tightly bound together. It is difficult for us to see, for example, that the proposition "Blank is a standard of length" is of a different kind from any proposition giving a particular measurement of length; or that the proposition "Blank are samples of the colors red and yellow" is of a different kind from any particular proposition stating that a given patch is red or is yellow; or that "I have a pain" is a proposition of a totally different kind than "He has a pain." The first proposition in each of these examples has no empirical basis or grounding (much less a causal status); it is rather the standard or norm by which we make empirical judgments. That is, if we lacked a standard of length, we would be unable to make any particular measurement of length in the way we are accustomed to doing. If the statement "I have a pain" were not accepted as incorrigible—as being, to a large extent, incapable of being contradicted—then the meaning of such propositions as "He has a pain" would be quite different. Where and how the line is to be drawn, for any particular phenomenon, between its empirical and logical features cannot be decided a priori, but only through an examination of the forms in which it occurs in our lives.

The sense of the term *logic* thus undergoes a metamorphosis in the later Wittgenstein. Logic is no longer correlated with the empirical, scientific world; it is no longer the structure or form that exists between language and reality. Rather, logic is what belongs to the descriptions of a language game: it cannot be absolutized. The later Wittgenstein does not abandon his Kantian predisposition (apparently inherited through Schopenhauer) to see meaning as logical.

But he has grasped that a *single* logical structure is necessarily an empirically grounded structure—grounded in a particular way of life or set of "hardened" (*erstarrten*) uses (W-OC, sec. 96). To adopt the conceptual structure supplied by Newtonian physics or any other science is but to project the "conditions of our preservation as predicates of being in general," as Nietzsche said. Thus, one of the main purposes of the later Wittgenstein's definition of meaning as use was to keep us from absolutizing certain concepts the way Hume, Kant, and the early Wittgenstein had done, to keep us from believing that certain concepts are absolutely the correct ones. The definition of meaning as use lets logic loose.

6

The later Wittgenstein was not a linguistic philosopher in any usual sense of the term (as G. E. Moore reported, "He did not think . . . that language was the subject matter of philosophy").[23] Nonetheless, he certainly was concerned to a large extent with the question, in Rush Rhees's words, "of how words mean" (W-RR, 55). To aid himself in answering this question, Wittgenstein fashioned, among others, two conceptual tools—the notions of *language games* and *forms of life*. As he employed these terms, they had at least three major functions. First, they allowed him to conceive of the meanings of words in terms of both the linguistic and nonlinguistic contexts in which the words occur. Thus, the first section in which the term *language game* occurs in *Philosophical Investigations* states: "I shall . . . call the whole, consisting of language *and the actions* into which it is woven, the language game" [emphasis mine] (W-PI, sec. 7). Similarly, the first section in which the term *form of life* occurs states: "To imagine a language game is to imagine a form of life" (W-PI, sec. 19).

For Wittgenstein, language and reality were inseparably connected—not in the sense that our linguistic categories determine reality, but in the sense that we cannot say anything about one without

23. W-PP, 257. See also W-PP, 324; W-WCII, 97; W-LC, 2, 3; W-PI, secs. 108, 649; Derek L. Phillips, *Wittgenstein and Scientific Knowledge* (New York, 1977), 40–41; Peter Winch, *The Idea of a Social Science* (London, 1958), 15; Hacker, *Insight*, 124; Hallett, *Wittgenstein's Definition*, 102, 108, 158, 163, 166, 195; William Donald Hudson, *Wittgenstein and Religious Belief* (New York, 1975), 8, 14–15; Bernard Williams, "Wittgenstein and Idealism," in Godfrey Vesey (ed.), *Understanding Wittgenstein* (New York, 1974), 86.

revealing some feature of the other. Language is grounded in a context of human behavior and actions: "It is not a kind of seeing on our part; it is our *acting* which lies at the bottom of the language game" (W-OC, sec. 204; *see* 110). Forms of life are just these ways of acting. As Finch says, "Forms of life are established patterns of actions shared in by members of a group."[24] These patterns of actions cannot themselves be conceptually justified (for they are the basis of all conceptual justification): "Why should the language game rest on some kind of knowledge? . . . You must bear in mind that the language game is so to say something unpredictable. I mean: it is not based on grounds. It is not reasonable (or unreasonable). . . . It is there—like our life" (W-OC, sec. 559). Or speaking of what constitutes an adequate test for the truth of our assertions:

> If someone is taught to calculate, is he also taught that he can rely on a calculation of his teacher's? But these explanations must after all sometime come to an end. Will he also be taught that he can trust his senses—since he is indeed told in many cases that in such and such a special case you *cannot* trust them? (W-OC, sec. 34)
>
> What *counts* as its test? "But is this an adequate test? And, if so, must it not be recognizable as such in logic?" As if giving grounds did not come to an end sometime. But the end is not an ungrounded presupposition: it is an ungrounded way of acting. (W-OC, sec. 110)

Although Wittgenstein said that the best way to approach the solution to philosophical problems is through an examination of the uses of words, he added, "That does not mean that I want to talk only about words. . . . Your questions refer to words; so I have to talk about words" (W-PI, sec. 120).

Wittgenstein talks a great deal about the uses of words because he thinks that doing so provides a good method for revealing the nature of the phenomena of which words are a part. In particular, such a method helps one avoid the trap—which linguistic and other philosphers fall into—of thinking of language as a sort of autonomous, conceptual process that points to an underlying, empirical reality. Language is an element of reality, not a third eye hovering outside it. Wittgenstein asks: "Did we invent human speech? No more than we

---

24. Henry LeRoy Finch, *Wittgenstein: The Later Philosophy* (Atlantic Highland, N.J., 1977), 90.

invented walking on two legs" (W-RPII, sec. 435). Elsewhere he says, "The term 'language *game*' is meant to bring into prominence the fact that the *speaking* of language is part of an activity, or of a form of life" (W-PI, sec. 23); and: "Words are also deeds" (W-PI, sec. 546).

The second major function that Wittgenstein's notions of language games and forms of life served was that they allowed him to conceive of meaning in terms of a loosely structured, logical framework or range of possibility. In the early Wittgenstein's view, the "old logic" was flawed because it treated logic as a system of laws that could be abstractly formulated and then applied to our reasoning processes; it presupposed a self capable of examining the grounds of its own possibility, an inner god that could reliably assure itself of what it could and could not conceive, that is, of what was and was not possible. For the early Wittgenstein, on the other hand, what was logical, what marked the limits of what was possible, was presupposed in our thought and language and could not be formulated by them; to do this would require another, extrahuman form of thought and language (W-T.2.0121). Logic could be shown by a correct logical notation, but this notation could not in turn describe itself. The early Wittgenstein writes: "The fact that the propositions of logic are tautologies *shows* the formal—logical—properties of language and the world" (W-T.612). He also says: "There is no such thing as the subject that thinks or entertains ideas" (W-T.5.631); and: "The subject does not belong to the world; rather; it is a limit of the world" (W-T.5.632).

In his later work, Wittgenstein radically changed his views from what they had been in the *Tractatus*. Nonetheless, important features in Wittgenstein's critique of the old logic are retained in his concept of language games: logic is the possibilities presupposed by or implicit in our use of language.[25] It is what is presupposed in our description of a language game: "Everything descriptive of a language game" he says, "is part of logic" (W-OC, sec. 56). And: "Understanding the description itself already presupposes that he has learned something" (W-RC, sec. 121).

To "do" logic is thus not to detach oneself from one's immediate

25. W-WCII, 12–13, 21, 99, 124, 138–39, 143; W-WCI, 54; W-PI, secs. 81, 90, 242; Hacker, *Insight*, 98, 103.

frame of reference, that is, to appeal to some rule or law that can be applied a priori. Logical status is context-dependent,[26] and to do logic is to be "self-conscious about all the possible uses of language."[27] Logic, Wittgenstein says, is rooted not in something that can be called an assumption or presupposition, but in a way of acting: "It belongs to the logic of our scientific investigations that certain things are in deed not doubted" (W-OC, sec. 342; *see* 401). Logic is something "animal": "I want to regard man here as an animal; as a primitive being to which one grants instinct but not ratiocination. As a creature in a primitive state. Any logic good enough for a primitive means of communication needs no apology from us. Language did not emerge from some kind of ratiocination" (W-OC, sec. 475). Logic is based on something nonlogical: "If I have exhausted the justifications I have reached bedrock, and my spade is turned. Then I am inclined to say: 'This is simply what I do'" (W-PI, sec. 217). And: "When I obey a rule, I do not choose. I obey the rule *blindly*" (W-PI, sec. 219).

But if logic is so concrete, so deeply rooted in the morphology of behavior, how can one even *talk* about logic? The answer is that one cannot talk *about* logic from a standpoint outside logic; what one can do is note the language game, describe it, and thereby *reveal* the logic: "Am I not getting closer and closer to saying that in the end logic cannot be described? You must look at the practice of language, then you will see it" (W-OC, sec. 501). Or, as Morawetz puts Wittgenstein's view: "Propositions of logic do not describe logic."[28] We thus make contact in Wittgenstein's later work with one of the essential tenets of his earlier work: that logic can only be shown, not stated. The reason, again, is that logic, being the structure of action, is also the structure of thought, because "thought is an event,"[29] in

26. Thomas Morawetz, *Wittgenstein and Knowledge: The Importance of "On Certainty"* (Amherst, 1978), 47.

27. *Ibid.*, 51.

28. *Ibid.*

29. W-WCI, 34. See also W-WCI, 26, 117; W-Z, secs. 101, 104, 105, 114–16, 125, 126, 605, 606; W-PG, 27, 114, 155, 160, 172. Thought is rooted in action, but it is not a "mental activity"; this phrase is misleading because it makes it sound as though thought were a special, mysterious activity. See W-BB, 6–7, 16, 43; W-PI, secs. 329, 332,

Wittgenstein's words, and is rooted in action: "If I say 'we *assume* that the earth has existed for many years past' (or something similar), then of course it sounds strange that we should *assume* such a thing. But in the entire system of our language-games it belongs to the foundations. The assumption, we might say, forms the basis of action, and therefore, naturally, of thought" (W-OC, sec. 411).

As in the *Tractatus*, Wittgenstein viewed meaning in terms of possibility, thereby both distinguishing and connecting the realms of Hume's relations of ideas and matters of fact. But his understanding of the nature of possibility—of what logic was based on—wholly changed. Meaning became for him not primarily cognitive, but rather normative, given not by what is possibly true or false, but by the rules or norms embedded in use, which can include, but is by no means limited to, cognitive elements.[30]

Finch brings this point out clearly in his discussion of Wittgenstein's concept of criteria. He begins by observing that "criteria are somewhat like the logical forms of the *Tractatus*, which establish possibilities of sense prior to the assertion of facts."[31] He then makes the all-important point: "Criteria . . . must be understood in a wider way than the *Tractatus* manner of speaking suggests, because criteria provide the loci for every kind of 'going wrong' (and not just the case of falsity). . . . Criteria by supplying what is accepted as correct ways of speaking give us what we may be wrong about, deceived about, under an illusion about. . . . However a criterion fails, it still sets up a usage which covers being right and also all these cases of being wrong because whichever way it turns out, we are right or wrong about the same thing or in the same way."[32]

The point is not just that we can't restrict our concepts of logic and meaning to cognitive statements, but that even if we accept that a proposition is "whatever can be true or false" (as Wittgenstein some-

---

p. 212; W-WCII, 54–55, 115; W-RPII, secs. 7, 18, 20, 184, 186, 187, 194, 213, 214, 220, 248, 257, 266, 565; Finch, *Later Philosophy*, 213, 215–216.

30. This is the dominant theme that runs through Wittgenstein's last work, *On Certainty* (W-OC).

31. Finch, *Later Philosophy*, 56.

32. *Ibid.*, 62, 57.

times did; see W-PI, sec. 136), what we call a proposition is more or less arbitrary, which is to say, in Wittgenstein's words: "what we call logic plays a different role from that which Russell and Frege supposed. We mean all sorts of things by 'proposition' and build up logic from that" (W-WCII, 12–13).

For example, examining a number of language games, Wittgenstein asks: "Now what role do truth and falsity play in such language-games? In the game where the child responds by pointing to colors, truth and falsity do not come in. If the game consists in question and answer and the child responds, say, to the question 'How many chairs?' by giving the number, again truth and falsity may not come in, though it might if the child were taught to reply 'Six chairs agrees with reality'" (W-WCII, 12).

The later Wittgenstein's definition of meaning as use thus forces us to give up any a priori distinction between what is empirical and logical, between the sayable and the unsayable, and between what can be cognitively justified and what can only be shown or revealed through description. These distinctions are, for the later Wittgenstein, always *there*, but always different. Indeed, no statement for Wittgenstein is intrinsically empirical or logical, whether it be "Two and two equals four" or "The sun will rise tomorrow": "*A priori* and empirical are not two kinds of propositions—the same expression can be an hypothesis or a proposition in a strict sense. So also a proposition can be *a priori* or empirical."[33]

One can legitimately say that a given statement is universally and necessarily true (or false), but only if one attaches the qualifier "by virtue of the way we have always used it." How the distinction between the empirical and the logical is drawn depends on the particular language games and forms of life of the people who are making it. Meaning is normative and logic is a "normative science."[34] Thus, Wittgenstein says: "If language is to be a means of communication, there must be agreement not only in definitions but also (queer as

33. W-WCI, 76–77. See also Hanna Fenichel Pitkin, *Wittgenstein and Justice* (Berkeley, 1972), 136.

34. W-PI, sec. 81. It is doubtful that Ramsey meant this phrase in a sense similar to that of Wittgenstein.

this may sound) in judgments. This seems to abolish logic, but does not do so" (W-PI, sec. 242). It does not abolish logic but transforms logic into the description of language games.

That is why Wittgenstein calls even mathematics an anthropological phenomenon: "What I'm saying comes to this, that mathematics is normative."[35] It is also why he would have regarded Hume's implied view that two and two equals four in any universe as senseless and why he relates even the concept of thinking to the norms of a way of life: "Now if we were to see creatures at work whose rhythm of work, play of expression, etc. was like our own, but for their not speaking, perhaps in that case we should say that they thought, considered, made decisions. That is: in such a case there would be a *great deal* which is similar to the action of ordinary humans. And it isn't clear *how much* has to be similar for us to have a right to apply to them also the concept 'thinking', which has its home in *our* life" (W-RPII, sec. 186).

Similarly, Wittgenstein emphasizes the normative character of our aesthetic judgments: "It is remarkable that in real life, when aesthetic judgements are made, aesthetic adjectives such as 'beautiful', 'fine', etc., play hardly any role at all. Are aesthetic adjectives used in a musical criticism? You say: 'Look at this transition' or 'The passage here is incoherent.' Or you say, in a poetical criticism, 'His use of images is precise.' The words you use are more akin to 'right' and 'correct' (as these words are used in ordinary speech) than to 'beautiful' and 'lovely'" (W-LC, 3).

He also emphasizes the normative character of our judgments about other languages: "We constantly judge a language from the standpoint of the language we are accustomed to" (W-WCII, 21). That we can even doubt is normatively grounded: "Why is it not possible for me to doubt that I have never been on the moon? And how could I try to doubt it? First and foremost, the supposition that perhaps I have been there would strike me as *idle*. Nothing would

35. W-RFM, bk. V, sec. 40; see also sec. 46. Wittgenstein is especially emphatic about the normative character of mathematics. See W-RFM, bk. I, secs. 9, 159, app. I, sec. 4; W-RFM, bk. II, secs. 18, 26, 28, 42; Hacker, *Insight*, 155; Phillips, *Scientific Knowledge*, 126.

follow from it, nothing would be explained by it. It would not tie in with anything in my life" (W-OC, sec. 117).

Thus, what human beings mean when they use language can't be detached from who they are and how they live: "I did not get my picture of the world by satisfying myself of its correctness; nor do I have it because I am satisfied of its correctness. No: it is the inherited background against which I distinguish between true and false."[36]

Wittgenstein's notion of language games is thus very different from the pedestrian concept it may at first sight appear to be. It entails the view that there exist loosely formed structures or systems of uses that provide the tracks along which meaning (and nonsense) run. Our thoughts and actions follow courses, exhibit forms, show patterns—all in a multitude of overlapping, intertwining ways. Such channels of meaning, however, are not things of a special nature (that is, subjective entities or processes added onto or accompanying phenomena); they cannot be explained or interpreted as though they were discrete substances any more than logic in the *Tractatus* could be stated. All explanations and interpretations are themselves part of a logical or conceptual framework; they are not explanations or interpretations of that framework.

For Wittgenstein, our perspective or point of view is not something that "gives" meaning to phenomena or events; the philosopher needn't rummage around in his mind for the right ideas or concepts (like Plato's philodoxers). Rather, the meaning is already there, embedded in the framework. That is why Wittgenstein declares: "We must do away with all *explanation*, and description alone must take its place."[37] After the early 1930s, by "explanation" (*Erklärung*), Wittgenstein means empirical, scientific, or causal explanation. The use of the word *description*, on the other hand, conveys Wittgenstein's conviction that meaning does not have to be invented or posited, but is simply there. "Don't think, but look!" he says, meaning we should

36. W-OC, sec. 94. For Wittgenstein's efforts to dissolve the division between mind and matter or between the mental world and the physical world, see W-OC, secs. 97, 98, 124; W-RPII, sec. 652; W-BB, 47; W-WCI, 80.

37. W-PI, sec. 109. See also W-RC, sec. 55. On the concept of interpretation, see W-PI, pp. 198, 201; W-PG, 23, 144, 147–48.

take off our conceptual blinders and see what is all around us (W-PI, sec. 66).

Like St. Augustine, whom he deeply admired, Wittgenstein believed that the philosopher must open himself to the meanings that permeate his existence; he must not close himself off from such meanings by objectifying them, by making that which *grounds* all interpretation and explanation itself *subject* to interpretation and explanation. Wittgenstein writes in *On Certainty*, which was composed during the last eighteen months of his life: "I really want to say that a language-game is only possible if one trusts something (I did not say 'can trust something')" (W-OC, sec. 509). Elsewhere in that same work, he says: "My *life* consists in my being content to accept many things" (W-OC, sec. 344).

7

The third major function served by Wittgenstein's use of the notions of language games and forms of life is that they allowed him to show how no particular language game or form of life could be absolutized. This point is closely bound up with Wittgenstein's concept of "family resemblance," which entailed a denial that the meaning of a word, for example, *game*, consists in what is *common* to all games. For Wittgenstein, there exists a multitude of overlapping connections or family resemblances between games, but no one element common to them all; any account of the meaning of a word must therefore take this complexity into account and not assume that there is a single element—usually thought of as a kind of ethereal, mental substance—that lies behind all instances of the phenomenon. The account of meaning as that which is common to all instances of the phenomenon necessarily objectifies meaning by separating it from those instances; what is common to all the phenomena cannot be any *one* of the phenomena. It must therefore be a special sort of substance in its own right.

But such a notion does not merely objectify meaning, it also absolutizes it. If meaning is that which is common to all the phenomena (and necessarily separate from the phenomena), then it is also neutral in regard to any *particular* phenomena. To understand is, therefore, to place oneself in an extraphenomenal, nonnormative position, whereas to be objective is to remove oneself to a privileged position common to all the phenomena. For Wittgenstein, by contrast:

> We want to establish an order in our knowledge of the use of language: an order with a particular end in view; one out of many possible orders; not *the* order. (W-PI, sec. 132; see W-NLPE, 305)
>
> We could say people's concepts show what matters to them and what doesn't. But it's not as if this explained the particular concepts they have. It is only to rule out the view that we have the right concepts and other people the wrong ones. (W-RC, sec. 293)
>
> Men have judged that a king can make rain; *we* say this contradicts all experience. Today they judge that aeroplanes and the radio etc. are means for the closer contact of peoples and the spread of culture. (W-OC, sec. 132)

But Wittgenstein opposes what could be called conceptual absolutism not just through his notion of family resemblance, but also through the use of a technique he refers to as the invention of "fictitious natural history." This technique is employed extensively in Wittgenstein's later writing. It consists of, first, imagining a form of life or a people whose manner of acting, seeing, calculating, thinking, hoping, etc., is radically different from our own; and, second, comparing such fictitious natural history to our own real natural history. Such fictitious natural history is not meant, of course, to be taken seriously for itself, but rather it is intended to throw light on the meaning of our own practices and beliefs.[38] By these comparisons, Wittgenstein tries to show that no concepts that man employs can be treated as absolutely the correct ones: "If anyone believes that certain concepts are absolutely the correct ones, and that having different ones would mean not realizing something that we realize—then let him imagine certain very general facts of nature to be different from what we are used to, and the formation of concepts different from the usual ones will become intelligible to him" (W-PI, p. 230; see W-Z, sec. 350).

What Wittgenstein is saying here is best understood as an expression of humility regarding man's situation and therefore precisely opposite in spirit (and content) to any form of relativism or conventionalism. Indeed, from Wittgenstein's point of view, the relativist, in

---

38. Wittgenstein says this explicitly in such passages as W-RPII, secs. 47, 578, 605, 606, 707.

maintaining that all differing points of view may be treated as equal in status, assumes that there exists a stance from which all points of view may be treated *as* equal in status (and once this assumption is made explicit, it becomes clear that relativism is just a disguised—and, therefore, especially dangerous—form of conceptual absolutism).

The normative concept of meaning, however, disallows such relativism:

> Being acquainted with many languages prevents us from taking quite seriously a philosophy which is laid down in the forms of any one. But here we are blind to the fact that we ourselves have strong prejudices for, and against, certain forms of expression; that this very piling up of a lot of languages results in our having a particular picture. (W-Z, sec. 323)
>
> If you say there are various systems of ethics you are not saying they are all equally right. That means nothing. Just as it would have no meaning to say that each was right from his own standpoint. That could only mean that each judges as he does. (W-RR, 101)

Wittgenstein's philosophical method encourages us when we use such words as *relative, conventional,* or *arbitrary,* to ask ourselves, Relative to what?, Conventional according to what standard?, Arbitrary by what norm? The point is that there is nothing *there* to be relative *to*; meaning *is* normative. That is to say, there is nothing outside the rules, norms, and values that justifies obeying or disobeying them, for they *are* the logical space in which we act and think:

> You can only get hold of the meaning of a word through the rule with which you use the word. . . . If you say that the rules of grammar are arbitrary, you perhaps expect some further set of rules to justify them. But these rules will then in turn need justification. Grammar is self-contained. . . . To say that the earth is not supported is exactly similar to saying that language is not supported (though we only speak of supporting where the earth is concerned, and not elsewhere). The whole chain of our reasoning is not supported any more than the earth is supported; the whole of grammar is not supported in the sense that a sentence is supported by reality. You can't in fact call language or grammar unsupported because there is no question of its being supported.[39]

39. W-WCI, 86–87, 104. See also W-WCI, 36, 39, 48, 49, 57–58; W-Z, secs. 357, 358, 431; W-PP, 278–79; W-RFM, bk. II, sec. 42; W-PG, 13; Finch, *Later Philosophy,*

Wittgenstein speaks of language and its rules of use as being arbitrary only to emphasize its logical, presuppositional, and nonempirical features: "Rules are arbitrary in the sense that they are not responsible to some sort of reality—they are not similar to natural laws; nor are they responsible to some meaning the word already has. . . . The objection that the rules are not arbitrary comes from the feeling that they are responsible to meaning. But how is the meaning of 'negation' defined, if not by the rules? . . . The rules constitute the meaning, and are not responsible to it." [40]

No one is more insistent than Wittgenstein that we are wedded to certain uses and practices (linguistic and otherwise) that we could not shake off easily or at all and that are therefore far from being arbitrary for us:

> Can I then not use words to mean what I like?—Look at the door of your room, utter a sequence of random sounds and mean by them a description of that door.
>
> Different people are very different in their sensitiveness about changes in the orthography of a word. And the feeling is not just piety toward an old use.—If for you spelling is just a practical question, the feeling you are lacking in is not unlike the one that a "meaning-blind" man would lack. [41]

It is for a similar reason that Wittgenstein finds the notion of a purely *invented* language so unappealing: "Esperanto. The feeling of disgust we get if we utter an *invented* word with invented derivative syllables. The word is cold, lacking in associations, and yet it plays at being 'language'. A system of purely written signs would not disgust us so much" (W-VM, 52).

Wittgenstein's opposition to relativism and conventionalism is thus ultimately grounded in his concept of meaning; relativism requires a reference point to be relative *to*, an object—material or mental—that lies outside the norms and rules of language. It is precisely such a concept of meaning as object (found in the views of comparative religionists, as well as of Hume and Kant) that

---

156–57; Barry Stroud, "Wittgenstein and Logical Necessity," in E. D. Klemke (ed.), *Essays on Wittgenstein* (Urbana, Ill., 1971), 447–63.

40. W-WCII, 4. See also W-WCII, 65–66, 69, 155–57; W-Z, sec. 320; W-PG, 186.

41. W-Z, secs. 184 and 5, respectively. See also W-Z, secs. 6, 375; W-BB, 57; W-PI, sec. 520.

Wittgenstein is everywhere concerned to combat: "We are up against one of the great sources of philosophical bewilderment: a substantive makes us look for a thing that corresponds to it" (W-BB, 1).

Wittgenstein's opposition to such a concept of meaning can be illustrated by his views on two closely related topics: the correspondence theory of truth and negation. His basic point in regard to the correspondence theory (which in Bertrand Russell's classic formulation states that truth is the agreement of belief and fact) is that what we recognize as fact and what we recognize as belief are not structured by a reality external to language. Rather, it is language that directs us to acknowledge what is a fact and what is not a fact—and therefore what corresponds to one. And this directing power of language is not a priori, but given through use and practice. For Wittgenstein, it is therefore perfectly acceptable to say that truth is the agreement of a belief with a fact, so long as it is understood that what reality is, is defined by the language game:

> If everything speaks *for* an hypothesis and nothing against it, is it objectively *certain*? One can *call* it that. But does it *necessarily* agree with the world of facts? At the very best it shows us what "agreement" means. (W-OC, sec. 203)

> What prevents me from supposing that this table either vanishes or alters its shape and colour when no one is observing it, and then when someone looks at it changes back to its old condition? "But who is going to suppose such a thing!"—one would feel like saying.
>
> Here we see that the idea of "agreement with reality" does not have any clear application. (W-OC, secs. 214–15)

Or as he says in the *Investigations*: "The proposition that only a proposition can be true or false can say no more than that we only predicate 'true' and 'false' of what we call a proposition. And what a proposition is is in one sense determined by the rules of sentence formation (in English for example), and in another sense by the use of the sign in the language-game. And the use of the words 'true' and 'false' may be among the constituent parts of this game; and if so it *belongs* to our concept 'proposition' but does not '*fit*' it" (W-PI, sec. 136). Which is to say that the truth or falsity of a proposition is not something *external to* the proposition; it can be distinguished but not separated from it.

If what is true or false, however, is given by the logical framework (or way of defining what agreement with reality is) in which we make true and false statements, then does not at least this logical structure correspond to something factual, such as the facts of nature? For Wittgenstein the facts of nature are themselves given by certain categories of language games and life forms. There are no absolutely correct concepts, simply because there are no absolutely correct facts of nature that we can identify as causes of those concepts. There exist, of course, correspondences between facts and ideas, but the basis of such correspondences is not empirical, but rather embedded in our language games: "The laws of nature . . . are part of language and of our way of describing things" (W-WCI, 79). Conversely, our language activities are as much a part of natural history as any other, more biological activity: "Commanding, questioning, recounting, chatting are as much a part of our natural history as walking, eating, drinking, playing" (W-PI, sec. 25).

Our propensity to view meaning as an object, however, underlies not just the correspondence theory of truth, but many common philosophical notions about negation (which is, in turn, connected with our notions about contradiction, excluded middle, and a host of other philosophical puzzles that cannot be examined here).[42] Wittgenstein writes: "It is sometimes asked, how can we negate a proposition? For if not p is true there is nothing to correspond to it; there is only something to correspond to p when p is true. What corresponds to 'the door is not open' when it is open? But there is a false analogy here; p does not correspond to *something*" (W-WCI, 52). In reality, "the grammatical rules applying to it determine the meaning of a word. Its meaning is not something else, some object to which it corresponds or does not correspond. The word carries its meaning with it; it has a grammatical body behind it, so to speak. Its meaning cannot be something else which may not be known" (W-WCI, 59). Negation must be understood normatively:

Negation, one must say, is a gesture of exclusion, of rejection. But such a gesture is used in a great variety of cases!

42. See W-WCI, 92; W-PI, sec. 352; W-PP, 302; W-RPII, sec. 290; B. H. Slater, "Wittgenstein's Later Logic," *Philosophy*, LIV (1979), 201–204.

Does the *same* negation occur in: "Iron does not melt at a hundred degrees Centigrade" and "Twice two is not five"? Is this to be decided by introspection; by trying to see what we are *thinking* as we utter the two sentences? . . . It looks as if it followed from the nature of negation that a double negative is an affirmative. (And there is something right about this. What? *Our* nature is connected with both.) (W-PI, secs. 550–51)

The answer, then, to the question posed above (If what is true or false is relative to the logical structure in which we make true and false statements, then does not this logical structure itself correspond to something factual?) is no. Logic, the normative basis of our assertions, does not correspond to something real, but *is* something real. Logic and the rules of grammar are, in this sense, as we have already seen, arbitrary: "One is tempted to justify rules of grammar by sentences like 'But there really are four primary colours.' And the saying that the rules of grammar are arbitrary is directed against the possibility of this justification, which is constructed on the model of justifying a sentence by pointing to what verifies it" (W-Z, sec. 331).

To say that meaning is normative is not to say that it is governed by the decisions and preferences of individuals. Rather, its "governor" is the forms of life in which it is embedded. Its freedom is a lawful one:

"So you are saying that human agreement decides what is true and what is false?—It is what human beings *say* that is true and false; and they agree in the *language* they use. That is not agreement in opinions but in form of life.

The rule governed nature of our languages permeates our life.[43]

Wittgenstein's value to the social scientist consists not in the terminology he introduced, but in the central conceptual insights entailed by his normative account of meaning. That account requires,

43. W-PI, sec. 550, 551; W-RC, sec. 303. For a few samples of the almost innumerable passages in which Wittgenstein discusses *rules*, a term he uses in a fashion closely related to that of *norms*, see W-OC, secs. 61, 62; W-Z, secs. 306, 320; W-WCI, 36, 44, 83–84, 92–93, 112; W-PI, secs. 31, 162, 201, 198, 217, 234, 235, p. 147; W-LC, 5; W-RPII, sec. 76; W-RFM, bk. I, sec. 164; W-RFM, bk. II, sec. 28; W-PG, 6, 14, 29, 52, 60, 68, 184. For passages in which Wittgenstein discusses the important point that a rule doesn't determine its own use (for that would be to separate the rule, and therefore meaning, *from* use), see W-PI, secs. 54, 68, 80, 81, 85, 125, 140, 165, 198, 201, 217, 292; W-RPII, sec. 682; W-NLPE, 291; W-RFM, bk. I, secs. 7, 8, 33, 20–22, 113–16; W-PG, 24, 80, 94, 163.

first, that we dispense with any across-the-board compartmentalization of reality into inner, subjective categories and outer, material
ones (a compartmentalization that is prominent in the works of
Hume and Kant, as well as in the *Tractatus*). For the later Wittgenstein, all these various dualities must be bridged, and we must
instead frame the distinctions we draw between the empirical and
logical features of phenomena within particular contexts or language games/forms of life. Doing this will help to keep us from objectifying meaning, since it will force us to "stay with" the phenomena and not go outside them in search of their sense and significance.

Second, Wittgenstein's normative account of meaning requires
that we admit with humility that what is *meaningful* to us will always hinge on what is *familiar* to us. Since the distinction drawn between the empirical and logical features of phenomena can be drawn
only *within* a given language game/form of life, it will be based *on*
that language game/form of life; it will derive ultimately from the
everyday uses or channels of meaning in which our concepts have
their home (and which in turn cannot have an empirical basis, because they are themselves the grounds on which we make any empirical assertion). That is why Wittgenstein throughout his writings
tries constantly to show that the meaning of our concepts—from
color to number to disease to human behavior to the soul—will ultimately have reference to a concrete human context. In all these cases,
we must not confuse the meaning of the concept with the empirical
explanation (however successful) of the phenomena that fall under
such a concept (scientific explanations may, of course, contribute to
the meaning of the concept, but here what contributes is not the empirical explanation as such, but the acceptance and use of the explanation within a social and cultural context). By confusing meaning
with empirical cause, the *normative* elements implicit in our concepts are obscured; we invest in empirical phenomena a sort of motive force to reach out and produce our concepts. Meaning then becomes an amalgam of fact and concept, a shadowy, ethereal process
that is *like* external phenomena, except that it goes on in a place
where no one can see it (in the mind). Meaning, therefore, is reduced
to a mental process contributed by the subject. For Wittgenstein,
by contrast, meaning cannot be contributed by the subject, because
the subject is already presupposed in any such contribution. As

Wittgenstein makes clear in his private language argument, as well as in his discussions of the possibility of feeling pain in other people's bodies, what we call the self has indeed no empirical basis, but is a conceptual feature of our life forms.[44] Wittgenstein's attack on the possibility of a "private language" is really an attack on a non-normative concept of meaning. A private language entails the ability to give meaning to words (and the sensations they stand for) in a context in which the terms *right* and *wrong* or *correct* and *incorrect* have no use (W-PI, sec. 258). But for Wittgenstein this would be to deny meaning altogether. Hence, there can be neither a private language nor a private self that employs such a language. What we *are* is bound up with the ways we act and think. How we understand the beliefs and practices of other peoples depends very much on our own beliefs and practices:

> We . . . say of some people that they are transparent to us. It is, however, important as regards this observation that one human being can be a complete enigma to another. We learn this when we come into a strange country with entirely strange traditions; and, what is more, even given a mastery of the country's language. We do not *understand* the people. (And not because of not knowing what they are saying to themselves.) We cannot find ourselves in them (Wir können uns nicht in sie finden). (W-PI, 223; *see also* W-RPII, sec. 700)

> I don't mean that as a matter of experience one can't understand a language game/form of life if he doesn't join in living. . . . Rather, I mean that I wouldn't say either of myself (or of others) that we understood manifestations of life that are foreign to us. And here, of course, there are degrees. (W-RPII, sec. 30)

> What makes human sacrifice something deep and sinister anyway? Is it only the suffering of the victim that impresses us in this way? All manner of diseases bring just as much suffering and do *not* make this impression. No, this deep and sinister aspect is not obvious just from learning the history of the external action, but *we* impute it from an experience in ourselves. (W-BUF, 16)

44. See W-PI, secs. 283, 410; W-BB, 52–54; W-RC, sec. 127.

III Nature and Culture
The Individual and Society

For Wittgenstein, as we have seen, the meanings of words are given by the rules or norms governing (but not rigidly dictating) their use, where *use* signifies necessarily public use and refers not just to a conceptual, linguistic sphere, but also to the life forms in which our concepts are grounded.

How can Wittgenstein's view of language be applied to the study of culture? Wittgenstein's normative account of meaning should be understood as a radical critique of the subjectivistic, empiricist accounts given by Hume and Kant. The crucial flaw in both these accounts is that they posit the source of our ideas and beliefs in a private self or consciousness. The test for determining the objectivity of our ideas and beliefs then becomes whether or not they correspond to the data of experience—which is to say, to empirical correlates in the external world. Those ideas and beliefs that do not so correspond—a category that includes, in large measure, our moral beliefs and judgments—are merely subjective or without meaning. At this point, however, the perspectives of Hume and Kant sharply diverge. For although Hume is content to give these merely subjective ideas and beliefs a quasi-illusory status, designating them as "feelings" or "sentiments,"[1] Kant devises an elaborate system to rationally justify the subjective basis of our ideas and beliefs.

There is thus an analogy between Hume's and Kant's philosophical systems and the views of comparative religionists summarized in the first chapter. Just as Hume and Kant gave our ideas and beliefs a subjective source in the self, counting as objective only those ideas and beliefs that had empirical correlates in the external world, the comparative religionists posit the basis of culture in the subjective processes of the individuals who make up that culture, counting as

---

1. In the case of our moral beliefs, Hume is, however, careful to say that they are the product of a "sentiment made universal in the species," and in one place even baptizes them "a priori" (H-EPM, 230).

necessary those universal forces and conditions in nature that are external to culture and that constitute its objective reference point. Hume was content to give our "merely subjective" ideas and beliefs a somewhat illusory status, tracing their source to the feelings and sentiments of individuals. In a similar fashion, Boas is content to give the "secondary" components of culture a somewhat illusory status, tracing their origin to the emotional processes of individuals. Kant sought to justify the subjective basis of our ideas and beliefs by rationalizing and universalizing them in the "structure of the consciousness." In a similar fashion, historians of religions grant our distinctively cultural beliefs and practices—religious, moral, artistic—a subjective status, but insist that this subjectivity is of a fundamentally rational and universal nature, being grounded in the components of consciousness. It would, therefore, follow from these parallels that comparative religionists are open to some of the same sorts of criticisms made of Hume and Kant.

As we have seen, Hume's logic and epistemology takes for granted that man as an individual, autonomous being is the fount of an unlimited number of ideas. What makes such ideas possible is their obedience to the law of noncontradiction; what makes them real or meaningful is their correspondence with empirical data. Implicit, and wholly unexplained, in Hume's logic and epistemology is an ontological priority—a hidden ontological priority—given to the only being who could be the source of these ideas: the self. At no point does Hume ask, as Kant and, even more, Wittgenstein ask, What is presupposed *by* such concepts and ideas? What concepts of existing and knowing are implied by the fact that we think in such and such ways? What indeed is presupposed in our very conception of the self? To none of these questions does Hume have an answer; for him, the self remains a constant and extremely reliable fund of ideas—a hidden pocket of infinity.

So it is also with Boas. His view of culture is erected on the foundation of a throughgoing subjectivism. On one hand, Boas says, "The activities of the mind . . . exhibit an infinite variety of form among the peoples of the world" (B-JAF, 1). He also writes: "The imagination of man knows no limits, and we must expect great variety in mythical beings and happenings" (B-ANA, 313). On the other hand, what gives such ideas meaning and reality is their correspondence with some sort of sensory experience: "There is hardly a single trait of all the mythologies that does not reflect naturally, by exaggeration or by contrast, the ordinary sense-experiences of man" (B-ANA, 346). Or applying the same perspective to language: "Since the total range of personal experience which language serves to express is infinitely varied and its whole scope must be expressed by a limited number of word-stems, an extended classification of experiences must necessarily underlie all articulate speech. . . . This trait of human thought and speech may be compared to the limitation of the whole series of possible articulating movements by selection of a limited number of habitual movements" (B-MPM, 208–209).

For Boas as for Hume, meaning must have an object—and when an external one can't be found (as in the case of our distinctively cultural beliefs and practices), then an internal one will have to do. Here, however, we see that the same objection made against Hume's formulation of the difference between empirical and logical truth applies to Boas' understanding of the difference between natural and cultural phenomena. In both cases, what is accomplished is a separation and not a distinction; cultural and natural phenomena are made to refer to two different domains or "spheres of reality"—one internal and mental, the other external and material—but no criteria are given by Boas for distinguishing between the two logically. Like Hume in regard to our nonscientific beliefs, Boas flits back and forth between an empirical and a logical understanding of cultural phenomena; he conceives of the "inner processes" to which such phenomena supposedly refer as a type of ethereal object—and thereby invests them with a status at once empirical and logical. It is, indeed, just such a confusion of the empirical and the logical that allows Boas to treat culture as both sui generis and secondary, as (1) autonomous and possessed of a status logically different from natural phenomena and (2) subject causally to external natural and historical forces and thereby possessed of an empirical status not essentially different from that of natural phenomema.

Of course, it may be argued that Boas does in fact give much cultural phenomena, as Hume gives the moral sentiment, a universal status—and in this way grasps, to some extent, the logical status of culture. The problem, however, is that although Boas gives many cultural phenomena a universal status, he infers very little from that status. Just as Hume's notion of meaning as a "mental content" restricted the development of his philosophy, so too Boas remained bound to a view of the meaning of cultural phenomena as grounded in material or mental objects. Neither thinker made a significant effort to see that if certain concepts and ideas are universal, then they may constitute the structuring elements of experience, rather than be results of such experience. Hume's and Boas' theories of human nature and of the sameness of the human mind amount to little more than a concession that certain types of ideas and practices are extremely widespread among different cultures—but neither of them on that account retreat from their adherence to an empirical criterion of meaning. What they do is regard these general facts of human nature as themselves contingent—and thereby avoid seeing them as elements of a logical framework by which our experience is interpreted. Logic for them (in contrast to Wittgenstein) embodies a pure, wholly abstract ideal of reason that must not be so much distinguished from experience as separated from it—drained of any admixture of the empirical. As Boas puts it, "In logical processes we find a decided tendency with the development of civilization to eliminate traditional elements" (B-MPM, 251). Elsewhere he says: "It is evident that the fewer the number of traditional elements that enter into our reasoning, and the clearer we endeavor to be in regard to the hypothetical part of our reasoning, the more logical will be our conclusions" (B-MPM, 223).

By positing the foundation of culture in hidden mental processes, Boas thus defines culture in a manner only superficially different from that in which nineteenth-century evolutionists such as Tylor did when they accounted for culture along the lines of a naturalistic psychology. The important difference between Boas' and Tylor's perspectives is that Boas is a great deal more skeptical than Tylor regarding the possibility of accounting for these processes scientifically. But what would give such skepticism force and depth—a logical and normative understanding of culture and belief—is missing in Boas' account, as it is in Hume's. The cultural evolutionists were in this regard more consistent than Boas; they rightly believed that if cultural phenomena had reference to mental processes occurring in the minds of individuals, then there could be at least no theoretical block to a completely scientific and rational account of culture.

2

Kant's views, it was argued, mark an advance over Hume's in that they make explicit the subjective understanding of possibility that is the foundation of the empirical criterion of meaning adopted by both philosophers. But although Kant explicitly identifies the self with the possibility of experience, it was further argued, his view of what determines the *bounds* of such possibility is still uncritical. He assumes that there is some one range of possibility against which some one range of contingency can be posited; he assumes that reality can be divided into two compartments, the phenomenal and the noumenal. Like Hume, he gives no real grounds for distinguishing between the empirical and logical features of phenomena other than the inherent power of the self to recognize or see the distinction.

Historians of religions' account of the nature of culture is parallel to Kant's account of the nature of our ideas and concepts in that the former give culture a subjective basis, but at the same time endow such subjectivity with a fixed and universal status. Historians of religions accomplish this by rooting the subjective nature of culture in an "other," noumenal world that is separate from that of the phenomenal world and is possessed of its own higher reality. In a manner quite analogous to that with which Kant sought through his Copernican Revolution to justify our scientific and moral beliefs by viewing them as rational and objective from a subjective frame of reference, historians of religions, despite their employment of Husserl's avowedly subjectivistic method of phenomenological analysis,[2] claim an objective status for their researches (SH, 224). Historians of religions, in the words of Gerardus van der Leeuw, seek to comprehend "the objective appearances of religion in the light of subjective processes."[3] Or as Eliade says, discussing the role of symbolism in religion: "The cosmological values of symbols enable

2. Historians of religions themselves insist that the *phenomenology of religion* must be distinguished from *phenomenology* in a philosophical sense. See BL-R, 8–9; BL-S, 5, 194; A, 58, 72, 108, 110–11; SA, 29; Ninian Smart, *Religion and the Sociology of Knowledge* (Princeton, 1973), 21; Michael Pye, *Comparative Religion: An Introduction Through Source Materials* (New York, 1972), 16–19.

3. Gerardus van der Leeuw, *Religion in Essence and Manifestation*, trans. J. E. Turner (London, 1938), 694.

[man] to leave behind the subjectivity of a situation and to recognize the objectivity of his personal experiences."[4]

Both Eliade and Rudolf Otto[5] provide accounts of religion and the sacred that mirror Kant's famous proclamation in the first *Critique* that "although all knowledge begins with experience, it does not follow that it all arises out of experience" (K-CI, 41, B 1). Thus, Eliade frequently argues that "religious meanings" originate with the natural world but do not arise out of it—that "the sacred is an element in the structure of consciousness, not a stage in the history of consciousness" (E-Q, i). Rudolf Otto, on the other hand, uses language that is even more explicitly Kantian. Thus, man's sense of the holy or numinous or sacred "issues from the deepest foundation of cognitive apprehension that the soul possesses, and, although it of course comes into being in and amid the sensory data and empirical material of the natural world and cannot anticipate or dispense with those, yet it does not arise *out of* them, but only *by their means*. They are the incitement, the stimulus, and the 'occasion' for the numinous experience to become astir."[6]

But the analogy between the views of Kant and historians of religions can be extended further. Just as Kant's account of the nature of our ideas and beliefs represents a significant but strictly limited advance over Hume's, the historians of religions' understanding of culture represents a significant but strictly limited advance over that of Boasian anthropologists. Historians of religions, in contrast to Boasian anthropologists, view culture not as a subjective residue left over when all empirical considerations have been taken into account, but as an a priori feature of man's experience. The *meaning* of cultural phenomena is not (for the historian of religions) to be viewed in terms of how well, or how poorly, it can be explained by empirical causes; rather, the meaning is a synthetic a priori feature of the phe-

4. Quoted in Guilford Dudley, *Religion on Trial: Mircea Eliade and His Critics* (Philadelphia, 1977), 17.

5. The differences between Eliade and Otto have occasionally been exaggerated (Dudley, *Religion on Trial*, 140). As Otto himself made plain, he was "on no account . . . a nonrationalist." See SH, 166.

6. Rudolph Otto, *The Idea of the Holy* (New York, 1959), 24. On Otto's deeply Kantian perspective, see pp. 42, 50, 65, 83, 189, 222, 296, 311, 318, 349, 372–73. Otto was heavily influenced by Schleiermacher; see p. 369.

nomena to begin with, to be found in and read out of such phenomena. But historians of religions largely negate their positive insights concerning the a priori status of the significance of cultural phenomena by going on to absolutize and objectify this meaning. They think that because such meaning is a priori, it must be universal to all cultures—a move that misses the creative implications of Kant's notion of the synthetic a priori. For the synthetic a priori must (that is, from a Wittgensteinian point of view) be seen in relation to experience, to be distinguished, but never separated, from it. To see the meaning of cultural phenomena as universal to all cultures is precisely to accomplish this separation. Once this is done, what a given cultural phenomenon truly is becomes a sort of substance (usually quasi-mental) inhabiting a sphere detached from that of the merely empirical—and such isolation not only objectifies meaning but also gives the realm of the empirical a fixed status, as though there were set conditions and needs that carried *their* meaning in themselves and that the relatively subjective meaning of culture must accommodate itself to. Historians of religions thus embrace, in their concept of culture, Kant's notion of the synthetic a priori, but are then unable to allow the meanings of cultural beliefs and practices to speak for themselves. Like Kant through his notion of analytic truth, they then seek to absolutize them. The end result is a dualism analogous to that of Kant's dichotomy between the phenomenal and the noumenal. The meaning of cultural phenomena is seen not as a presupposition *of* experience, but as inhabiting a sphere isolated from it, isolated from the realm of natural and historical processes.

3

It was as a critique of these subjectivistic and empiricist accounts of culture that the normative concept of culture had its origins. The main feature of this concept, as we saw earlier, is that the meaning of cultural phenomena is grounded neither in external natural processes nor in the internal mental processes of individuals, but rather in the rules, norms, and values governing (but not rigidly dictating) practice and belief. The sources of such norms are nonsubjective and nonempirical. They cannot be known *prior* to empirical investigation, but neither can they be defined *in* empirical terms. Rather, they exhibit a certain range of possibility of belief and practice.

Wittgenstein's normative account of meaning has a threefold relevance to the study of culture. First, just as language cannot be understood apart from the form of life in which it occurs, man's cultural activities cannot be understood apart from the natural and historical processes in which they occur. We must avoid the temptation to etherealize culture and to see it as issuing from certain higher acts of consciousness removed from the conditions of life. Rather, to imagine a culture is to imagine a natural and historical setting for it.

Second, culture is not something that must be taken to be all of a piece with natural and historical processes; it is also that which exhibits a certain logical framework or range of possibility. It is the description of this framework in terms of norms or rules of practice and belief that reveal (not constitute) the meaning of cultural phenomena. The social scientist, however, will be capable of grasping this meaning only if he first opens himself to it. He will not be able to do so if he confuses it with any empirical (including causal) explanation or subjective interpretation of it. The social scientist must grasp meaning as a logical space in which we move, as a range of possibility rooted in use and practice.

Third, the social scientist must not make the mistake of thinking that there is any one, privileged perspective from which to understand the nature of cultural phenomena, the mistake of thinking that there is an extracultural stance common to all particular cultures. Just as Wittgenstein invented "fictitious natural history" so as to disprove the presumption that certain concepts are absolutely the correct ones, the comparative religionist must interpret *real* natural history without presuming that there is some *one*, correct standpoint from which to do so. Even the effort to define culture can in this respect be harmful. It can be harmful if the definition refers—as many definitions of culture and religion by anthropologists and historians of religions do—to extracultural conditions, needs, or existential states. Culture is best "defined" in the way Wittgenstein "defines" game—by pointing to examples of particular games and noting their differences and similarities.

4

Let us turn now to an examination of the problem of the relationship between culture and natural processes. According to Tylor's use of the term *culture*—a use that has had great influence on comparative religionists—the meaning of culture is very close to that of *civilization*; culture is thought of less as a process than as a *state* grounded in certain fixed mental capacities intrinsic to man and not shared by animals. In what way does the normative view of culture dispute this concept of culture? Comparative religionists' concept of culture is inspired by a well-intentioned effort to give culture autonomy; by conceiving of culture as subjective in nature, comparative religionists wish to sharply separate *culture* from the empirical conditions culture is subject to. The problem, however, is that all such a conception succeeds in doing is transforming culture into a special, quasimental *object*, with the result that a separation but not a distinction is effected between cultural and natural processes.

Consider, for example, the concepts of compassion, vengeance, and cruelty. What does a comparative religionist, an anthropologist, or a sociologist mean when, in the course of describing, for example, sacrificial rites, initiations, acts of sorcery and witchcraft, puberty rites, or penal codes, he uses the adjectives *compassionate, vengeful,* and *cruel*? One thing he clearly does not mean, most people would agree, is that there is something inherent in the action, considered as such, that makes it compassionate, vengeful, or cruel. For to maintain this would be very much like saying that the action in the picture considered earlier—in which a person was shown holding a knife to another's throat—could be labeled good or bad just on the basis of one's looking at it. Of course, we can, and very often do, depict actions that, by virtue of the artistic conventions employed, we reflexively call compassionate, vengeful, or cruel. But in all cases, it would be at least possible to interpret the picture differently. The bare action does not tell the whole story, but must have a human feeling or sentiment added to it that will make it truly compassionate, vengeful, or cruel. This is also why animals cannot feel such emotions; they lack the capacity to add or give meaning to the bare actions.

Against this account of the meaning of compassion, vengeance, or cruelty, two points should be made. The first is that in associating the meaning of those terms with some internalized feeling or capacity, we are failing to distinguish between our concepts of compassion, vengeance, and cruelty and the phenomena that could be said to fall under such concepts. An example of this within our own culture that is instructive to examine is the debate on capital punishment. Most people who participate in this debate—even those who give prominence to the issue of deterrence—certainly do not treat it as a purely factual one. Most arguments for or against the death penalty have what might be called an "edge." Proponents are wont to give long, grisly accounts of murders, whereas opponents are wont to give long, grisly accounts of executions. Proponents defend the right of people to satisfy their desire for retribution, claiming that such a response to murder is both natural and justified. Opponents, on the other hand, defend a different sort of response, one they maintain is just as natural and ultimately far more justified than vengeance: compassion for one's fellow human beings, especially those confused and sick enough to take another's life.

The question, however, now arises, In associating compassion and vengeance with certain emotional states, do such arguments for or against capital punishment give us a clear idea of what compassion and vengeance *are*? The answer is no, for the conceptual basis—the standards and norms—by which we would gain such a clear idea, is lacking. Of course, it is true that vengeance and compassion are natural to man, but it is also true that they are natural to him as a *cultural* being, not as an *animal* being. They are concepts that apply, in a strict sense, only to humans.

What this means is that vengeance and compassion cannot be taken for granted the way we take for granted the behavior of animals or our own physiological responses. It is questionable what *constitutes* acts of vengeance and compassion. Not only do their meanings vary from culture to culture, but even within our own modern society it is not always clear what being compassionate and vengeful signify. Why, for example, should refraining from executing a brutal murderer be called an act of compassion? And why should actually executing him—*taking* his life—be considered retribution or compensation? Where is the payment? Where are the goods?

The point here is not that there aren't answers to the questions, but that there is nothing self-evident about the nature of compassion and vengeance that will be of help in finding them. The answers we give will depend on the standards of justice and morals we adopt (which will, in turn, depend loosely on the norms of the society and culture in which we live). We will not adopt such standards on the basis of our compassionate or vengeful feelings. Any act of compassion or vengeance *presupposes* a code of law and morality; otherwise it would not be—in common with all animal behavior, no matter how gentle or violent—compassionate or vengeful to begin with.

To argue for or against a certain standard of justice and morals on the basis of man's emotional responses to crime is senseless, for we only have these responses in a fully human sense—which is to say, we are only compassionate and vengeful—once such a code is operating.

Arguments for or against the death penalty are, therefore, conceptually confused in that they uncritically identify compassion and vengeance with empirical phenomena—emotional states and feelings—and do not articulate the conceptual basis by which such phenomena have been so identified in the first place. In our everyday discourse, it may be perfectly appropriate to make such assumptions, to accept compassion and vengeance as givens. But in a debate on the legitimacy of a certain law—a debate that is about the concepts of compassion and vengeance if it is about anything at all—it is not appropriate.

A similar point can be made in regard to comparative religionists' descriptions of the practices and beliefs of the cultures they study. Suppose, for example, a researcher were to describe—without elaboration and in that matter-of-fact way that characterizes so much writing in the social sciences—the Eskimo practice of leaving their elderly to die, as cruel or lacking compassion. In what way is such a description inadequate? Not in the sense that it is false (for it may not be), but in the sense that it has been arrived at uncritically. In most cases, what the researcher will have done is lift a foreign culture's practice out of its context and set it down, so to speak, in the context of his own culture, where it quite naturally elicits an emotional response that prompts us to label it as cruel. What is wrong with describing the Eskimo practice in this fashion is not that a value judgment has been made, but precisely that it has not been made. The researcher has failed to cultivate a critical consciousness in himself of the norms and values such descriptions are based on.

In labeling the Eskimo practice of leaving their elderly to die as cruel, the researcher has thus committed a twofold fallacy. First, he has failed to distinguish between the empirical and conceptual features of any act we would call cruel; he has, that is, failed to articulate the norms or values that would justify calling any given act cruel. Blind to the values and standards of his own culture, he has plunged "double-blind" into a foreign culture; his failure to cultivate a consciousness of the normative basis of his own classifications has rendered him powerless—conceptually impotent—to grasp the normative basis of other peoples' classifications. He thinks, at least implicitly, "Well, being cruel is being cruel." It is a certain emotional and internalized state that can be "grasped" independent of the norms and values of the culture and ways of life of the people involved. But it is precisely those ways of life that give such emotional states meaning—which allow him to legitimately call them cruel or compassionate or vengeful—in the first place.

Here we get a hint of how closely linked our understanding of the practices and beliefs of other cultures is to our critical consciousness of our own practices and beliefs: it is only by means of the latter that we get a "handle" on the former.

5

In equating the meaning of such terms as *compassion* and *cruelty* with internalized states and feelings, we are not simply failing to distinguish between the empirical and logical features of the phenomena involved, we are also separating different types of phenomena in an illegitimate way. We are, that is, drawing a line between nature and culture, between animal and human behavior, in a way that is conceptually confused—in a way that ignores that nature is, after all, a cultural (and social) concept.

But how can this be, since I have just been insisting that we distinguish between what is natural to man as an animal being and what is natural to him as a cultural being? The question betrays the need we feel to have some very concrete (empirical) *basis* for distinguishing between animal and human behavior, when in fact although the distinction is always *there*, it is always different, and an empirical basis is exactly what we do not have for it. The difficulty, in other words, comes down to this: we must always sharply distinguish between the empirical and logical features of a given phenomenon, but must never objectify this distinction and transform it into a separation between phenomena of different types, whether it be material versus mental, or animal versus human.

What basis, for example, do we have for saying that animals are not compassionate, cruel, or vengeful? Even if scientists were to discover very clear and discrete physiological and neurological differences between humans and animals, even if evolutionists were to find out that a particular feature of the nervous system appeared at the very moment that human beings came upon the earth, these differences would not by themselves explain the radically different ways in which we view animal behavior and human behavior. The meaning of what we call vengeance, cruelty, and compassion is not dictated by nature—or by physiological processes human or animal—but by human action and psychology embedded in social and cultural contexts. Animals cannot feel vengeful or compassionate, because they do not, by definition, have access to such contexts. The concepts of vengeance, cruelty, and compassion *can*not apply to them.

"But if we carry this sort of reasoning far enough, we'll conclude that there is no basis for distinguishing between the behavior of man and that of insects."

Well, what *is* the difference between a man and a bug? Consider the question often asked in one form or another by children: What goes on inside a bug when it crosses from one side of the room to the next? The "adult," philosophically informed answer to this question is: When the bug starts walking, it does not "decide" to do so; nor does it, having started, "intend" to reach the other side. What happens is that it simply walks and, a short time later, finds itself on the other side of the room. This answer is, however, misconceived. It is misconceived because it tries to use words like *purpose* and *intention* in a context in which they have little or no application. Of course, we *do* say that some types of animals engage in purposeful, intentional behavior—a cat stalks, an ape reaches. But a bug? The background essential to the words *purpose* and *intention* having a use is missing; there is not enough continuity between the life forms of insects and humans for us to supply such a background in anything but a whimsical, playful way (though the fact that we do so at all is significant). If there does not exist the possibility that an insect engages in purposeful, intentional behavior (if an insect is not capable of purposeful, intentional behavior by virtue of the definitions or established usages of *purpose* and *intention*), then it makes just as little sense to deny that insects so behave as to affirm that they do.

Of course, one is inclined to object here: "But why should we distinguish between the impossibility of something occurring and the denial that it does in fact occur. Don't they really amount to the same thing? Aren't you just splitting hairs?" It is essential to make such a distinction. For if we confuse possibility with fact, then we will be inclined to think of purpose and intention as inner objects (or states or processes) that, for some reason, man possesses but insects do not (and there will, accordingly, always exist the possibility that insects *do* have them, but that this fact has been ingeniously disguised—a disguise or "secret" that scientists will someday unravel). It is not just the meaning of cultural phenomena that we misunderstand, but also *ourselves*; it is as though we want to assure ourselves that we are indeed very different from bugs. In doing so, however, we are not content to let those differences stand in all their immensity. We want, in addition, a reason, a *hard* reason, for them, and so we posit a mental entity to account for them. But in doing this we actually bring about a lessening of the difference between man and insect by (1) making the basis for such a difference something unseen and inner—something that one can never *quite* grasp or visualize (such as a brightly colored object that exists in perpetual darkness)—and (2) conceiving of this difference as empirically grounded—so that there will always exist the possibility that it will someday be discovered that, contrary to what was previously thought, insects really do engage in purposeful, intentional behavior, *i.e.*, that they undergo the same mental processes we do. By contrast, Kafka, in his story "The Metamorphosis," made critical use of the immense difference that exists between our concepts of man and insect to achieve a certain dramatic effect.

A similar lessening of the differences between man and other forms of life is unwittingly brought about by the view that animals are in some sense equivalent to machines. The idea is that animals act on reflex; their behavior is physiologically, biochemically, and environmentally determined. Men, too, act on reflex, but they also have an extra "something" that allows them to view themselves from a standpoint outside their own mechanical reflexes. It is not difficult to trace the sources of this peculiar view. Animals lack the capacity to express certain feelings commonly found among humans. We would never say, for example, that a dog who greeted his master in a friendly way really held a grudge against him, but didn't want to show it. We would not say this even if on some subsequent occasion the dog bit his master and ran away. Hypocrisy is just not a concept that we *allow* (in anything but a fanciful way) to be applied to dogs. The reason for this is not to be found in what dogs are, in fact, observed to do; it is to be found in our concept of what dogs can and cannot do or feel. When someone says that animals act mechanically, that is, on reflex, he is on the one hand taking note of a real difference that exists between humans and animals and on the other exaggerating this difference in an unjustified way (for, clearly, we do attribute feelings to animals—though more so to a dog than, for example, a fish). What leads us to exaggerate in this way is the presumption that the difference between man and animals must consist in some single, clearly definable quality or attribute—a presumption that is, in turn, connected with the tendency to view the difference between man and animals as empirically grounded (*i.e.*, in this case, as a sort of mental capacity added to a mechanical apparatus—a soul on a stick, so to speak). We blind ourselves with an "essential" difference while failing to take note of concrete ones. To view certain types of animals as sharing, in a limited way, human emotions is not a primitive view characteristic only of non-Western civilizations; it was common in the seventeenth century (when Descartes lived), and it is common today. It will be always be common so long as man shares his environment, to some degree, with animals.

"But if we carry your sort of reasoning far enough, we will end by concluding that there is no real difference between man and a block of wood." But what is the difference between a man and a block of wood? Is it that the former thinks and that the latter does not? Or is it that the former has a soul and the latter does not? Why shouldn't we say that a block of wood, or a stone, has a soul—as some "primitive" peoples are inclined to do? Do we possess *evidence* that this is not the case? Even when we speak of men having souls, we do not appeal to what would in most cases be regarded as evidence. Men do not *have* or *possess* souls, as they do a house or a car; the word *soul* signifies what, in part, man is. Or to put this in a different way: if man has a soul, then that soul is written all over him. To say that man has a soul is to point to a form of life and action that is absent in the case of inanimate objects. Man's soul is neither inside him, in his mind, nor outside him, on his body; rather, it permeates his actions. It is the same with consciousness and the ability to think; only under certain conditions does it make sense to speak of these at all. To say that a block of wood doesn't think is harmful, because it gives us a picture of man as a block of wood that *does* think.

Ironically, it is the same conceptually confused way of separating man from animal, or man from inanimate object, that lies at the basis of our tencency to think that there could be a computer that behaves and thinks like a human—even to the point of endowing it with a "self-consciousness" such that it believes it *is* human.

What immediately comes to mind, of course, when such a possibility is suggested is the question, In a world where *machines* can believe they are human, what would it be like for a *human* to believe he or she was human? How, indeed, would we know that we ourselves weren't robots—or at least androids? For we would no longer be able to rely, for such "knowledge," on the testimony of our own thoughts and feelings; rather, we would have to be "tested" by some more objective, scientific criterion. This test would serve the purpose of proving not just to others but also to *ourselves* that we were human.

Is, then, the notion of a machine believing it is human an incredible one? Certainly not in an empirical sense. Why shouldn't we be able to program a machine to believe what we want it to believe? It seems reasonable to suppose that any limits to our ability to do this are technical—and therefore capable of being overcome in time.

But is this supposition, in fact, reasonable? To see that it is not, consider the argument of Norbert Wiener's *The Human Use of Human Beings*. The book, which has had a strong influence on people's thinking about computer technology, maintains that learning in human beings is similar to that in digital computers, in that both take place by a process Wiener calls feedback. Through such a process, the human being or machine can vary his or its responses in accordance with the ever-changing input received from the environment.

It is due to this ability, according to Wiener, that both humans and computers can be taught to behave "purposefully"—that they are able, for example, to perform such complex tasks as driving a car. Simple organisms, by contrast, are limited by their own conditioned reflexes; they can respond to environmental stimuli only in accordance with what actually does—often contrary to expectations—in fact happen. In this sense, Wiener concludes, we can build purpose into machines.

What Wiener and many others fail to note in making such arguments, however, is that a machine can be taught (at least theoretically) to drive a car only because we ourselves already know, in a more or less complete fashion, what it is to drive a car. It is misleading to say that a machine, like a human being, responds to actual, unexpected situations; rather, it responds to what actually happens only *within* a certain range of expectations—a range that is defined by us and that we call driving a car. If we could not define this range, then we could not construct the program that would direct machines to drive cars.

This is, however, exactly the situation we are in when it comes to programming a machine to believe it is human. Computers can be taught to do whatever we can define clearly and completely enough to write a program for—which is to say, whatever we can express in binary symbolism. They cannot, however, be taught to do what we ourselves do not have discrete knowledge of—and that includes the ability to will, intend, and be purposeful. That is because purpose, intention, and will do not, in their more important uses, refer to any particular action or actions, but to the concepts that govern human actions in general. Although we can, of course, give many examples of purposeful and intentional behavior that are uniquely human, they would serve merely to characterize what human purpose and intention are. They would not serve to circumscribe conceptually or define analytically the nature of purpose and intention. For that nature is, to a large extent, human nature, and human nature is something that we *are*, that we exhibit and express, not something that we "know." To build a computer that could act and think "humanly," we would have to be able to see ourselves from an extrahuman standpoint. That is—unless we are going to deny we are human—a logical impossibility.

It is no more possible for a machine to be human than it is for an animal to be mechanical—and therefore totally unlike humans.

"But what about man's capacity to use language—or, more generally, to symbolize? Surely you will not deny that this radically and clearly distinguishes man from animals? Even in the earliest, most primitive sorts of cultures, we find this capacity demonstrated, as for example in tribes practicing totemism, in which an object or representational figure is adopted as the emblem of the tribe. This emblem symbolizes the tribe as a whole; it points to an order of reality distinct from that of the natural order, in which the empirical properties of the thing being used as an emblem are transcended. What is seen at the level of totemistic cultures becomes more marked in our own modern culture. It is not as a piece of cloth that we value the flag of our country, but for what that piece of cloth symbolizes. It is this capacity to symbolize that forms the basis for our own use of linguistic signs. What are by themselves mere scratches on a piece of paper or sounds transmitted through the air are given life and meaning through man's unique capacity to symbolize."

Certainly, man's use of language distinguishes him from animals; but what needs to be critically examined is the status of that distinction. The above account is, in this regard, badly misleading, for it makes it seem as though a symbol were something existing alongside or affixed to the representational object or sign, yet in no way partaking of its natural properties.

Consider the example of the soldier who, in battle, risks his life to save his country's flag. One might like to say here that certainly the soldier is not risking his life for a mere piece of cloth. That means, presumably, that the soldier would not rush back into battle if it were only his shirt or his pants that were at stake. Yet, there is surely something unarbitrary about the fact that flags are made out of cloth. This fact, after all, allows them to be easily carried, to be hoisted high (so that they can be seen by friends and foes alike)—and to flap in the wind. "But none of this is essential to what a flag is as a symbol or representational object." Here the demand exceeds the capacity to produce, for if we insist on treating a flag as a symbolic representation that transcends any and all of the uses to which it is put, then we will be left with a concept of flag that is wholly abstract and ultimately unfamiliar to us. Given such a concept of flag, one might reason that pebbles can be used symbolically, so why couldn't a "flag" consist in a pocketful of pebbles carried in a soldier's pocket—and to justify this, one could stipulate that all the soldiers had been informed beforehand that the pebbles were *there*.

Compare the assertion that what a flag represents and what a flag is as a natural object refer to two different orders of reality with the following account by Rilke of a flag being carried into battle:

> He is running a race with burning halls, through doors that press him close, red-hot, over stairs that scorch him, he breaks forth out of the raging pile. Upon his arms he carries the flag like a white, insensible woman. And he finds a horse, and it's like a cry: away over all, passing everything by, even his own men. And then the flag comes to itself again, and it has never been so kingly; and now they all see it, far in the van, and know the shining, helmetless man and know the flag. . . . But, behold, it begins to glow, flings itself out and grows wide and red. . . . Their flag is aflame in the enemy's midst, and they gallop after.[7]

Quite rightly, we reject the suggestion that a flag is a mere piece of cloth. But it is important, in doing this, to ask first, Just what do you mean by a "mere piece of cloth"? For then we will see that a flag is not a mere piece of cloth *not* because a flag as a symbol is something essentially different from a piece of cloth as material object, but because the sorts of uses that might be included under the phrase "piece of cloth" are not generally those that would be included under the term *flag*. Such a meaning cannot be reduced to the material properties of a piece of cloth—but neither does it point beyond itself to an "other" order of reality. That is why it is wrong to characterize the symbolic representations of primitive peoples—as seen, for example, in the practice of totemism—as more crude and less "truly symbolic" than our own. When a primitive tribe expresses, through the adoption of an emblem as the totem of its tribe, its kinship with the animal or vegetable world, or when it regards certain objects as sacred and others as profane, that is not to be explained by saying that material elements still cling to that tribe's use of symbols (and that therefore they are at a less advanced level than we are). Such an explanation derives from a misunderstanding of our own uses of symbols as detached from the practices, activities, and life forms in which they occur.

---

7. Rainer Maria Rilke, *The Lay of the Love and Death of Cornet*, trans. M. D. Herter Norton (New York, 1959), 65.

It is at the level of man's use of linguistic signs, however, that we are most inclined to view his capacity to symbolize as abstract and disembodied. Indeed, the difference between the symbol and the spoken or written sign is so striking that the tendency to regard the symbol as mental and ethereal is almost overwhelming. To combat such a tendency we might keep in mind Wittgenstein's comment in the *Tractatus*: "In order to understand the essential nature of a proposition, we should consider hieroglyphic script, which depicts the facts that it describes. And alphabetic script developed out of it without losing what was essential to depiction" (W-T.4.016).

We should not, however, think of language as a logical *picture* of reality—as being connected to reality by a common logical structure—but rather as comprising the systems of uses or channels of meaning within a given context or life form. The picture has a certain *form* that we recognize that real objects conform to. The form is given by the use. Consider *red* versus *a sample patch of red*; in some cases, we could say the former replaces the latter. Then language would be a "picture of reality"—it is the use that shows this. But a logical picture? No. For it is forced to say that, in every case, the use of language is in some sense pictorial.

Although Wittgenstein in the *Tractatus* was correct in viewing language and reality as connected by a logical structure, he failed to grasp that this logical structure is one that can be given only in terms of practice and use. Instead of thinking of a linguistic symbol as a pictorial element added onto a linguistic sign, we should think of it as the use of such signs in particular contexts. And this will help to make explicable why modern man, quite as much as primitive man, becomes so attached to the linguistic signs (such as proper names) he in fact employs—notwithstanding the symbolic function of such signs. It explains why even minor changes in our conventions regarding language can affect us deeply; why it is impossible to "translate" much poetry; and why, when a person sees his name printed in a newspaper, it does not occur to him to say, What does that have to do with me? It's only my *name*.

Some say that the sign is dead until we give it life and meaning.[8]

---

8. "Das Pergament, ist das der heilge Bronnen, Woraus ein Trunk den Durst auf ewig stillt?" (Parchment—is that the sacred fount from which you drink to still your

But in fact, once having learned a language, oral or written, we *cannot* react to it as though it were dead (though the necessity consists in the system of language and its accompanying *Lebensform*, not in the thought processes accompanying the language). Consider an Englishman looking at a word on a printed page—say, *cow*—and trying to prevent himself from recognizing it by putting his fingers in his ears so he will not "hear" the word. The meaning of a word is something that cannot be, so to speak, shut out.

To highlight the organic character of our languages, it might be useful to think of them as systems of gestures, akin perhaps to the sign languages used by deaf people. What such a comparison emphasizes is that to conceive of language organically—to liken a word to a gesture—in no way diminishes the symbolic force of language. For although some of the sign languages used by the deaf are described as crude (the American Sign Language, for example, is based on a grammar different from that of English), no one would claim, I think, that they lack the capacity to perform symbolic functions. What we would say, rather, is that certain of the gestures used by deaf people can be understood by persons not trained in such a language—that is, those gestures similar to ones used in our day-to-day intercourse—whereas other gestures cannot be understood (similarly, certain signs in a pictorial script can be understood by anyone, because they are literal pictures, *i.e.*, they employ the artistic conventions with which most of us are familiar, whereas others require special training to be recognized as pictures of something. In what exactly consists the difference between the gesture that everyone understands (say, that of pointing) and the gesture that is employed for specialized purposes by deaf people (say, that which signifies thinking)? Is it that the former is more concrete and less symbolic than the latter? How could this be, for both are, after all, gestures? We might think of the gesture for pointing as more natural and literal than that for thinking, just as we might think of the pictorial representation of a house as more natural and literal than the pictorial representation of thinking. What defines this difference are the uses of these symbols—which are, in turn, tied to the natural

---

thirst forever?) Goethe, *Faust*, trans. Walter Kaufmann (New York, 1963), I, 107, lines 566–67.

history of man—not anything in the signs or gestures themselves (or in the things they represent). Different gestures play different roles, just as different linguistic signs play different roles. But although the roles that both words and gestures play can be radically different, a word can no more leap outside its own system of uses to describe itself than can a gesture.

"But certainly there are general distinctions that can be drawn between what we call nature and what we call culture. All men, for example are bounded by certain natural conditions—that they must die, nourish themselves, keep warm, and so forth. These conditions act as the limits within which all men must move."

It is true that we are not, in general, at a loss to find initial conceptual footholds into other cultures (though, very often, a lot of dirt is kicked away in the process). To explain this, however, as comparative religionists do, by saying that all cultures are subject to certain conditions, though different cultures react in different ways to those same conditions, is misconceived. For if all cultures are subject to the same conditions—we might note in the manner of the *Tractatus*—then it can only be *shown*, not *said*; it is embodied in those elements that are common to all cultures. When we say, "All men must die," and use this sentence in such a way as to mean that all cultures must deal in some way with the universal fact of man's morality, then we are talking—in the *Tractatus* sense of the word—nonsense. (The "fact" of man's mortality is part of the face that man, as man, presents, embodies, is. Man knows exactly as much about death as his cultural beliefs and practices show he knows.)

It is important to understand that the statement "All cultures are subject to certain universal conditions" is true only tautologically. What evidence would we deem admissible to support the contention that such and such a man did *not* die? The statement "All cultures are subject to certain universal conditions" is an a priori requirement whose only real function is (conceptually) destructive; it allows us to become meaning-blind to the norms and standards of the cultures we study. We, as it were, see through the particular practices and beliefs of the culture we are confronted with, reading them in the light of certain empirical facts or realities. But it is the conceptual framework that establishes the nature of such facts and realities, not vice versa. Without cultivating a consciousness of that conceptual framework—and in the study of culture, this means necessarily the conceptual framework *both* of our own culture and of the one we are studying—we are being uncritical, applying without "looking" (as Wittgenstein said) our own concepts and norms to other cultures.

When we feel that we have a certain conceptual foothold in a foreign culture—although such a feeling should itself be viewed critically and suspiciously—then that tells us something about *our* culture and *that* culture (not something about the conditions that the two cultures, or that all cultures, are subject to). What it tells us is that our concepts can be compared with (likened to and contrasted with) those of another culture. Although all cultures are, indeed, linked, this linkage is an a priori requirement whose significance shouldn't be misunderstood—*i.e.*, it says nothing empirically about the so-called nature of man. The linkage, in other words, is genealogical (like Wittgenstein's family resemblances between games). The fact of such interconnections does not signify that there exist certain conditions that all cultures are subject to, or that there is a single, essential difference that separates man and beast, or even man and inanimate nature. What there is, rather, is a large family of differences that extend over the entire range of living and nonliving processes. That culture is embedded in, and does not exist apart from, natural processes can be seen in the inescapably anthropomorphic forms that all culture takes. It is not just in fairy tales that man endows animals and natural objects with human qualities; the data of comparative religion show that man's gods are almost always given some kind of human form (and this is true even of one of the supposedly more transcendent religions, Judaism). The point here, however, is not so much that man has projected human categories onto nature—that he has conceived of nature in his own image—but that he has conceived of himself, of culture, in nature's image. Culture must be understood as a form, or an embodiment, of nature; the forces that lift man as a cultural being "above nature" are themselves natural forces. Culture is a recasting or refinement of animal nature. In the same way that we must not think of man's consciousness as providing an absolute, once-and-for-all distinction between man and animal, we must not think of culture as being able to transcend the limits of nature. In doing so, we only ignore all the particular differences that demarcate culture and nature and let ourselves be blinded by the glare of an illusory one. Culture is an entity molded of the materials of nature.

The concept of culture adopted by comparative religionists as a static entity founded on the internal capacities of man's subjective life must therefore be rejected. What this means is that any effort to explain the significance of cultural phenomena causally must also be rejected. *Since* culture is so deeply embedded in nature, we cannot speak of the natural forces of either the internal or external environment as determining culture. For once we rid ourselves of the notion that what is cultural corresponds to some sort of subjective object, there will be nothing *there* to determine. The point is not just that culture can't be reduced to natural forces (as the evolutionists of the last century and the materialists of this one would have it), but also that the sphere or limits within which cultural processes go on cannot be *defined* by natural processes (as Boasian nonnaturalists would have it). Culture is too much a part of nature for the line we draw between the two to have a fixed status; to describe a culture is to describe a natural and historical setting for it. Which means that although cultures may be *characterized* according to their natural conditions, they cannot be so *categorized* (or defined). Rather, such natural conditions are themselves a part of all cultural life and are in no sense its grounds.

6

At this point, it would be helpful to clarify some of the issues and problems concerning the dichotomy between the individual and society. One of the principal views to be found in the works of Emile Durkheim, the great French sociologist, is that the individual is the product of society. According to this view, society is not a mere collection of individuals; rather, it is impelled by forces and possessed of characteristics that radically transcend individual experience. In proposing this account of the relationship between the individual and society, Durkheim was trying, I believe, to combat the idea (widespread in his time, as in our own) that society is a mere artificial construct imposed on, and standing in essence opposed to, a pre-existing substratum of individuals. Rather, Durkheim wished to bring society and the individual together—to see them as mutually dependent.[9]

His formula that the individual is the product of society, has not, however—notwithstanding its great influence in all spheres of sociology—been well regarded. And with good reason. To say that the individual is the product of society may effectively close the gap between the two, but does nothing to dispel the artificiality that still attaches to the concept of society. So long as society is divorced from nature, so that social needs and the needs of the individual as a natural being refer to two opposed spheres of reality, then the claim that the individual is the product of society will only give society as an artificial construct more power, not make it less artificial—or less potentially monstrous. The split between the individual and society must therefore be viewed in the context of the split between nature and culture, for it is the latter that generates a conception of society as a subjective, artificial entity whose real substance is the individuals who compose it. In the same way that culture as a subjective entity is opposed to natural processes—processes that man can, potentially, master—so too society as an artificial entity is opposed to the needs of the individual as a natural being. In this fashion, man's mastery over nature turns against him and becomes malignant. The same concept of culture as a subjective entity standing apart from natural phenomena, when viewed at the level of the relations between man and man rather than between man and nature, becomes a "group mind" that turns against the individual—and absorbs him. Durkheim's view that the individual is the product of society only gives (though, I think, in opposition to Durkheim's intentions) the monster more power, and does not make it less monstrous.

To provide a satisfactory resolution to the split between the individual and society, we must first become clear on the status of the terms *individual* and *society*. Once this is done, the individual will emerge not so much the *product* of society as its *presupposition*.

Let us consider, first, the status of the term *society*. In using this

9. See Emile Durkheim, *The Elementary Forms of Religious Life*, trans. Joseph Ward Swain (New York, 1915), 243, 302, 470; Emile Durkheim, *Sociology and Philosophy* (Glencoe, Ill., 1953) 33–34, 45, 48, 57–59, 146, 165; Kurt H. Wolff (ed.), *Emile Durkheim: A Collection of Essays* (Columbus, Ohio, 1960) 36, 183, 194; Stephen Lukes, *Emile Durkheim: His Life and Work* (New York, 1972), 11, 15–18, 32–33, 219, 340, 414, 507.

term, we do not oppose, implicitly or explicitly, one sphere of reality to another; society is not like a play put on by actors whose real lives may be quite different from those that they portray on stage. Rather, *society* is the term we use to refer to collective actions and behavior. Such collective action and behavior (as seen, for example, in religious practices) does not have a basis outside itself; it is not subject to forces, naturalistic or nonnaturalistic, that operate from without. Rather, such forces are embedded *in* society. (But this doesn't mean— as Durkheim is usually interpreted to contend—that religion is a projection of society; it would be far more true to say that society is a projection of religion. The point is that religious beliefs and practices *are* social; they are one of the forms—the most important form, as Durkheim believed—that society takes.)

To speak, then, of the function or purpose of society can be misleading. It can be misleading if such functions or purposess are taken as extrasocial, for in this sense, society really has no purpose— whether it be utilitarian, psychological, or metaphysical—precisely because it is the substratum or basis in which these purposes arise. Any such purposes (for example, to produce more efficiently; to serve as a psychological shield against death; or to embody some archetypal, sacred reality and repudiate man's profane existence) are simply characteristics of society. They reflect the development and nature of *particular* societies; they do not shape society from without. Hence, their status cannot be extrasocial. Indeed, insofar as man's needs are particular to a given society, they are characteristics of that society and do not have an extrasocial status. Insofar as man's needs are universal and thereby operative in all societies, they form part of the meaning or definition of *society*; their status is analytic. The very fact that such needs are universal indicates that they cannot be separated from our concept of society to begin with. It is therefore nonsensical to give them an extrasocial status or to speak of them as acting causally on social phenomena. We would like to feel that there is some cause or condition or purpose waiting in the wings that can be lowered at any time to explain and make sense of social processes. In fact, human action has no sense or logic other than that which can be read directly from the action (though it must be remembered that human action has historical depth). Since social action or behavior is the most basic form of action there is (a human action that had no

links to any other human action would be a contradiction in terms—
i.e., it would not be human), it follows that society is the source of its
own *revealed* logic and meaning. There may be some a priori text or
script (naturalistic or metaphysical) by which the play of society un-
folds, but we are ourselves actors *in* this play and therefore cannot
experience it *as* a priori. Our only knowledge of what happens will
come from closely observing what goes on around us—though we
should know at the same time that such observations are themselves
part of the play. Society is a play with no spectators.

Two points, then, must be kept in mind regarding the term *society*.
First, the development or nature of society is dictated by "the imma-
nent consequences of its own development."[10] Second, what we call
society is not a composite entity; the boundaries between what we
call society and nature cannot be demarcated so that the functions of
society can be isolated and encapsulated vis-à-vis nature. Natural
and social processes form a continuum; our concept of nature is after
all a *social* concept. It is therefore a misunderstanding to say that society can be defined with reference to natural processes; there is in
reality no such thing as "society in general," but only an array of different types and kinds, closely or distantly related. We form our concept of society on the basis of the types we are closest to. The term
society has the same status as does Wittgenstein's *language games*; the
different types of societies form a kind of family tree, with many
overlapping characteristics but no single one in common. Moreover,
although there exists no abstract standard of society against which all
particular societies can be matched, there does exist a basis of comparison in the characteristics of the societies themselves. By such a
comparative method, the kinship between different societies can be
expressed as a kind of family tree. Just as culture is not an extrasomatic state akin to civilization, society is not an artificial construct
imposed upon a preexisting substratum of individuals. What we call
society and culture are much more organic processes than achieved,
mental states; there are not a multitude of separate, discrete societies
and cultures, but rather many different kinds—all of which belong
to the same family. That there should be no discernible similarities

10. This phrase is borrowed from Albert Pierce's thoughtful essay, "Durkheim and
Functionalism," in Wolff (ed.), *Collection*, 154–69.

between two particular societies or cultures does not contradict this scheme any more than would a lack of discernible similarities between a person and one of his ancestors; the values held by different societies and cultures are related in sometimes close, sometimes distant ways. They are related through what might be called a historical genealogy.

The second term that needs to be clarified is that of the *individual*. In this light, it is useful to consider Wittgenstein's attack on the possibility of private language games (usually referred to as the private language game argument). A *private language* is characterized by Wittgenstein as one whose individual words "refer to what can only be known to the person speaking; to his immediate private sensations. So another person cannot understand the language" (W-PI, sec. 243). By a private language, Wittgenstein means not a language that has been derived from or is in some way based on a public language and just happens to be used by an isolated individual; he means a language *not* so derived, one that *cannot* be understood by another because the objects to which its words refer are seen only by the individual involved.

The central issue addressed by the private language game argument is this: Does there exist an empirical check for our use of langauge? Do our words gain their meaning, their significance, simply by their reference to sensations, perceptions, and sense-data—to a type of experience or evidence that (in the Humean sense) appears before the mind's eye? And closely related to this issue is another: Do our ideas and beliefs have a subjective origin in the self? For if language is the result of a mediation that occurs between, on one hand, a private self or consciousness, and, on the other hand, the data presented to this self, then the problem of how we can ever be directly acquainted with anything outside our own skulls—how consciousness can be sure that it is observing a realm that is *not* consciousness—raises its monstrous head. In such a manner does the attack on empiricism lead inevitably to an attack of subjectivism.[11]

Wittgenstein's attack on the possibility of a private language

11. On this point, see Andrew Oldenquist, "Wittgenstein on Phenomenalism, Skepticism, and Criteria," in E. D. Klemke (ed.), *Essays on Wittgenstein* (Urbana, 1971), 398.

should not be construed as an attack on the possibility of genuinely private (or, better, personal) experience. Rather, his effort is to clarify, in a manner similar to that of Durkheim's, only more successfully, the status of such private or personal experience.[12]

Wittgenstein's numerous (and extremely elegant) arguments against the possibility of a private language will not be summarized here.[13] However, his basic line of reasoning is that the subjectivistic account of the origin of our ideas and beliefs depends on an empirical criterion of meaning; the notion of a discrete, self-contained mind requires discrete, self-contained data that it can be presented with and, hence, interpret. But such an empirical criterion of meaning is naive, since the facts do *not* speak for themselves but presuppose a conceptual or logical framework. It is not our sensations alone that give the languages we use, or could possibly use, meaning. Rather, the meanings of words are normative, grounded in a *Lebensform*, or system of practices and activities.

The notion of a private language exhibits a confusion that causes us to mark a separation, not a distinction, between the empirical and logical features of phenomena. What is being separated in this case is the self (a quasi-empirical, quasi-conceptual entity) and the world of other selves, or the Other. What is not being distinguished is our concept of the self and the empirical phenomena (such as sensations) that exhibit or manifest this concept. The notion of a private language entails the principle that the self is constituted independently—at least in a logical sense—of the Other. But really, the same concept of self applies to both; sensations and reflections (I feel . . . ; I think . . .) presuppose this same logical basis. Hence, the very idea of one self "at war" with other selves (as Hobbes would have it) has no clear sense, for the two enemies get their supplies—owe their existence to—the same source.[14]

12. See Henry LeRoy Finch, *Wittgenstein: The Later Philosophy* (Atlantic Highlands, N.J., 1977), 51, 245.

13. See W-PI, secs. 243, 275, 279, 289, 293–96, 314, 401; W-Z, secs. 87, 545, 549, 554–57, 560, 567, 595, 599; W-WCI, 99; W-BB, 4–5, 12, 45, 49–50, 52–53, 61, 67; W-RC, secs. 57, 83; W-LC, 69; W-PG, 48, 50, 99, 100, 106, 180; W-NLPE, 273, 279, 287, 290, 291, 314.

14. See W-PI, secs. 253, 283, 286, 312, 404; W-NLPE, 312–13, 277, 298; W-Z, sec. 536; W-WCII, 17–18; W-PG, 105.

From Wittgenstein's perspective, the *I* is neither an object nor a metaphysical essence: it is a mode of expression that sits at the foundation of all our actions and thoughts. That is why if we wish to know something about ourselves, the best way we can acquire such knowledge is to observe others: "Do not ask yourself 'How does it work with *me*?' Ask 'What do I know about someone else?'" (W-PI, 206). Or: "I give myself an exhibition of something only *in the same way* as I give one to other people" (W-Z, sec. 665).

Wittgenstein does not reduce (in the manner of behaviorists) mental processes to physical ones; rather, he maintains that neither can act as a reference point for sense or meaning. The only reference is action: "To say 'I have a pain' is no more a statement *about* a particular person than moaning is" (W-BB, 67). Elsewhere Wittgenstein writes: "Other people cannot be said to learn of my sensations *only* from my behaviour, for I cannot be said to learn of them. I *have* them. The truth is: it makes sense to say about other people that they doubt whether I am in pain; but not to say it about myself" (W-PI, sec. 246). Our subjectivity is so deeply embedded in our way of life that there can be no question of giving criteria for it: "My attitude towards him is an attitude towards a soul. I am not of the *opinion* that he has a soul" (W-PI, p. 178).

It is by keeping in mind Wittgenstein's intent to keep the *I* free of the object-language we customarily use (and at the same time ground this *I* not in something ethereal or metaphysical, but in a form of life) that his puzzling contention that is is possible to feel pain in another person's body can be understood. What we mean by *I* has no object; rather, it constitutes in part the frame of reference by which we judge the truth or falsity of statements. Therefore, there is nothing logically impermissible about saying, "I feel pain in his tooth." Since the *I* is not a something (or more precisely, is neither a something nor a nothing) defined by its presence in something else (for example, a body), it makes no sense a priori (though it may make a great deal of sense a posteriori) to deny that it is or is not present in any object. The reason we do not feel pain in another's body is empirically, not logically grounded. On the other hand, it *is* a logical truth that I cannot feel *his* pain:

A has a gold tooth means that the tooth is in A's mouth. This may account for the fact that I am not able to see it. Now the case of his toothache, of which I say that I am not able to feel it because it is in his mouth, is not analogous to the case of the gold tooth. It is the apparent analogy, and again the lack of analogy, between these cases which causes our trouble. . . . It is conceivable that I feel pain in a tooth in another man's mouth; and the man who says that he cannot feel the other's toothache is not denying *this*. The grammatical difficulty which we are in we shall only see clearly if we get familiar with the idea of feeling pain in another person's body. For otherwise, in puzzling about this problem, we shall be liable to confuse our metaphysical proposition "I can't feel his pain" with the experiential proposition, "We can't have (haven't as a rule) pains in another person's tooth." (W-BB, 47)

Wittgenstein's purpose in all this is to get us to stop objectifying the *I*. For in the modern sensibility, the *I* becomes an object in the way that we normally treat the *he* as an object—as a person or thing we refer to. We even think that to preserve the integrity of the *I* we must treat it *as* an object. The communal system of practices and activities (upon which the *I* is grounded) come to be conceived of in opposition to the *I*—an object defending itself against a collection of other objects. As a result, the sense that we are part of a collective process—that even our deepest and strongest feelings are rooted in others—is lost. That is why anthropologists and comparative religionists in general have a hard time understanding those beliefs and practices of foreign cultures that manifest their concept of the self in different forms than ours do (think, for example, of the ways in which masks and names are treated, or of the witch doctor's ability to help or harm someone by manipulating a few sticks).[15] We have become so attached to our own concept of the self—to the particular sorts of criteria and experiences that count *as* the self—that we feel conceptually impotent when confronted with such practices and beliefs.

As another way of bringing out the nature of the distinction between the empirical and logical features of the phenomenon of the self, Wittgenstein discusses the topic of solipsism.[16] For Wittgenstein, the case of the solipsist is highly instructive because the solipsist *partly* grasps the nonempirical status of the self. When the solipsist

15. See Daniel Lawrence O'Keefe, *Stolen Lightning: The Social Theory of Magic* (New York, 1982), 25–62, 263–328.

16. See W-NLPE, 281–2, 297–300; W-PP, 311; W-WCII, 22.

says, "All experience is unreal except *my* experience," he, as it were, beats his wings against the walls of the fly bottle, but fails to see the way out. He affixes that which we call the self to a particular body or mental state (his own) and detaches it from all others. But if the solipsist were to carry through his reasoning consistently, he would see that his suggestion lacks sense. The phrase *his own*, as used above, has no meaning. For in a world where there is only one person to which the terms *I* and *mine* can legitimately be applied, there can be no use for these terms at all. Instead of saying, "I have pain," one might just as well say, "There is real pain," and signify all other occurrences of pain by the statement "There is apparent pain." When the solipsist says, "All experience is unreal except *my* experience," he wants to deny the reality of the experience of others, to deny that these others are the possessors or owners of their experiences. But if this is true, then it is also true that the solipsist cannot be the owner or possessor of his experiences either—which shows the futility of trying to affirm or deny such a thing in the first place. That which we call a person is an expression or embodiment of our concept of the self. It is therefore senseless to regard such a person or persons (whether they be solipsists or Cartesians) as having control or possession of—as having an absolutely privileged position in regard to—this concept.

Suppose there was a solipsist king of virtually unlimited power who had managed to convince all his subjects that the only experiences that were real were those affixed to his own person. In such a case, any harm inflicted on the king would be regarded as—one might say, quite literally—a calamity for the whole country. The suffering of all others, by contrast, would be met with indifference (more precisely, the concept of suffering could not be applied to anyone but the king, just as we ordinarily do not think of ants as suffering). One is tempted to say here, "The king would have total power." If one means by this statement that the physical and mental states of the king would be catered to with an unlimited amount of attention and care, then certainly it would have some validity. But on the other hand, if one is referring in this statement to the king's capacity to will, to intend, to be purposeful—those ways in which we denote the exercise of the functions of the self—total power is exactly what this king would *not* have. For such a self would belong quite as much to the lowliest subject as to the person of the king (compare the combination of powerlessness and omnipotence that seems to attach to the famous).

The case of the solipsist is instructive because the mistake that he makes is simply a more extreme version of the mistake that all of us make when we regard experience as potentially private. To regard experience as private is to ground it empirically within the mental processes and states of the individual. Most of us admit, of course, that each individual can have his own private experiences—whereas the solipsist, more consistently, declares that there is only one *real* kind of experience. Both, however, commit the same fallacy: they attempt to define the self empirically. *That* certain sentences ("I feel pain") cannot be contradicted points up a feature of our concept of the self; but the employment of such sentences should not mislead us into thinking that the self has a private, empirical basis. That is why it is so important to sharply distinguish between the meaning of *I* and the proper name associated with the *I* (let us say, in this case, HM). HM refers to my physical and mental states, which can be empirically defined; it is the enactment of our concept of self—and is thus not possessed or owned by anyone, including myself. Although HM may influence and shape the *I* (what the *I* is can be read out of the actions and behavior of HM and other persons), neither HM nor any other set of initials in any sense *creates* the *I*. Rather, as one might say, the *I* is a kind of inheritance that we may diminish or increase, but that we cannot ignore. It is a *social* inheritance.

7

All of this brings us to the problem of the relation between the individual and society. By speaking of the self as a social inheritance, I wish to emphasize the interdependence of our concept of individuality and the social framework in which individuals live. The characteristic feature of what we call individuality resides not in the private behavior of the person—in his subjective consciousness—but in his social behavior. Moreover, the term *private* must be sharply distinguished from the term *personal*; what is private is necessarily nonsocial, whereas what is personal can occur only in a social context. The point here may be expressed in part by saying that the personality is socially defined, so that one "reads oneself"—literally, learns about oneself—in the faces, gestures, and words of others. It is from others that one learns one is possessed of a particular drive, intensity, purpose—or that one is easy and vacillating, or meek and shy. To all these attributes is attached a certain *value*. One becomes conscious of oneself through the process of being valued or even "appraised" (one tells a joke and others laugh; one solves a problem that no one else can; one "sees oneself" listening or acting considerately or sensitively, *in* the responses of others).

One could say, "Some people are just *naturally* kind, considerate, mean, avaricious." But such a judgment is not usually held *by* everyone about the *same* person (the different perspectives of a mother, employer, son). Even in those rare cases in which such a judgment does seem to be held by everyone, to say, "Such and such is just naturally . . ." is to say, "It is natural in this society . . ." or "The behavior of such and such serves as a paradigm of what we mean by . . ."

But it is not just that one reads oneself in others; one also reads others in oneself. An examination of one's own motivations and feelings will often reveal much that is socially significant (hence the reason an artist or philosopher, working in isolation, can penetrate to truths of a universal nature).

Consider the concept of self-interest—in which someone is, for example, interested only in himself or uses others to gain his own ends (such as increased wealth or increased prestige and power). Why does a person *want* such things? What does he get out of them? It sounds here as if I am saying, "Money or social position is not of intrinsic value." But this means nothing. The monk who lives in the monastery denies himself certain worldly pleasures. But he does not deny their value in the sense that someone might deny the value of a bag of trash; the monk is not indifferent to worldly pleasures any more than the self-seeker is. One might say, "To discover that sort of indifference, it is necessary to journey conceptually outside the culture and society in which both the Christian monk and the self-seeker live." So does the Buddhist, who counsels not repudiation of worldly pleasures, but indifference to them, or the North American Indian who gives away all his worldly goods in a potlatch—do *they* have a different attitude toward money and worldly power than we do (than does either the Christian monk, at one extreme, and the self-seeker, at the other)? Different, yes—but with many links, too, if one compares, for example, the potlatch with gift-giving in our society.

An egotist is only an egotist *in* a society: a self-seeker desires wealth and power for himself, but only after a social value has been placed on them. Still, it is not right to say, "Money or a given social position has no intrinsic value." Rather, one should say, "Their value obtains from their being part of a way of life shared by people."

The personality, therefore, is not a single, composite entity that *has* social experiences; rather, it is made up of these social experiences in such a way that precedence is given to certain parts over others. The parts of the personality are in a constant state of commanding and yielding to themselves, and this state cannot be seen apart from the social experiences that are its occasions. The personality as a whole has a single, central authority no more than does society as a whole. But on the other hand, just as an intelligible description or logic can be read out of social processes, so too the various parts of the personality may be controlled so as to operate smoothly and in conjunction with one another. There may be a harmony of the personality, though not a single, central authority residing over all the parts (for any such authority would constitute just another part). We may control and "master" ourselves from within, but we cannot know or see ourselves from without. As Nietzsche said, "Your true nature does not lie within you deeply concealed, but immeasurably high above you." [17]

It is the illusion that there can be such a central control or authority that induces us to think that the self—that which constitutes our concept of individuality—can be empirically defined in terms of private experience. For to conceive of the personality as a single, central authority (rather than as a harmony of parts, as did Plato in the *Phaedrus*) is to detach and to objectify it, to see it as a special, ethereal substance opposed to the more material, organic functions of the personality. But this is little more than a form of self-tyranny, a way of reducing the multitude of aspects of the person to mere servants and slaves of a dictatorial master—a "mental master" that uses the desires and inclinations of the individual as data for its "programs"

17. Friedrich Nietzsche, *Schopenhauer as Educator*, trans. Adrian Collins (2 parts; New York, 1964), II, 107.

(and like all tyrants, this one is always in danger of destroying the slaves on whom its existence depends).

The point here (and for that matter, in Wittgenstein's discussion of private language games) is not to deny the individual his capacity for private experience, but rather to cultivate a critical consciousness of our concept of privacy. When the individual maintains the integrity of his private experiences, and defends the self-sufficiency and independence of his own consciousness, what he is really doing is wrapping himself in a kind of haze that no one can penetrate. The fuzziness that the individual experiences when he turns within himself is the fuzziness necessarily produced when the individual pushes to the borders or limits of his public personality and attempts to grasp this personality. The effort cannot be successful; the individual can at best create another aspect of himself, but can never grasp himself as a whole. But in pushing his own view of himself as far as he can go, the individual stumbles across an important truth: that the plunge to within is really a plunge into a communal depth, into the substratum and basis of social life as we know it. The forms of the self are nature's way of "publishing" itself, as Emerson and Thoreau and E. B. White realized. So that the plunge into a communal depth is also a plunge into the nature of individuality, for it is indeed the latter that social life presupposes. The individual, like the universal needs and conditions imposed by nature, is a necessary presupposition of society. The individual—that is, the different types of individuality to be found in different cultures (and within the same culture)—is nothing more than the *form* that society takes, the "face" not so much that it wears but that it presents and is. (Durkheim maintained that society can be more than the sum of its parts; this is true, but only to the degree that it is also true that society can be *less* than the sum of its parts).

It is thus by understanding that at the heart of the deepest, most private parts of ourselves lies a public experience open to view that the falseness of the dichotomy between the individual and society is exposed. The dichotomy is based ultimately on the view that individual and social behavior or action are of two radically different kinds; the individual thinks, wills, and intends, whereas society does none of these things. But such a dichotomy quickly collapses when the ethereal, rarefied account of the nature of individual consciousness is put aside and such consciousness is grasped as an integral feature of the personality that cannot be objectified. What that consciousness is can be described only in terms of the way it expresses itself—in terms of the actions and behavior of the individual within a social context. It is precisely the plunge into the deepest, most private parts of ourselves that brings to light the organic, intrinsically expressive nature of the personality. What we do in taking such a plunge, in trying to find that substance or object that lies at the heart of the self, is experience the limits of that self. We run back and forth along the walls and ceiling of a glass building, banging our heads until we finally realize that what we truly are can only be enacted, not known. The meaning of individual actions, often thought to be seated in certain mental processes of intention and will, must be understood as seated within a nexus of social conduct and circumstances that can only be described, not explained or interpreted. At that point, the illusory quest for the heart of the self is abandoned, and consciousness is experienced as a tool in the formation of our total personalities (a tool that, however, we do not so much control as—given the development of the proper skills—we *use*). What we imagined to be utterly private is then brought to light, and we see that how we use our consciousness is indistinguishable from what the consciousness *is*. We see that consciousness does not shape the personality from the outside, but instead manifests itself as part of the personality from within. It is therefore not necessary to plunge to within to find our true selves; rather, it is necessary to keep reaching out to make this true self. The notion of the self as a form of action or expressive state means that we continuously *become* what we *are*.

What is true of the personality is also true of society, for the latter is also continuously forming itself. Society is not a subjective entity defined by reference to natural processes (and therefore of a fixed nature) any more than the personality is a consciousness defined by reference to physiological processes. The effort to defend the integrity of the individual's private experience is analogous to the effort to defend the integrity of certain universal and necessary conditions that all societies are subject to; both are prompted by the desire to find an independent grounding (for the personality or for society) in the empirical world. But that which we call the personality and that which we call society both include naturalistic functions—functions that are not separate from but are integrated with the total structure of society and the personality. When the individual acts to exercise control over himself (which means he acts to harmonize the various parts and functions of his personality), he necessarily exercises a social control as well. He acts "alone" only *within* society. Society is the play, the individual a performance.

IV   Meaning and Morality

The phrase "That's a value judgment" is often used in a sense that makes it nearly synonymous with phrases like "That's subjective" or "That's a private matter" or "That's a matter of personal feeling." Certainly, modern philosophers and social scientists—including Hume, Kant, and comparative religionists—have been more than a little affected by such a tendency to view what we call values as pertaining to (and ultimately rooted in) the private concerns of the individual and his subjective states of consciousness. In what follows, I maintain that this tendency is harmful and should be resisted, that we must, in a sense, turn our backs on the connotation of the word *value* as subjective. For if, as I have been arguing, meaning is presuppositional and is rooted in use and practice, then conversely what we call values (whether moral or nonmoral) have a preeminently logical status. Just as it was contended in the two previous chapters that meaning is intrinsically normative, so now in this chapter, it is contended that our norms and values are intrinsically meaningful.

But to understand this point of view, certain misconceptions concerning the relation between facts and values, or what is often called the fact/value dichotomy, must first be cleared up.

In addition to Hume's distinction between logical propositions (expressing relations of ideas) and propositions of a factual or theoretical character (expressing matters of fact), there is a third category of propositions that he distinguishes: moral statements. As in his treatment of factual beliefs, Hume's examination of moral beliefs or "pronouncements" (as he is inclined to call them) has one overriding purpose: to show that they are nonrational.[1] The argument is that

---

1. See Barry Stroud, *Hume* (London, 1977), 185. Hume has been widely regarded as a precursor of emotivism. See D. G. C. MacNabb, "Hume," in *Encyclopedia of Philosophy*, IV, 87; Antony Flew, "On the Interpretation of Hume," in V. C. Chappell (ed.), *Hume* (New York, 1960), 283; W. D. Hudson, "Hume on Is and Ought," in V. C. Chappell (ed.), *Hume*, (New York, 1960), 299.

morals derive from neither of the two sources of reason that he recognized: relations of ideas and matters of fact.

On the one hand, moral statements for Hume are distinct from those expressing relations of ideas, because such relations are found just as much in material things and animals as in men—and surely, Hume reasons, no one would be so absurd as to apply our moral precepts to animals and inanimate objects. On the other hand, moral statements are distinct from those expressing matters of fact, because there is nothing *in* the objects of experience, in the mere situation alone, that would conduce to moral judgment; whether or not the physical act of killing, for example, is viewed as justifiable homicide, murder, or a display of heroism does not depend on anything in the act itself (B-THN, 468).

For Hume, the object of moral belief is human action, but "actions are, by their very nature, temporary and perishing" (B-EHU, 98). It follows, therefore, that "actions themselves . . . are never consider'd in morality" (B-THN, 575).

But if moral judgment does not depend on reason as it is concerned either with matters of fact or relations of ideas, then on what does it depend? The answer that Hume gives is: feeling or sentiment. If one were to look for what the nature of vice consists in, for example, "You never can find it, till you turn your reflexion into your own breast, and find a sentiment of disapprobation, which arises in you, toward this action. Here is a matter of fact; but 'tis the object of feeling, not of reason. It lies in yourself, not in the object. So that when you pronounce any action or character to be vicious, you mean nothing but that from the constitution of your nature you have a feeling or sentiment of blame from the contemplation of it. Morality, therefore, is more properly felt than judg'd of" (H-THN, 468–69).

Though a motive can lead to or cause an action, it cannot be identified *with* such an action. Rather, it is subjective and internal: "'Tis evident, that when we praise any actions, we regard only the motives that produced them, and consider the actions as signs or indications of certain principles in the mind and temper. The external performance has no merit. We must look within to find the moral quality. . . . All virtuous actions derive their merit only from virtuous motives" (H-THN, 477, 478).

If it is true that moral qualities are distinct from any external action, then it follows, *a fortiori*, that they are also distinct from any fact or statement of existence (whether it be scientific or metaphysical). It is the latter distinction that is the basis for Hume's famous dichotomy between *is* and *ought*, or fact and (moral) value. Reason consists in "the discovery of truth or falsehood," which in statements expressing matters of fact is "the agreement or disagreement of belief and fact." But since the objects of moral belief—human actions—do not express what is truly moral (they are merely external) and, besides that, are "temporary and perishing," a moral belief has nothing to correspond to; it is a detached, self-enclosed sentiment or feeling and cannot represent reality the way a factual belief can:[2] "Now 'tis evident our passions, volitions, and actions are not susceptible of any such agreement or disagreement; being original facts and realities, complete in themselves, and implying no reference to other passions, volitions, and actions. 'Tis impossible, therefore, they can be pronounced either true or false, and be either contrary or conformable to reason" (H-THN, 458).

What is my principal objection to this account of morals as grounded in feeling and sentiment? It should be noted first that although Hume does not give our moral beliefs an empirical status, he still regards them *in the light of* an empirical criterion of meaning. For Hume, it is, indeed, the *failure* of such beliefs to satisfy this criterion that characterizes their nature. Thus, Hume, in his treatment of moral belief, assumes the same criterion of meaning as in his treatment of factual belief—that there be an "impression" to which the belief corresponds. Only now, instead of applying his "razor" and actually looking for such objective data to which our moral beliefs might correspond, Hume assumes from the start that they can't be found. He feels justified in making this assumption, because the objects of moral belief—human actions—are temporary and perishing and therefore could not possibly serve as an objective reference point the way empirical data *possibly* (but not, as it turns out in many cases, *actually*) could for factual beliefs. Then, on the basis of this *assumption* (which, in his analysis of certain factual or theoretical beliefs, came only as a *conclusion*), Hume posits the nature of moral

2. See Stroud, *Hume*, 159.

belief as an internal sentiment or feeling. Since he has never given up his concept of meaning dictating that an idea, to be rational, must be empirically grounded in an observable mental content, he has no problem applying this criterion to the moral sentiment and concluding that it is nonrational. The theory of meaning by which Hume denied the objectivity of many factual beliefs is used to deny even more strongly the objectivity of moral beliefs. And it is precisely from this stronger denial that the dichotomy of fact and value derives. A factual belief is *relatively* more objective than a moral belief, because of the possibility of its being empirically grounded. But a moral belief does not even contain the possibility: "Though an appeal to general opinion may justly, in the speculative sciences of metaphysicians, natural philosophy or astronomy, be deemed unfair and inconclusive, yet in all questions with regard to morals, as well as criticism, there is really no other standard by which any controversy can be decided."[3]

Hume's uncritical account of logical truth, in sum, has dictated his account of moral belief. His separation of factual and logical propositions prepared him for a similar separation of factual and moral propositions. Through the former separation Hume was prevented from recognizing that what we call logic is a presuppositional component of the factual and the empirical, not a kind of proposition that corresponds to a special sort of process or "act of understanding." Given such a lack of recognition, it followed that Hume would also fail to see that what we call values (whether moral or nonmoral) were embedded in and presupposed by the facts, not by a special kind of proposition corresponding to subjective, nonrational processes. Hume failed to grasp the logical character of morals because he failed to grasp the normative character of logic. Through his superstitious view of mathematics as inhabiting a privileged, extra-human domain, Hume was saved from making his account of logic *explicitly* subjectivistic. But there is, nonetheless, a core of subjectivism in his account of logic, and this core expands and becomes manifest in his treatment of morals. What we find in Hume's bifurcation of facts and values is thus the same bifurcation—only rendered

3. Quoted in Frederick Copleston, *A History of Philosophy* (9 vols.; New York, 1964), V, 153.

explicit—in his account of logic and facts. The contrast in both cases is between a "kind" of proposition that can only be justified (explicitly for morals, implicitly for logic) by reference to subjective processes.

In turning now to Kant's moral theory, we find a much more critical account than is found in Hume's. Kant grasps, at least in part, the logical character of moral belief and does not allow an empirical criterion of meaning to dictate completely his view of the status of moral belief. Nonetheless, his bifurcation of reality into two realms— phenomenal and noumenal—largely negates the positive aspects of his theory. This can be seen as follows.

In the *Critique of Pure Reason* (which deals principally with theory of knowledge), Kant sought to establish a rational foundation for the laws of the natural sciences by conceiving of them as synthetic a priori judgments whose sources are the structural elements of our consciousness. But precisely because such judgments are elements of the structure of our consciousness of the sensory world, Kant reasoned, they cannot be applied to the nonsensory world; the traditional propositions of metaphysics have no foundation comparable to those of the natural sciences. This does not mean that such an other, noumenal sphere doesn't exist; it just means we shouldn't claim to have scientific knowledge of it. What Kant did, then, in the *Critique of Pure Reason*, was not just to provide a rational foundation for the laws of science, but to create a "vacant place"[4] where the truths of metaphysics had been. As Kant said: "I have found it necessary to deny knowledge in order to make room for faith. The dogmatism of metaphysics is the source of that unbelief, always very dogmatic, which wars against morality" (K-CI, 29, B xxx).

In the *Critique of Practical Reason*, which deals with moral theory, Kant fills this vacant place not with any propositions or assertions that claim to be knowledge in a scientific sense (for this would be just to repeat the mistakes of traditional metaphysicians), but with what he calls "practical postulates" (K-CII, bk. II, ch. II, sec. 3)—that is, the traditional metaphysical notions of God, immortality, and free will, presented now not as providing the basis for speculative conclusions about the sensory world, but simply as being demanded by the

---

4. K-CI, 24; see also 360–61, 378–79, 427, 498–99; K-CII, xvi, 50; K-G, 85–86, 91–92.

reality of morals. Since Kant did not show in the *Critique of Pure Reason* that the traditional dogmas were false, but only that they could not be *proven* to be true, he has left himself space to reintroduce them under a different status—provided first that he can show that morality demands such postulates. Kant's reasoning might be expressed as follows: The traditional metaphysical propositions were invalid because they were applied outside the confines of their own proper domain. Metaphysicians thought that they could be used speculatively to extend our knowledge of matters of fact. But if we now recognize and accept this limitation, and at the same time recognize and accept "the reality" of morals and its need to be grounded in an objective law, we can give morality a noumenal basis without contradicting what we said in the first *Critique*. Reason in its speculative capacity must indeed be empirically grounded, but reason in its practical, moral capacity requires a basis in the noumenal sphere. We never said after all that the Ideas of reason were not objective, but only that they were not knowable. And in morals we are not claiming to "know"—in a strict sense—anything.[5]

Is Kant's account of morals, then, a subjectivistic one? Certainly it is not subjectivistic in a Humean sense. For although Kant has sharply differentiated between what Hume called matters of fact and moral pronouncements—between scientific knowledge and moral belief—he has not reduced the latter to the "human, all-too-human" level of feeling, but rather, has elevated it to a level suprahuman.[6] Kant, in other words, has posited the foundation of morals not in the "merely" universal and necessary conditions of man's experience—in the realm, that is, of human nature—but in an extra-human, noumenal sphere that lies outside what man can ever know

5. On the relation between the two *Critiques*, or between practical and theoretical reason, see K-CI, 18–19 (B x), 26 (B xv), 28–29 (B xxix–xxx), 61–62 (B 29–30); K-CII, 3, 5–6, 12, 15, 18, 25, 29, 44–48, 50–51, 56, 67, 92, 95, 108–109, 125–26; K-G, 23–24, 33, 43, 44, 78–79, 80–86, 89–90, 91–92; Norman Kemp Smith, *A Commentary on Kant's "Critique of Pure Reason"* (New York, 1962), 78, 169, 170, 428, 452, 500, 511–13, 515, 560–61, 569–70, 571–73; Lewis White Beck, *A Commentary on Kant's "Critique of Practical Reason"* (Chicago, 1960), 11, 37, 39, 40, 43–44, 47, 48–50, 66–68, 72, 77, 83, 95–96, 110.

6. See K-CI, 174–75 (B 167–68); K-CII, 9, 18, 32; K-G, 28–29, 32–33, 34, 35, 43–44, 48–49, 52; Beck, *Commentary*, 49–50, 54, 71, 72–73, 84, 101–2; Smith, *Commentary*, 570–72.

or experience (however much such experience may imply the existence of this sphere). Kant's characteristic way of referring to this extrahuman sphere is as that which pertains not just to man, but to all rational creatures. The idea is that the human—which contains an admixture of the sensuous—is not purely and wholly rational.

But although Kant's account of morals is not subjectivistic in a Humean sense, it certainly is subjectivistic in that it posits the foundation of morals in the freedom and autonomy of the self.[7] Only Kant gives such freedom and autonomy a radically different status than Hume gives them; they are not mere affairs of sentiment, but have a suprarational source. Kant departs from Hume's moral perspective not by adding an element of objectivity to morals (though in the second *Critique* he claims he does), but by adding an element of rationality.[8] The fundamental difference between Kant's and Hume's moral theories—as between their epistemologies—is indeed this issue of rationality. Both agree that morality is subjectively grounded; only Kant insists that this subjectivity is highly rational—an objective subjectivity, so to speak—whereas Hume is content to see it as subjective in a nonrational and emotional sense. The differences and similarities between their moral theories can be traced, I think, to the differences and similarities between their views of reason. Both adhere to a detached, analytical concept of reason. But whereas for Hume this concept is simply assumed and not explicitly justified, in Kant it is formulated in the notion of noumena. It is indeed in Kant's moral theory that his view of the nature of reason finds its clearest expression (K-G, 39–43). Both Hume and Kant objectified logic by setting a realm of the logically necessary or conceiv-

7. Kant insists in many places in the second *Critique* that he has given morals an objective basis. However, this contention must be understood in the context of the first *Critique*; Kant's "objectivity" is really an objective subjectivity. See K-G, 73–74, 93; K-CII, 22–23, 25; K-CI, 67 (A 23), 71 (A26), 76–78 (B 49–52), 82 (A 42), 123 (B 122), 139–40 (A 113–14), 310 (B 370–71), 319 (B 385), 327 (B 397), 333 (A 349), 354 (383–84), 439 (A 490–91), 435 (B 512), 613–14 (A 771–72); Smith, *Commentary*, 82–83, 96, 101, 103, 153–54, 272–74, 293–94, 500–502, 560–61; H. J. Paton, *Kant's Metaphysic of Experience* (2 vols.; New York, 1936), II, 453–54.

8. K-CII, xi, xvi, 63–64, 73, 79, 88; Beck, *Commentary*, 40, 41; W. H. Walsh, "Kant," in *Encyclopedia of Philosophy*, IV, 317; G. J. Warnock, "Kant," in D. J. O'Connor (ed.), *A Critical History of Western Philosophy* (New York, 1964), 310.

able against a realm of contingency; by so defining and fixing the realm of possibility, it became plausible to say that what gives such merely possible or conceivable ideas reality or meaning is their correspondence with empirical data—that is, with impressions (Hume) or intuitions (Kant). But since there can be no such "evidence" for moral belief, the latter must be purely subjective (Hume) or identified with the realm of the possible (Kant). In the latter case, morality is given a superior status to that of science, but only by being placed in a special, isolated sphere whose perimeter is *defined* by science.[9]

2

Both Hume and Kant, thus, sharply differentiated between the realms of knowledge and morality, facts and values, *is* and *ought*. Their motivations for doing so, moreover, were basically similar: they sought the preservation of morals. Faced by the steady encroachment of science into all walks of life, Hume and Kant, as well as numerous other philosophers and social scientists (including Wittgenstein in the *Tractatus*), felt it necessary to isolate morals within a separate sphere of reality or at least domain of human conduct. Only in this way could what is characteristically human—man's ability to distinguish between right and wrong (which is, in turn, grounded in his free will and capacity to intend)—have a place at all in a world filled with facts and causal relations.

The fallacy in Hume's and Kant's endeavors, however, should by now be clear. To isolate moral value within a separate sphere is not to preserve it from the facts, but to transform it into an imitation of them. What was argued earlier concerning meaning applies quite as much to moral meaning as well. Intention and free will are understood either as *concepts* (in which case it is just absurd to say that man has them or doesn't have them, and that without them there would be no morality—as though one could go about losing or finding concepts) or they are understood as mental processes (in which case they cannot be what constitutes our concepts of moral judgment—a con-

9. See K-CII, 113, 24–25. The formal character of Kant's theory of morals is exhibited throughout the second *Critique* and *Foundations of the Metaphysics of Morals*. See K-G, 6–7, 19, 26, 49–50, 68–69, 92–93; K-CII, 24–25, 32, 33–35, 48, 63–64, 70, 78, 82, 95, 113, 119.

tention that would hold even if it were documented by psychologists that moral judgments were always accompanied by characteristic mental processes, for such documentation would still say nothing about what it *means* to make moral judgments). As long as we sharply distinguish the two senses in which we use the terms, we will not be tempted to see them as referring to special sorts of empirical processes, which man somehow in the course of evolution developed but animals did not. We will likewise not be tempted to segregate morals within a certain domain of reality or sphere of human conduct; the moral life will not be something that goes on in that interior room of the soul Edith Wharton spoke of. Rather, it will be seen as embedded in or running through the thoughts and actions of our everyday life; it will be totally open to view.

The point, then, is not that there is no such thing as a fact/value dichotomy, but that there are two different ways in which it must be taken if it is to have validity. The first is in the sense in which the distinction between facts and values (whether moral or nonmoral) simply refers to what I have been calling the empirical and logical features of phenomena. In this sense, the distinction is without content—that is, it does not refer to two different domains or areas of social existence (for example, scientific and religious), but cuts across both of them. Within each domain, we can distinguish between fact and value (or rule, norm, standard, paradigm—the context will dictate the appropriateness of the term used). An account or description of values will give or show the meaning of the phenomenon in question, whereas an account of facts will enable us to posit causes and make predictions of an empirical nature. The relationship between value and fact is similar to that between a standard or rule of use and any empirical conclusions drawn on the basis of that standard. Thus, one could say (to use a favorite example of Wittgenstein's), "I designate *this* the color sample red," and then proceed to identify particular colors as red (or not), based on the sample. The designation of "*this*" as "the color sample red" is not an empirical definition; rather it is the normative basis by which we justify empirical statements about red. Similarly, "Thou shalt not kill" is a norm or standard on the basis of which a certain behavior might be judged. Different as these sorts of statements are, both advance rules or norms by which human behavior or activities are governed. The rules or norms are read out of our use of the term and in this way define a certain range of possibility of experience. Such norms cannot be known prior to experience; nonetheless, once they are established, they gain a status radically distinct from such experience. Although different norms or standards can obviously come into conflict, no experience can contradict a norm or standard—that is, no identification of a color could show that the color sample for red is not red, and no observation of behavior could show that it is really all right to kill. Either one accepts the norm or doesn't accept it. If the norm is altered, or if it is rejected or accepted, this cannot be caused by a new experience, for it is the norm that determines what is perceived as new. Norms, standards, and values do change, of course; their status shifts back and forth on the borderline of logic and the empirical (the "logic" of a way of life is continually evolving). But no empirical explanation could ever adequately account for such evolution.

The second way in which the fact/value dichotomy may be taken is not as a distinction between the empirical and logical features of phenomena, but as a reference to different norms rooted in different sorts of activities within a given culture. Obviously, this is the way many people think about the difference between, for example, what a scientist does and what a theologian does (the former is presumably concerned with facts, the latter with values). There is certainly a sense in which this is quite legitimate; there is, after all, a tremendous difference between scientific assertions and religious assertions. Thus, it might be said that although both scientific and religious beliefs contain normative elements, such elements are in greater supply in the latter case than in the former; religious statements are empirical and more meaning-filled. For example, "God created the world" is not meant to urge us to go on an archeological dig, but to enjoin us to live—to think and to act—in a certain way or in a certain light. It legislates a way of life. Religious and moral statements thus approximate a form of action far more closely than do factual statements; they are more concerned with laying down rules than making predictions from them. For this reason, they permeate our lives in a more thoroughgoing way than any science could. In contrast to scientific statements, which rely on the controlled laboratory environment for their validity, the sphere of religion is encompassing.

But though there exist such clear and important differences between scientific and religious activities in our culture, these differences must be framed with reference to the culture in which they occur; they gain their meaning from that culture and therefore must not be given an extracultural status. The point is not to confuse the culturally based difference between kinds of practices and activities with the logical distinction between norms and facts. The fact/value dichotomy, as it is employed by social scientists and philosophers, is harmful because it does just that; it invests with logical force—or absolutizes—a contingent, culturally based difference and then applies it to situations, contexts, and cultures in which it may have no place. What *we* mean by religion and science, or mental and physical phenomena, or free will and mechanical cause, are not necessarily what other peoples mean—if, indeed, they have any counterpart to these concepts at all. On the other hand, if the distinction between fact and value is taken as a distinction between the empirical and logical features of phenomena, then it is indeed—in a sense—absolute, though without substance. How or in what way the distinction is made depends on the phenomena and forms of life in which it is made; *that* it can be made is, however, a constant. The distinction, though perhaps always different and always changing, is nonetheless always *there*.

Let us now examine the first sense in which the fact/value dichotomy may be taken—that is, as a distinction between the empirical features of phenomena and the logical features of phenomena. The main point I want to make is that whatever *kinds* of social practices (*i.e.*, scientific or religious) we associate factual and moral beliefs with—and however sharply we wish to separate such practices—we must not think that it is something inherent in what is often called the object of those beliefs that allows us to separate them. The idea might be expressed in the following way. When Hume declared, as he did at the beginning of the *Enquiry Concerning the Principles of Morals*, that "disputes with men pertinaceously obstinate in their principles are, of all others, the most irksome," and when Kant lamented, as he did in many places in the *Critique of Practical Reason*, that the rationalization of our moral precepts is a far more difficult task than that of our theoretical ones, they were both presupposing a difference in moral and factual beliefs, a difference that most of us have come to accept as natural and that is often thought to explain why moral disputes, far more than factual disputes, are likely to arouse our ire. Whereas factual disputes can be resolved by appeal to evidence—and therefore can be cut short before inflaming the disputants—moral disagreements allow for no such quick and easy resolution. People might argue very heatedly over the precept "Thou shalt not kill" (for example, in regard to its application to abortion), but it is difficult to imagine arguing in such a fashion over the claim that "The boiling point of a given liquid is x degrees."

But now it must be asked, Is it really the possibility of an appeal to evidence that makes factual assertions more resolvable than moral assertions? Or is it that in the case of factual contentions we agree to adopt certain procedures and conventions that allow for such evidence to be used? The point is closely related to the point Wittgenstein made about the assumptions implicit even in so basic a method of instruction as ostensive definition. What Wittgenstein's analysis in general encourages us to do is pay attention to the large number of assumptions we make in statements like "The boiling point of this liquid is x degrees" or "The length of that stick is x feet." What we assume is the validity of certain methods of measuring: we act in a way that presupposes that the mercury will not fluctuate randomly, or that the ruler will not undergo changes in length while being used. If these assumptions were not made, if these procedures were not adopted, it would be impossible to resolve even such straightforward factual assertions as those above. On the other hand, it is easy to imagine certain definitions and standards being adopted such that disputes about abortion could be easily and simply resolved. That *we* do not so resolve them says something about *our* difficult and complicated mode of life; it is not necessarily grounds for concluding that moral disputes are of a special—"irksome," as Hume says—character.

As a historical example illustrating this same point, consider the famous dispute between Galileo and the churchmen who would not look through his telescope. It is misleading to say they would not look because they didn't trust their own senses. Rather, they would not look because they didn't trust the *telescope*—that is, because they thought the instrument would give them a distorted view of the heavens. This distrust, judged in the context of even our own time and culture, was a perfectly reasonable one. As any modern laboratory scientist would agree, all scientific procedures and methods must be subjected to the sharpest scrutiny before they can be relied on; their capacity to deceive and misinform (to the extent that an entire scientific theory or hypothesis can be constructed on the basis of false evidence) must be kept constantly in mind by the conscientious researcher. That modern science has been able to produce so much of what we call objective knowledge is due to the fact that it has been able to develop reliable procedures and methods of measurement, which has in turn depended on its use of the controlled laboratory environment. Both scientific and religious assertions are normative, however different a role we may assign such norms in our culture. Or, to put it in another way, what is problematic about scientific knowledge is not its nature but its *place*.

To differentiate between moral and factual beliefs by saying one can be empirically supported, the other cannot, is misleading because it makes it sound as though the differentiation were due to fixed properties intrinsic to moral and factual beliefs. The emphasis is being put in the wrong place; it is not *that* a factual belief can be empirically supported that makes it factual, but that such beliefs are grounded in practices and activities for which empirical evidence is readily available. Similarly, one should not say that a moral belief is a belief that cannot be empirically supported, but rather that a moral belief is a belief that we allow, in contrast to factual beliefs, to be thrown radically into question. The statement "It is permissible to allow children to suffer needlessly," however repugnant, has a degree of "sense" that the statement "Oranges are normally purple with red polka dots" does not. To say that a moral belief is a belief that can be radically thrown into question is to emphasize that what *makes* a belief moral is not a property inherent in it (*i.e.*, what it refers to), but rather the sorts of circumstances in which it is used.

For a churchman at the time of Galileo, the orders "Do not look through the telescope" and "Do not have sex with that woman" were perhaps not of such radically different sorts as we are likely to believe. This shows why it misses the point to say to the churchman, "Just go ahead and look; then you'll see there's no harm in telescopes." For we would not argue against someone counseling abstention from sex that the other person should just go ahead and try it.

There is a continuous flux and interchange between what we call moral and factual beliefs; both gain their sense or meaning—their normative basis—from the form of life in which they arise. Anything that affects that form of life will affect their relationship with one another. That is why revolutionary scientific theories such as those of Freud and Einstein, though presumably dealing with the factual realm only, can have a very strong moral impact as well: they change our way of life, our way of believing and acting, and this cannot fail to affect our values, too.

3

Thus, our factual beliefs, quite as much as our moral ones, are normatively grounded, and it is therefore misleading to distinguish between the two by saying that the former can be empirically supported and the latter can't. Still, there is obviously a clear difference between what we call facts and what we call values—and it is even possible to describe the nature of this difference in general terms.

I said above that a moral statement may be radically questioned, whereas a factual one may not. What I mean by this is that moral contentions direct themselves to a more basic level of behavior or action than do factual ones. There is frequently no controlled laboratory environment, no agreed-upon methods of testing, to check the validity of moral assertions, precisely because it is the methods of testing that are at issue. Moral contentions are such that it is our own eyes, ears, hearts, and minds that are the subjects of what is being contended. Although both moral and factual beliefs are grounded in use and practice, factual beliefs in a sense call a halt sooner than do moral beliefs to the questioning of norms or standards. A scientist will in no way throw into question the fact that we can use our eyes to observe. But a moralist can say with good sense: "Our eyes were created for a purpose. We should or should not use them in this or that way." The moralist will try to define the nature of man or the world, asking, Why? The scientist asks, How?

For this reason, moral belief, though united to factual belief, is more basic than the latter because the sphere with which it deals is more encompassing and more directly concerned with human conduct. In the case of factual assertions, one might say: "I believe such and such to be the case. Now let us agree to test this in the following way." But in the case of such statements as "It is wrong to kill" or

"The soul is immortal," it would be pointless (though not impossible or even difficult) to set up such tests; the statements are themselves expressions of norms and do not, as in the case of factual statements, presuppose a norm. In the case of factual assertions, it makes good sense to set up a controlled laboratory environment to test their validity; the laboratory defines the range of the norm, the limits of what is being surveyed. But in the case of moral assertions, the range cannot be so circumscribed; a "controlled laboratory environment" can be set up only at the cost of making ourselves perpetual subjects. No amount of self-experimentation will ever get us closer to *moral* knowledge; our contentions will achieve only the status of belief. This is why in the case of factual issues, it is useful and sensible to entertain hypotheses, even when one is skeptical of their truth; whereas it makes no sense to pretend to believe in God (so as not to offend him just in case he does exist) or to pretend to believe in the immortality of the soul (just to make sure one doesn't wind up going to hell if there is one). Morality, as Kant stressed for the wrong reasons (because he believed its status was absolute), is not hypothetical; it carries its justification in itself and has the same logical status as a deed. When one believes something factually, one can, as it were, consider, reconsider, retract, and even deny the belief simply by changing one's opinion—though presumably on the basis of evidence. But when one "believes" something morally, the situation is more complex, since it is not so much a matter of changing one's opinion as changing *oneself*—and the course of action one has taken. To try to retract a moral belief is a little like trying to undo a mile one has run by walking backwards.

Logically speaking, a moral or religious belief *is* an action, even a performance (like one's thoughts, it stands naked before the eyes of God). That is why a large number of the tales of creation and other myths of primitive peoples end with the statement "And this is why today we do (or are) such and such." What is at stake is not any explanation or interpretation of the nature of the world, but the way one lives *in* it—and this is conveyed not by the espousal of a belief, but by the performance of a ritual. Similarly, many Jewish and Christian rituals (Passover, Communion) are linked with events that one signifies belief in by recounting—a recounting that takes the form of a ritual. The point here is not that the belief is subsidiary to the ritual, but that it is *part* of it. Moral and religious beliefs always direct themselves toward actions—either to preserve them, or change them, or introduce others—in such a way that the belief cannot be meaningfully separated from the action.

Compare the holding of a religious belief with the making of a resolution—for example, to stop smoking two weeks from today. In each case, under certain conditions, and in regard to certain people, we are inclined to say that his believing in the doctrine or his resolving to stop smoking means nothing. We are inclined to say this because neither the belief nor the resolution seems to have any result (*i.e.*, his espousal of religious precepts is hypocritical; he never stops smoking); neither seems to show itself in his behavior or actions. When one genuinely and significantly makes a resolution to do something, one simultaneously begins to carry it out (just as when one holds a religious belief, one does not wait for the consequences of that belief, but embraces them at that moment). Resolving to do something determines what will be done only in the sense that it is part of the doing; it does not determine what will be done from an external standpoint. A person does not get wet by merely approaching a river; he must jump in.

As another example, consider very briefly the debate on the issue of abortion. This debate is often presented as one involving the conflict of two principles—one maintaining the right of women to have control over their own bodies, the other maintaining the absolute value of human life in however early or incipient a stage. These principles are of course important, but to represent the conflict between abortionists and antiabortionists as one primarily of belief or principle is insufficient. Neither the principle of women's "rights" over their own bodies nor the principle of the value of all human life makes sense when seen in an absolute sense—that is, when taken apart from any possible application. Rather, each must be taken in conjunction with a way of life; one legislates for certain "freedoms" conferred on the individual by modern medical and other technologies, the other legislates against these freedoms on the basis of traditional values. Both the positions are equally "moral" positions that carry their justifications within themselves. What makes the debate on this issue so bitter and emotional is that there is no really neutral standpoint from which one can judge the legitimacy of the arguments made. One lacks agreement as to what would constitute evidence "for" or "against" abortion (the proabortionist, pointing to the suffering of the mother and her unwanted child, and the antiabortionist, pointing to the death and apparent suffering of the fetus, are both seeking to empirically justify positions whose grounds are nonempirical).

Moral assertions orient themselves, in a direct and spontaneous way, to a practice, behavior, or form of life, whether to preserve, change, or introduce a new one. Factual assertions, on the other hand, although ultimately grounded on a practice, are hypothetical in nature; they direct themselves to the acquisition of more or better information based on or assuming the establishment of a practice. Factual assertions must therefore be—if they are to have sense—circumscribed; their range of application must be defined. Morality and religion, by contrast, survey the whole range of human behavior; there is nothing *as* behavior or action that they are not interested in. They gain their sense or meaning directly from the practice or form of life of which they are a part.

For Hume and Kant, it will be recalled, the object of moral belief was, properly speaking, human behavior—and precisely for this reason could never attain the sort of objectivity of factual belief that had as its object empirical evidence. For these thinkers, consequently, moral belief emerged as a kind of weak imitation of factual belief—one that had no basis in empirical reality and needed to be given a special, subjective reality. But so long as we keep in mind that all our beliefs, factual and moral, are normatively grounded, we can avoid this stultifying picture and grasp that the real distinction between factual and moral beliefs is that the latter play a more direct and fundamental role in our lives—even if the conclusions made on the basis of them are, necessarily, less precise. The sense in which moral and religious beliefs are prior to factual ones might be expressed in the following metaphorical way.

When someone says, "Truth consists in the agreement of a fact and a belief," it is as though he were drifting along a river and had suddenly declared, "At such and such a time, such and such will be seen on the banks," and then (when his prediction had been borne out) taken the view that such a "fact" was a feature of reality, not realizing that what made his prediction correct was not just what the bank looked like, but the speed of the current that carried him to that part of the bank at that time. What is verified in all correspondence theories of truth is the method of verification—a certain rate of flow.

A moral judgment, on the other hand, is to be recognized by the distinctive velocity it contributes to the flow; a moral act (a creative moral act) is an accelerated one. It causes society to move in a different pattern, at a different speed, and thereby alters riverbed and banks in ways that could not have been predicted. It narrows and widens the channel, makes more shallow or deeper the water. It gives to society a new velocity, and in this sense changes reality.

A moral act does not correspond to reality, but alters, preserves, or even adds on to it. Whereas epistemology finds its basis in what is and has been (those deposits that are the present functional and structural components of society), ethics is directed toward what will be—toward the future states of society that dictate what it becomes. So that even if morality stands helpless before the actual, existing state of affairs, it is ultimately prior; for it is not only responsible for the past, but is *at this moment* shaping the structure of society.

4

If, then, culture is a current or stream of action, then the values of that culture (moral and nonmoral) are what *steer*. The question, however, must now be posed, According to which directions? Is the way a culture develops arbitrary, the product of circumstances that may or may not have obtained? Does what we call a culture consist of practices that are conventional in nature, that could be replaced by other practices serving the same function or purpose, so that whether a culture develops a given practice or not is fortuitous, independent of any necessity intrinsic to that practice? And if the answer to these questions is no, then how can such an answer be made consistent with the account given above of the logical priority of values over facts? For if our values are not grounded in "something factual," then what is to *control* their development, to prevent them from taking off in any direction and forming channels in remote places of the earth, so to speak? These questions all hinge on the issue of cultural relativism, about which two points should be made.

The first is that even the most extreme relativist must admit to the existence of certain "boundary conditions" that accompany the development of any culture. No one would claim, for example, that a culture could develop independently of all economic conditions, just as no one would claim that all men are not subject to biological conditions (*i.e.*, the aging process). But it is important to be clear on our use of the term *boundary conditions*, which is in fact a dangerous and misleading one. This point will be discussed in more detail in the next chapter, but suffice it to say for the moment that when we use such boundary conditions (*i.e.*, the fact that man must eat or the fact that man must die) in order to explain or interpret man's cultural behavior, then we use them in an illegitimate sense. If, for example, in the process of examining the cave art of the Paleolithic hunter, one comes to the conclusion that this is a form of hunting magic that, however aesthetically pleasing, is meant to serve basically the same function or purpose that is served when a modern-day farmer gets on his tractor, then clearly the concept of boundary conditions is being misused. For what serves as a necessary and universal substratum of all cultural life cannot meaningfully link any particular practices of different cultures. The Paleolithic cave artist and the farmer on his tractor do not necessarily have *any* similarity or point of contact with one another (and this contention would hold even if it were definitely established that cave art was a form of hunting magic). We "know" that all cultures are subject to economic necessities only in a very special sense—in the sense that we do not know what it would be like for a culture *not* to be subject to economic necessities. (The closest we can get is to imagine an extremely rich culture whose people did not have to ever worry or even think about their economic needs; but what we would imagine a rich culture to be is clearly related to what we call a poor culture, which is, in turn, based on what we call "economic need"). To say "All cultures are subject to economic need" is, in a sense, a confession of ignorance; it is like saying, "This is all we know or are familiar with." It is therefore useless as a means of understanding a particular cultural practice. We must remember that when we use the term *boundary conditions*, we mean that these conditions are like the banks of a river that perhaps determine the direction in which the river flows. But because we are ourselves *on* the river, and therefore *subject* to the conditions that the banks impose on us, we have no way of calculating their effect; we *see* that we are subject to forces outside ourselves, and that everything that we call cultural is dictated by such conditions. But we do not *know* in an explanatory sense what those conditions are, because we do not *know* anything else but them.

The second point that should be made is related in an indirect fashion to the first. It hinges on the two different ways we understand the term *cultural relativism*. On the one hand, this phrase can be taken to refer to the fact—for it is a fact—that cultures vary a great deal in both their values and modes of life and that there is no limit we can impose, from a theoretical point of view, on the range of such cultural variability (though we can, and do, say that such and such forms are seen, others are not). The second, and quite distinct, way in which the term *cultural relativism* can be taken is in the sense that all cultures are equal in status—that there is no particular cultural form or variation that can legitimately be regarded as superior to or more favored than any other. For example, in viewing two cultures—one with a barter system as the basis of its economy, the other employing paper money—we would not be justified in coming to the conclusion that one economic system was better than the other. We might judge, of course, that one economic system had certain advantages the other did not. But the workings of the system as a whole could be judged only within the context of its own culture and the demands and conditions that that culture imposed. In judging that one economic system is better than another, we would ultimately become involved in evaluating the culture as a whole—and since this is clearly illegitimate, we must refrain from any such judgments and regard all cultures, as well as all forms of a given cultural or social practice, as equal in status.

These two ways of understanding the term *cultural relativism* may seem consistent with one another, but in fact there is a very important sense in which they are not. For to insist that all cultural forms and practices (for example, the economic systems of different cultures) be regarded as equal in status is to assume implicitly that there exists a standpoint from which such forms and practices may be regarded *as* equal in status; it is to view the economic systems of the cutlures as serving ultimately the same basic function or purpose—say, the distribution of wealth in the society—but in different ways. Now, it is true of course that if we *define* the economy of a society as the method by which a society distributes its wealth among the members of society, then all economic systems will have this purpose or function of the distribution of wealth in common. But here what is in common has the same logical status as the boundary conditions referred to above; to identify this common element is to say *nothing* about the economic system of any particular society. Rather, it is simply to convey what we *mean* by the term *economic system*. Similarly, to say that all societies must have some means of the distribution of wealth will not in any way characterize a particular society; it will simply convey what we *mean* by a *society*. When we view differing cultural forms and practices as equal in status, we are really objectifying the meaning of those forms and practices—that is, we are positing such meaning not in the particular forms and practices we are confronted with, but in some ethereal element that is common to all such forms and practices. If we define *economic system* as the method of distribution of wealth and view the barter system of a particular society as economic, then it is to say *nothing* about such a barter system if we say that it is the method of the distribution of wealth.

To regard all cultural forms and practices as equal in status is to try to adopt a standpoint outside any particular form or practice; it is to treat what *grounds* any attempted explanation as an element to be explained. "We use paper money; they exchange goods." Such a comparison will yield points of similarity and difference. But when we say, "Both methods accomplish the same purpose, though perhaps in different ways," we talk nonsense, for there is no society or culture that could *not* have such a purpose.

To acknowledge the extreme and, from a theoretical point of view, unlimited variability of cultural forms and practices, on the other hand, is not to deny that all societies as we know them must have some method of the distribution of wealth; for the use here of the terms *extreme* and *unlimited* variability *presupposes* some method of distribution of wealth. Although we readily acknowledge that a system of barter has enough in common with our own method of exchanging wealth for both to be called economic systems, we might not say the same of other, more bizarre practices that did not seem—to us—to have any method or consistency in them (even if we admitted at the same time that goods *did* wind up being distributed). To speak of the unlimited variability of cultural forms is therefore to speak of it given our concept of such cultural forms: at some point we would be forced to say, "What these people are doing here has nothing to do with what we call an 'economic system.'" Unlimited variability can exist—in a sense—only within limits. At no point should we try to extract, to detach and treat as an object, what is common to all forms of economic activity; rather, this common element *shows* itself in how we use the phrase *economic system*.

To acknowledge the variability of cultural forms and practices is therefore not to commit oneself to a position of cultural relativism in the proper sense of the term. For in the proper sense of the term, cultural relativism involves the adoption of an unacknowledged standard or framework *outside* the differing cultural forms. It is just the latter that the recognition of cultural variability denies. Different forms cannot be relative to one another, because there is nothing there—outside them—to be relative *to*. Nor can they be the product of "mere convention"—for this phrase implies a purpose or function that is *not* conventional. Nor can they be arbitrary, for their meaning can be understood only within the context of their society and traditions. And these latter are not arbitrary, for there is no nonarbitrary element outside them in relation to which they could be arbitrary.

5

The question of the arbitrariness of our values, however, is bound up with another issue besides that of relativism. This is the issue of the rational basis of morals—the question of whether or not morality is derived from reason.

Hume, who argued that no one is ever impelled to perform a moral action on the basis of a reasoned argument, thought that it was not. Reason for Hume was passive, concerned with matters of truth and falsity, whereas morality was active, concerned with matters of right and wrong—and between the thought and the act, the idea and the performance, there was no bridge (or at least none that had a rational foundation). Hume's conclusion was that since reason cannot precipitate moral action, such action must be impelled by a nonrational sentiment or feeling "made universal in the species."

To such a conclusion it can be replied that although it may be true—given Hume's account of reason—that no one is impelled to perform a moral action on the basis of a reasoned argument, it is certainly true that we are very often impelled to perform a moral action on the basis of someone *making* a reasoned argument. In this latter case, by whom and under what circumstances the argument is made—as well as the argument itself and what counts as a reasoned argument—become very important. It is not that a feeling must be added to a reasoned argument in order to make us act, but that in every moral action based on a reasoned argument, there is a context and situation presupposed by the action and argument. A proposition concerning the evils of war is likely to be understood differently if advanced in present-day Beverly Hills, California, than if it were advanced in post–World War II Germany. In the latter case, it might be reasonable to argue that extreme measures be taken to guard against the possibility of war, whereas in the former case it might not.

It is not any element of rationality implicit in an argument that impels us to act (morally or otherwise), but rather the argument's *reasonableness* (meaning both the argument itself and the context in which it is made). So that when Hume declares—in contrast to, for example, Kant—that our principles do not derive from reason, he is right in the sense that they do not derive from any idea or concept *as such*, but wrong in his conclusion that they derive from a nonrational sentiment or feeling. The idea or concept gains its life from the surroundings in which it is made; it is supported and given justification by these surroundings. If we cannot say that an argument or principle is reasonable on such a basis, then when can we?

For Hume and Kant, it will be recalled, what is characteristically moral about an action must lie outside the action proper; such is the basis of the ethical nonnaturalism of both philosophers. Of course, this characteristically moral element which must lie outside the action proper is for the two philosophers quite different. For Hume it is a nonrational feeling or sentiment, whereas for Kant it is a "pure," suprarational idea of reason. Nonetheless, both agree that what makes an action moral must be something more than the action itself—and that to take any other view is to involve oneself in some form of what G. E. Moore was to later call the "naturalistic fallacy."

The role of intention in moral belief will be discussed later, but for the moment suffice it to say that the view of morality suggested here (as neither rational nor nonrational but reasonable) denies, in opposition to Hume and Kant, both that something more must be added to an action to make it moral and that this involves one in any kind of naturalistic reduction. My basis for denying the former is the account of the logical or presuppositional character of our values given earlier. Meaning, as was argued, is normative. What we call moral meaning is nothing mysterious or essentially different from any other (nonmoral) kind of norm or value, but rather only a norm that plays a particular (and quite distinctive) role in our culture. Thus, the same basic view of the rationality and logic of our values given earlier can be taken in regard to our moral values as well. Morality is logical in character; it is the grammar of action, the form and shape of life's flow. As such, it is neither something added to action nor something that can be reduced to it; it is the form of action.

Consider the following example: We are presented with a photograph that shows a young woman taking part in a bank robbery. She has an automatic weapon in her hand, which she is pointing at several guards while her accomplices shout instructions at the bank tellers. Clearly, in most cases we would judge the action depicted here as morally reprehensible. But what if we were then told that a year before the photograph was taken, the woman had been abducted by a terrorist organization (the members of which were now her accomplices), had then been tortured, sexually assaulted, and brainwashed? Would we not see this same picture in a very different light? And wouldn't it be possible for us to judge the action in the photograph as (legal questions aside) morally *un*reprehensible— though such a judgment would depend on such matters as whether or not anyone had been harmed in the robbery and what her attitude was now (as given by what she said and how she acted)? This example shows that the process by which we judge an action to be morally reprehensible is not one (as Kant thought) of applying an apodictically certain moral principle *to* an otherwise morally neutral action. For clearly, there are many cases in which it is not morally reprehensible to break the law (or to lie, "cheat," or kill): Kant's notion of a categorical imperative as the foundation of morality is much too simple and one-dimensional to do justice to the ways in which we actually behave and think. Were Gandhi's acts of civil disobedience morally reprehensible? Or even the law-breaking actions of American western outlaws and other Robin Hoods throughout the world, many of whom have been viewed, by the community at large, as heroes?

But although it is not a principle of reason added to an action that determines its moral character, still less is it, as Hume maintained, a feeling or sentiment added to an action. That we regard a morally reprehensible action with a different feeling than we do an action that is not morally reprehensible is certainly a "fact" that, in particular cases, might be demonstrated. But such a fact is at best only one element of a total situation that cannot by itself determine the moral character of the deed. We might for example feel sorry for a criminal while harshly condemning his actions—or conversely, feel no sympathy for him and yet judge his actions as excusable. Of course, what is said here of the feelings with which we regard the actions of a criminal hold even more strongly for the feelings of the criminal himself.

Different situations and activities have their own different sorts of logic or reasonableness, and it is the latter (as well as the history and society that are the source of such reasonableness) that determines whether or not, as well as how, we judge any particular action as moral. One might call the method by which we grasp the moral character of our actions *moral description*—as opposed to the more general term *logical description*, which encompasses both moral and nonmoral norms. Although moral description (like logical description) gives the possibilities of behavior, the set of rules and norms according to which people behave, it never does this in a strictly a priori fashion but only after the practice and behavior have been observed. In the same way that logic doesn't dictate language use (it only reads out a structure from examination of certain uses), so too the categories of moral description do not dictate practice.

The *ought* of moral description is thus logically prior to the *is* of any action; at the same time, however, it is bound to it. Rules follow application, not vice versa. The *is* is not empirical in the usual (philosophical) sense, but is rather a continuing current of activities. As such, the rules that moral description yield never quite catch up with this current—with this continuous series of actions. Therefore it is not necessary to assign the moral logic or meaning of our actions to a category that is apart from such actions, even though the two are distinct. We hoist our lives up with the lever of value, but what comes up on the other side is unpredictable. The pilot shouts out directions, but he is not always heard through the roar of the waves—nor is he, when heard, always obeyed. Life is larger than logic—even moral logic.

6

Morality, then, is the form or structure of action and can be identified neither with any subjective feature grounded in the self, nor with intentional, mental processes that precede or accompany action. This view of morals is at odds not just with the views of Hume and Kant, but, it is probably fair to say, many of the dominant trends in ethical philosophy that have taken shape in modern times. It therefore becomes very important to address the issue of the intentionality of moral belief.

For this purpose, the aid of Wittgenstein can be enlisted. I do not want to examine in any detail Wittgenstein's views on the nature of intention, except to make clear that, as always, it is not Wittgenstein's purpose (any more than it is mine) to ask whether or not there really is such a thing as intending.[10] Rather, his purpose is to examine actual cases in which the term is used and by this means characterize its nature—which is to say, the range of ways in which it is used. The point that Wittgenstein comes back to repeatedly in such examinations is that when we intend to do something, we always intend within the context of an established practice or activity. For example, Wittgenstein notes that we could not intend to play a game of chess unless there were such a thing as playing chess. Moreover, when we use the word *intention* in sentences such as "Only he knew what he intended to do," this simply shows how we use the word—that is, what our *concept* of intention is. What is conceptual cannot be empirically defined in terms of an inner psychic process. For if *intention* could be defined this way, then it would make sense, at least in certain cases, to say of a person lowering a club on someone else's head that he did not really intend to hit him (that he was perhaps think-

10. See W-BB, 32; W-PI, secs. 205, 247, 337, 644, 659; W-CII, 33, 49, 53; W-RPII, secs. 115, 116, 175, 242, 274.

ing about something else and not paying attention to what he was doing), or to say that a cat stalking a bird was not really intending to kill it.

The point here might be expressed as follows: If intention is taken in its usual modern philosophical sense (to be contrasted, as Wittgenstein makes clear, with how people actually use the word) as a private mental process separate from any act that follows this process, then intention, according to the view of morals I am suggesting here, far from being the basis of morality, can have nothing *necessarily* to do with it. For consider where such an understanding of intention leads. If intention is private in the sense that a person knows he is intending to do something only by virtue of some hidden, subjective source within himself, and at the same time, all morality is based on such intention, then morals become not only subjectively based, but also intrinsically unknowable, at best to be inferred from the announcement or report of the intention. And how, if morality is unknowable, could anyone ever exercise moral judgment? If we decide or judge what is right and wrong on the basis of an intention *in* ourselves or inferred from someone else, then any such decision or judgment cannot derive from the circumstances or actions performed; its grounds must be a hidden, mental process. It is a contradiction to then posit a standard or norm by which the action is judged.

If, on the other hand, we view the intention as embedded in the situation, and therefore not removed from, but a part of, the action, then intention will certainly be an intrinsic feature of morality— though it can never encompass or adequately express by itself moral meaning. Consider, for example, a cashier working in a store who has shortchanged—by mistake—one of the customers. In many cases, we would not judge such an action to be morally reprehensible, because, for example, we might have concluded that the cashier did not perform the action on purpose; he did not shortchange the customer with the *intention* of doing so. His action was therefore a nonmoral one.

But now a few questions need to be asked about this apparently straightforward way of distinguishing a moral from a nonmoral act. First, how do we *know* whether or not the cashier committed the mistake unintentionally? And one answer to this question might run as follows: There are many ways in which we could judge whether the person had committed the act intentionally or not—by certain facts about the person, for example. If it turned out that the cashier did not know how to add or to subtract, we would be unlikely to judge he had committed the error intentionally. Or if the manager of the store were a lunatic and had ordered his employees never to calculate but only to guess at correct amounts of change to be returned to customers, we would again be unlikely to judge that the cashier's mistake was intentional. Or still another way of making such a judgment would be on the basis of what the cashier himself said were or were not his intentions—but in this case we would be faced with the problem of deciding whether or not he was telling the truth. Ultimately, we can never *know* but only infer the intentions of another person.

In response to which it must be demanded, "But then how does the person himself know whether or not he has committed the act intentionally?" And the answer to this cannot be: "Well, he just knows. He has a subjective certainty of it." For if that were true, then the locus of moral belief would not be so much in the self as nowhere. Morals would have as their basis an exchange of statements none of which could ever be confirmed, denied, or—because there would be nothing to agree *about*—made to agree with one another.

The correct answer to the above question is therefore that a person judges his own intentions on the same general basis as we judge them. It is only under certain circumstances, within certain constraints and norms of behavior, that a person states with confidence what his intentions were or are. Place him in unfamiliar circumstances, or deprive him of knowledge that he assumes as a matter of course—of, for example, the ability to add or subtract—and he will lose such knowledge of his own intentions. The point being, of course, not that he will not know what he was intending, but that he will not be able to intend at all. The capacity to intend assumes self-knowledge, which in turn assumes certain circumstances public in nature. Intentionality is therefore embedded in a situation, not in a person's mental processes. A person's mental processes are only one—of course, very real—component of such intentionality.

This discussion of intentionality should, I hope, clarify not just that to intend is to intend *in* a situation, but why philosophers so commonly misunderstand this point, why they are so inclined (since Abelard) to remove intentionality from any context and posit it as a hidden mental process in the psyche of the individual. This reason is tied to the earlier discussion of the fact/value dichotomy. For in conceiving of intention as a mental process, what we do is take certain circumstances and forms of behavior as fixed, then posit meaning and intention within an isolated, subjective sphere. We take as fact the moving substratum of our way of life, and to avoid a reductionistic view of morals, we fix on one aspect of this way of life—the mental life—as nonfactual and what is able to give meaning. But in reality our mental processes do not have a status any less factual and empirical than any other aspect of our actions and behavior; as such, they are incapable of carrying the load of meaning, especially moral meaning, that we wish to dump on them. Moral meaning, as the structure and logic of our actions, cannot have as its source an empirical process—not even a mental one.

Moreover, what has been said here of the effort to transform intentionality into a mental process and thereby make it the ground of moral beliefs and actions can also be said of the efforts of Hume and Kant to make happiness and obligation the characteristic features of morality. When Hume finds the essence of morality to consist in a "feeling of agreeableness" or moral sentiment made universal in the human species and actuated by utilitarian considerations,[11] or when Kant declares that only what imposes an absolute obligation or duty on the individual without regard to any intrinsic rewards or benefits is truly moral, both are positing the foundation of morals in man's mental capacities. It is not, of course, that happiness and obligation are irrelevant to moral conduct, but rather that they cannot be seen as embodying the meaning of such conduct. The eudaemonistic or ob-

11. *Utilitarianism* may be generally defined as the ethical doctrine that the rightness and wrongness of actions are determined by the goodness and badness of their consequences. Such a role of the consequences of actions in moral judgments may seem at odds with Hume's subjectivism, which specifically denies that the characteristic feature of moral belief can be found in its object—that is, in human action. But Hume was a utilitarian not in that he defined moral qualities in terms of their usefulness, but in that he viewed the harmful or beneficial consequences as *one* (not the only one) of the sources by which the "moral sentiment" is aroused. See H-EPM, 172–73, 179, 219, 230, 235–36, 243, 272–75, 296, 281, 234.

ligatory character of morals is a feature not of the mental state of the individual, but of the actions that the individual performs; happiness and obligation are not *causes* of moral behavior. They are its results; they are ways of characterizing particular moral actions. Similarly, the rationality of morals does not stem from the calculation of the benefits or advantages accrued to the individual or society by moral behavior, nor does it stem from the nature of the obligation or duty that the individual must a priori accept and act under. The rationality of morals, as was noted earlier, is a feature of moral action itself—which is to say, of particular kinds of actions. Moral behavior does not have a rational source; it is the source of the rationality of morals.

This point must be seen in relation to the earlier discussion of the individual versus society. Individual action is moral action insofar as it embodies, reflects, or challenges certain socially held, publicly displayed values. Individual action is not moral insofar as its sources are purely subjective, insofar as what the individual does is the product of a purely "free" choice that he might just as well not have made. The most important component of the moral behavior of an individual is not what he decides voluntarily to do, but what he does (voluntary or not) that will be incorporated—ranked, measured, judged— into the larger social sphere. A person's behavior becomes interesting and moral insofar as it reflects a way of life—and this can never be a matter of purely voluntary acts, acts that the individual, as individual, intends, for it is impossible for a person to fashion for himself that which wholly permeates his existence. Even when individual conduct doesn't merely reflect social values but also changes old, or fashions new, values, it still must have its grounds in a way of life that is logically prior—which is presupposed by what we call individual conduct. The moral meaning of our acts encompasses a sphere wider than that occupied by the cognitive judgments we bring to them.

It is for this reason that so much of the discussion of modern ethical philosophers bypasses the really fundamental moral questions. For what these discussions hinge on is the nature of the motivation—whether rational, irrational, or utilitarian—that impels an individual to act morally. Such an emphasis can only obscure the real issues at hand. *That* people act morally is a fact that needs to be accepted; they do not "act morally" only after having made a decision or having gone through this or that kind of reasoning (or lack of reasoning). The propensity of the ethical philosopher to view the subject of morals as an arena of private motivation is harmful in that he never steps outside this arena to see where the real decisions are made—in the public and personal (not private) life of the individual. The individual, as individual, habitually and quite naturally interprets as fact what is social value; he does not throw into question certain forms of behavior that are the environment in which his private concerns take place. He may even think that what is moral about his behavior is not his participation in this environment of a way of acting, but rather the subjective, mental processes that precede and accompany his actions. But for ethical philosophers to accept this view betrays superficiality. To find the basis of morals in those factors that motivate the individual to moral action is like assigning an absolute value to the cost of a particular item in an inflated, or deflated, economy. What the individual does as an individual can never be important in identifying the significance of moral acts; the actions of the individual are important insofar as they are the product of certain generally held moral sentiments or beliefs (or insofar as they combat such sentiments or beliefs). It is the social, cultural, and religious framework within which the individual acts that defines the nature of his acting in this or that way.

To make significant statements, then, about the moral behavior of a given individual in a given situation, we must not postulate certain principles—whether they be, for example, utilitarian, emotivist, intuitionist—that the individual may then act on. Rather, we must examine the moral content of the environment in which that individual in fact lives; in this way we will be in a position to understand what is happening on a moral level in the situation.

The objection, however, might now be raised that if the moral behavior of the individual can be judged only in terms of his social environment, would it not be possible to morally condemn or praise a person circumstantially—that is, on the basis of, for example, a mere "accident of birth." And in that case would we not be obscuring—once again—the difference between what is moral and what is nonmoral?

Although it is true that we do not make moral judgments about people on the basis of accidents of fate or fortune, how we judge and what we judge to be mere fate or fortune is bound up with our morality as a whole. Values are associated with certain types of circumstances, but these types are themselves defined by ever-changing forms of human behavior. To say, therefore, that one circumstance plays a role in defining value is to say simultaneously that there is no circumstance that is not in some way capable of being redefined, no circumstance whose role in our lives may not be elevated or degraded.

The fact is that we *do* judge people, in part, on the basis of their circumstances. In estimating the moral integrity of a person, or the worth of his actions, we do not eliminate everything that is incidental or circumstantial to the formation of his character. If we did this, we would eliminate his character altogether. It is true, of course, that we often take circumstances into account in estimating moral worth, but this does not mean that we do not allow them to play a role in our estimations. It means, indeed, just the opposite: that we *assign* the circumstances a role. Natural endowment or social position is not simply neutralized and prevented from influencing in any way our moral judgment; how we posit a quality as nonmoral forms part of the structure of our moral judgment. To give circumstance a role or place in this structure is therefore not to judge the individual for what he has no control over. For insofar as the individual has control over anything, it must be control over his actions and circumstances. Admittedly, such control will be partial; as an individual, he will be, to a large extent, locked into a certain range of circumstances. Experience carries with it limitations. But these limitations cannot be "bracketed" morally, for to do this is to bracket life itself and therefore transform morals into a set of empty and abstract beliefs. Circumstance, accident, and natural endowment may impose unfair and unequal constraints on us, but such constraints must be accepted and used, not denied. Circumstance can no more be segregated from moral worth than can the particular culture and historical time period in which one lives. A moral life is possible only on acceptance of a trust in the particulars of one's life. Character, moral character, is fate.

A further objection, however, might now be raised—that if the moral behavior of the individual is so organically related to his social environment, then is not a principle that many have seen as the very foundation of all morals—the a priori value or sanctity of the person—negated? I am not negating such value, but am only trying to show it does not have an empirical basis. The grounding of morals in action requires that all a priori principles (whether they be the moral sentiment of Hume or the practical postulates of Kant) be left behind. But the point of this conclusion is not that some individuals have no value and should be treated, as it were, like animals. It is to specify the conditions under which the individual does, in fact, gain value and to point out that if this value is detached from a social form of existence—a way in which people relate to one another—then such a value will become abstract and meaningless. A person, as the ancient Greeks and many other peoples believed, is a person only *in* a society. Value must be shown, must be manifested concretely, or else it will perish in its first test.

Certainly, there is no lack of "tests" in which this can be seen to happen (consider Alyosha's first, emotional response to Ivan's account of the general who tortured and killed a young child for accidentally mistreating one of the general's dogs in Dostoyevsky's *The Brothers Karamazov*). It is in cases in which there is some doubt whether an individual should be granted the full status of "person" or, alternatively, in which significant numbers of people ("welfare bums") seem to make no positive contribution to society and live like parasites that the understanding of the individual as having an a priori value independent of any social form of existence will break down. For people will tend to feel that such an a priori value does not (fully, at any rate) apply in some cases; they will revert to their own "selfish" interests and (we who are inclined to judge *them* would say) treat others inhumanely and cruelly. To say here, "Such and such has abused a freedom" can be misleading, for it must be considered where the culprit got his freedom in the first place. The point is not that individuals do not act freely, but that the line between the "free" and the "unfree" can be marked only with reference to particular circumstances. Freedom is not the opposite of constraint or authority, but is rather its daughter (just as the phenomenon of willing exists only when there is resistance and difficulty). No human action is free from social pressures; all are, in part, the product of or a response to them. But when we judge someone unworthy and deny him certain basic rights (which we, in principle, grant to everyone), we are saying at bottom that this person was "free" to act in such and such a way and did not. That is, we hold up a distorted and vacuous notion of the basis of moral behavior, and then, in situations in which we are offended by a particular person, we turn this idea against him, ignoring the fact that very few of our own acts are free, that our "virtues" are inextricably linked to the beneficial social influences we have come under the sway of.

The fact is we do judge people unfairly—that is, according to factors that are more or less beyond their control. This is inescapable because it is only through social achievement (of one sort or another) that virtue is recognized. Such achievement is perhaps never mere accident, but it is always partly that. The concepts of free will and the a priori value of the individual have a harmful effect when they hide from us our own need to judge morally, to *be* moral creatures. By the improper use of such concepts, we say to ourselves that there exists in all people a certain level of needs, rights, and privileges that must be dealt with in a nonmoral way, whereas value differences between people or cultures have a status subjective and private. We do not want to operate by a standard that discriminates (or rather, we do not want to admit this). But would a standard be a standard if it did not discriminate? Such a standard *can* be used to deny people certain privileges (though it is always open to us to object that this is a misuse of the standard). But an explicitly adopted standard does not—as an implicitly adopted one tends to do—*blame* as well as discriminate. Its discrimination is *controlled*.

All of this brings us to the last point that should be made here: that the effort to ground morality in the intentional mental processes of the individual is closely linked to the view that moral principles must be universal, applicable equally to all peoples. Of course, my point is not that there is no such thing as universal moral principles, but that the contention lacks clear sense.

It should be noted, to begin with, that such a contention is embraced not just by such ethical nonnaturalists as Hume and Kant, but also by naturalists as well. The main difference between the two is that the former make explicit what is only implicit in the latter. Which is to say: when naturalists calculate in utilitarian fashion the various "benefits" and "advantages" that presumably lie at the source of our moral beliefs, they assume a universal standard without which such calculation would be impossible (they *necessarily* do this, since all measurement requires an instrument of measurement, which in turn requires a standard). Hume's lengthy arguments for a moral sentiment make exactly this point—that ethical utilitarianism makes sense only when it is grounded on some prior, innate capacity to make moral discriminations. His theory of the moral sentiment is a way of rendering explicit this fact.

Why does the contention that there are universal moral principles lack sense? Consider the assertion—which is often made by philosophers and social scientists alike—that "there is a universal prohibition against murder."[12] Insofar as it is being maintained here that our concept of murder can be compared (likened and contrasted) with the concept of murder embraced by other peoples, I of course have no objection. For even if it were to turn out that the two concepts were so different that it would be questionable whether or not it was legitimate to call them both a concept of *murder*, still one could say that although they were not the *same*, they were related and, therefore, a comparison taking into account both similarities and differences would be justified.

But when philosophers and social scientists say that there is a universal prohibition against murder, they mean something quite different, something more than this. They mean that there exists some feeling or attitude or belief toward killing that is the same for all cultures. And what is the same here cannot consist of the actions performed by men and called murder, for these actions are, of course, very different (it is readily admitted—and it would be absurd not to do so—that not every act *we* call murder is regarded as such by other cultures). What is "the same" must therefore consist in something *apart* from any of the particular actions involved; it must be something internal that goes on in the mind or consciousness. But what is the status of this internal event? It is in the possible answers to this question that the sense of the contention that there is a universal prohibition against murder breaks down. For if this internal event has an *empirical* status, then it can have nothing to do, one way or the

12. Patrick H. Nowell-Smith, "Religion and Morality," in *Encyclopedia of Philosophy*, VII, 153.

other, with what we or any other culture calls murder (since what we or any other culture calls murder is a concept, not a fact).

If, on the other hand, this internal event is given a conceptual status, then what is being called a "prohibition against murder" must have reference not just to internal actions occurring in the mind, but also to external actions occurring in the social world. Clearly, the meanings given to these actions vary a great deal among different peoples, making it is implausible to say, a priori, that such a prohibition against murder must be universal. What must be determined before such a conclusion is reached is whether or not the different cultures really have the same concept of murder—and this can only be done by examining their social practices and beliefs. It is in relation to these practices and beliefs, and only in relation to them, that the words *the same* have good sense, just as it is only after criteria for identity are established that we can legitimately talk about certain beliefs being universal or not.

When, nonetheless, philosophers and social scientists talk so uncritically about the universality of moral beliefs, what they are doing is ignoring the cultural meanings embedded in foreign practices and beliefs and substituting their own, more familiar ones. What allows them to do this without apparently meeting contradiction by the facts is their confused view of the meaning of a "prohibition against murder" as a quasi-empirical, quasi-conceptual entity. For such a view permits them (1) to ignore the phenomena (*i.e.*, the practices and beliefs of other cultures) as they present themselves and to claim instead that what really constitutes a moral prohibition against murder is hidden and internal and (2) to impose their own cultural concept of murder on other cultures without examining *its* basis in a set of practices and beliefs.

There are few more seductive and potentially harmful contentions than those involving the universalization of our moral principles. It is the essence of morals to discriminate, to rank actions and types of behavior in a hierarchy or, at least, an unequal arrangement. The requirement, on the other hand, that our moral principles be universalized is promoted by an urge to deny the inequalities intrinsic to human behavior (or at least *our* human behavior), an urge to impose a separate, purified logic on life and to condemn what does not conform. The principle of universalization serves as one of the main props for this purified logic.

A principle can be universalized only when it is abstracted from all particular applications of the principle. Once abstracted, it becomes something separate that dictates to, rather than being read out of, human actions. The result is that the manifold differences in behavior that always form the basis of people's moral behavior—what they value and what they do not, what they feel should be ignored and what they feel should be paid careful attention to—are denied or at least glossed over. If people do not actually behave according to a priori rules of morality, it is sometimes reasoned, then this is not the fault of the rules (which are universal), but of the people. In this way, our moral principles become divorced from what people do.

7

If what I have been calling the "moral meaning" of our actions arises out of those actions and is not imposed on them by a disembodied, intentional self, then what role is there for the traditional notion of virtue, which is closely linked to the idea of "the virtuous man" and (according to some accounts) posits the basis of morals in the individual? The answer to this question is that the role of the traditional notion of virtue in the conception of morals being suggested here is a very large one, except that virtue must be thought of not as, in the modern sense, a kind of haze that accompanies the individual, but rather in terms of the Greek word *arete* (often translated "virtue"), with its connotations of a "doing" or a practice, activity, or art. Once this is done, there will be little temptation to associate virtue with a mental state; rather, virtue will be that which is embodied in human actions. The self, though denied a position or role as the basis of morals, will attain an even more fundamental one as its form. Virtue is not an inward process or state; it is, by nature, public and open to view. At the same time, however, the self can never be a spectator of its own virtue, because it is itself part of the picture. The self is indeed an *exhibition* of virtue; we mold ourselves and our conduct, but we do this from the inside out. Above all, we must do away with the notion of the self as an entity that peeps out from its corner to judge what is virtuous and what is not, that rushes out from time to time to do what it calls a "good deed" and thereby lines the cabinet of its mind with trophies. For virtue is not a pose that the self adopts; it is not earned, much less rewarded. It is a working, and a reworking, of the materials of ourselves (ethics as the aesthetics of character).

It follows, then, that it is very misleading to speak of self-knowledge in a moral sense. That is not, however, because values are subsidiary to facts, but rather because they are their basis. In the most fundamental way, we must remain ignorant of ourselves, for we are at once artists and works of art. Our consciousness, our thoughts and beliefs, are displays of character and virtue. How then could we use them to understand, to "know" ourselves? The dictum should not be "Know thyself" but rather "Become thyself."

To put this notion of virtue into perspective, it might be useful to see what bearing it has on one of the topics of ethical philosophy discussed at length by Hume, that of the question of man's inherent selfishness or benevolence. Hume took the position, at least in his later ethical writing, that man's conduct cannot be reasonably explained with reference only to his self-interest. Rather, a moral sentiment essentially disinterested with regard to the self must also be postulated. Although Hume in his first major work, the *Treatise*, describes this disinterested moral sentiment as simply the effect of a mechanical association of ideas, the perspective is much more generous in his later writings. Benevolence is an inherent part of man's nature.

It is interesting to note that this apparent shift in Hume's perspective is analogous to a shift in Kant's works. Kant, in his first *Critique*, justified the objectivity of science by grounding it in the empirical world (thereby implying that the assertions of religion and morals had a subjective status only), but then, in the second *Critique*, attempted to diminish the force of this argument by speaking of the "practical postulates" as objective. For both Hume and Kant, man's beliefs are rooted in his subjective consciousness. But because such an account seems to undermine especially man's *moral* beliefs (which lack empirical data to support them) a deus ex machina, in the form of inherent benevolence, or the practical postulates, must be called on to save the day. Only in this way can the integrity of virtue be preserved.

The view of morals put forth here requires no such rescue work. Since man's knowledge and behavior are rooted, in the first place, in his actions as a moral being, morals have no need of Hume's sentimentality or Kant's suprarationality to help them out of a difficult position. Man's conduct cannot be inherently selfish, because the self is nothing more than the form of actions in a public context. The self has reference to such actions; its actions, virtuous or otherwise, do not have their source in a mental, abstract entity. But at the same time that it must be denied that selfishness is an inherent part of man's nature, it must also be denied that benevolence and altruism are inherent. Man does not benefit others by sacrificing himself; all actions, including those of self-sacrifice, are *expressions* of self. When a mother sacrifices herself for her children, or a soldier sacrifices himself for his country, each gives expression to his or her character and personality. Calling their actions acts of self-sacrifice should not mislead us to believe that what they *are* is somehow capable of being negated, any more than calling an action selfish should mislead us to believe that anything can somehow be added to what a person is. In both cases, we have the misleading picture of a substrate (the self) accruing and denying itself benefits. But that we call giving money to the poor altruistic and stealing money from the poor selfish is not determined directly by what the self acquires or denies itself in the two cases; it is determined by the social and moral meanings we attach to those actions (for example, the giving of one's possessions to others can, in some cases, be characterized as selfish, as were the potlatches of North American Indians). The self is not denied or enlarged in such acts, because what the self is—as well as the concept of virtue, to which it is closely related—is expressed through those acts.

I am not denying that to be selfish and to be benevolent refer to different actions. Rather, I am emphasizing that they *do* refer to actions and, as such, have their reference in a context of both self and others. What would it be like to be selfish (or benevolent) in a world in which there were only one person? The terms would lose their meaning. Selfish acts and benevolent acts do not have reference to a universal standard of benefits and standards; they are ungrounded forms of action that mutually imply each other. The self does not escape the self when it is altruistic, nor is the Other denied in acts of selfishness. Selfishness is the ground of benevolence, as benevolence is the ground of selfishness. It is therefore misleading to characterize man as essentially selfish or essentially benevolent. (Aristotle grasped this in his notion of "the great-souled man.")

The refusal to ground morals in the mental or intentional processes of the individual is thus not equivalent to banishing the self from the sphere of morals (as if that were even conceivable). The behavior of the individual is still the fulcrum or reference point on which morality turns. But now, instead of virtue consisting in an intention or special mental quality *added to* the action of the individual, it derives from those actions themselves, from the form that they take. Thus, any effort to say what virtue is will not be able to avoid discussing at length, as Aristotle did, examples and instances of virtuous acts. What is at issue here is the cultivation of an attitude of innocence toward the subject of morals; we must stop seeing our behavior as dictated by some behind-the-scenes belief or rule.

But now the question arises, What of the traditional "beliefs" of religion that were affirmed by metaphysical philosophers to be the basis of morals and were denied this very status by Hume and Kant, the latter refusing to make morals dependent on unproved and unprovable religious dogmas and preferring instead to see their basis in a disembodied self? To answer this question, a point similar to the one made about the self as the basis of morals needs to be repeated: a belief can never be the foundation of morality, but at best one of its components. Thus, if religious beliefs are taken in a detached, subjectivistic sense, then the arguments of Kant more or less apply: such beliefs arise out of morality and are dependent on it. But if, on the other hand, religion refers to a way of life, the crucial element of which is practice, not belief, then morality and religion cannot be sharply separated. The two alternatives might be thought of in this way. In the first case, the dogmas and associated beliefs of a given religion are a sort of picture presented to the individual. The benefits and selling points of this picture are clear: it offers the individual an explanation of the nature of his existence—both where he came from and where he will go—and instructs him in a mode of conduct. The individual, for his part, may approach this picture and study it from all sides before accepting its explanations or not. In the second alternative, however, the situation is different. The individual does not view religion as a picture or explanation to be assented to or not; he finds himself in the picture (he is presented with "an offer he can't refuse"). Once in the picture, he no longer views its elements statically, but begins to see them move: he is himself part of the current. Any sort of mental assent he gives to the religion will not necessarily be of crucial importance; it will be just one of a series of actions that he performs in the religious life, or current, he now finds himself in.

The point is that although religious belief is of a radically different nature than scientific, factual belief, it is different not in the sense of lying in a subjective, "as if" sphere that never makes contact with empirical reality. Rather, it is different in that it lies closer to the heart of what all our beliefs are founded on, being the basis of all human action and forms of social and cultural life. The sacred history of the five books of Moses, for example, was obviously not put forward in the spirit of a scientific hypothesis. Nor was it put forward as an account wholly lacking in objective reality. It is a "history"—a story, if you will—told from the viewpoint of one of the principal characters in the story. Thus, it is certainly true that if religion is understood not as a picture to be looked at, but rather as one to put ourselves in, it does serve as the indispensable foundation of morals. It does this not by giving us a competing view or alternative to the scientific one, but by providing us with a means and a way of life, something that science (founded on the controlled laboratory environment) is incapable of doing.

A similar point can be made in regard to our concept of faith. Faith is not a detached belief that can be picked up or dropped; rather, it signifies a trust and acceptance of one's environment and one's self that is manifested in—that permeates and cannot be separated from—everyday existence. Faith is not opposed to reason; it is the grounds from which all reason issues (that is why we must be careful not to transform faith *into* a reason). That is, I think, what medieval thinkers had in mind when they self-consciously sought "reasons" for what they already believed on faith. Such a perspective must be contrasted with the modern one, which views faith as a subjective certainty, a mental and emotional state of the individual disconnected from all matters of reason. The latter notion of faith takes as its basis the concession wrung from science that the nonexistence of God cannot be proven. Its source can be traced to a feeling of despair that God has retreated so far behind the scenes, behind the scientific world of appearance and mechanistic laws, that we can no longer make contact with him except by plunging within, by indulging ourselves in some utterly private experience that will somehow break down the barriers that our way of life, our public behavior, has put between us and God. No wonder that such a faith has often let the winds of its impatience with and fear of reason whip itself up into a blustering faith! It was Nietzsche who discerned this situation most clearly; God had perished not from mere lack of belief, but from lack of a society and way of life in which God could be manifested.

Faith, then, in the sense in which I am using it here—a sense characteristic of non-Western and early religions as well as the monotheistic religions—denotes primarily a trust and acceptance of life's situation, a situation that one doesn't choose, but that one is born into and that forms the conditions of all experience, mental or physical.

Such acceptance and trust entails, first, that we not try to "deny ourselves" by separating ourselves from the particular circumstances that we are born into and that accompany us wherever we go: our family ties, social relations, culture, economic status, natural abilities and liabilities—that whole myriad of attributes and qualities that we are inclined to feel are external to "who we really are." The self, far from being independent of all these externals, could not exist without them; all acts of will and intention require them, require a resistance, a limitation, a horizon. The self is indeed most itself when it feels itself bounded—defined, but not limited, by its actions. Indeed, in inventing a self apart from all externals, we only add to the list of things that encumber us. The self is something neither external nor internal, neither a physical object nor a mental object; it is the form of action in the world. Everything lies open to view, including our deepest, most complicated thoughts. The attempt to see the self as something apart from its actions is an attempt to deny the nature of the self; but the denial only defeats itself. In the same way that the making of a resolution to do something can be effective only by being itself a part of the doing, so too the effort to conceive of the self metaphysically cannot be successful, but can nonetheless be accepted as an action that is one of the components of the self. To conceive of the self as a form of action is not to deny anything; it is rather only to witness that the light or meaning of our actions does not have a subjective source.

Second, and perhaps more important, faith entails the acceptance of our own passions and desires—a trust and belief in ourselves and in the grounds of our existence. As moral beings, we must never try to diminish such passions and desires, but only increase them. As Goethe said: "I hate everything that merely instructs one without increasing or directly quickening my activity."[13] Or Plato: "I only wish ordinary people had an unlimited capacity for doing evil, for then they might have an unlimited capacity for doing good" (Crito 44d). None of which is to say that we should give free vent to our emotions; it is to say that the commonwealth of our desires should be governed as a republic, not a dictatorship. As such, no emotion— even if it justifies itself as rational—should be allowed to take full control; the rationality of our emotional lives consists in the proper balance achieved among all our passions. In the same way that the logic of our moral behavior runs through all our deeds, both good and evil, so too the logic of our personalities runs through all aspects of who we are, from the most spiritual to the most corporeal. And of course, as in the case of the logic of our moral actions, the logic of our personality is nothing we can formulate and apply in a detached way; the logic of our personality is something that must be embodied and lived. Any control over it is necessarily from within, as an artist controls his creations by mastering the techniques by which they are formed. What we call virtue, then, is the form of our passions, the ground and logic by which they are expressed. In the same way that, on a social level, moral meaning is the logic that runs through our empirical existence and all the factual beliefs we formulate about it (that set of assumptions about human behavior without which our present form of life would be inconceivable), so too the operation of

13. Friedrich Nietzsche, The Use and Abuse of History, trans. Adrian Collins (Indianapolis, 1957), 3.

our passions and emotions must be grounded in that logical substratum we call personality. Virtue, as the directing force of our personalities, heightens, not diminishes, our sensory awareness by shaping it in particular forms. Self-knowledge, in this sense, is not an abstract reasoning, but a bringing to fruition of our passionate natures under the guidance of the hand of virtue.

V   The Causal Fallacy
Cultural Anthropology
and Comparative Religion

Conceptual difficulties manifest in traditional formulations of culture and morality are exhibited by a variety of disciplines, ranging from the physical and biological sciences to the study of culture and religion. The disciplines can be placed into two major groups, according to the type of fallacy they are associated with.

One type of fallacy, which will be discussed later, is characteristic of historians of religions and consists of defining cultural and, especially, religious phenomena according to a universal prototype or essence. Through such a definition, historians of religions invest certain features of man's subjective awareness with logical force.

The other type of fallacy, with which this chapter is concerned, is mainly (though by no means exclusively) characteristic of Boasian cultural anthropologists. It hinges on the status we give to the word *cause* and consists in investing empirical data in the external world with logical force.[1] As an introduction to some of the philosophical issues involved in this type of fallacy, Hume's views on causality will be discussed.

What were Hume's views on causality? It should be noted, to begin with, that for Hume the belief in causality is a very important one, for it is by virtue of causality that all scientific laws and principles are justified. As he says, "All reasonings concerning matters of fact seem to be founded on the relation of Cause and Effect. By means of that relation alone we can go beyond the evidence of our memory and senses." (H-EHU, 26).

Hume opens his discussion of causality by noting some of the features by which we are inclined to say "*x* caused *y*," including con-

---

1. Wittgenstein had a clear grasp of what I am calling the "causal fallacy," though he did not emphasize its application to the study of culture. W-WCII, 33; W-RC, secs. 51, 317; W-PP, 315–16; W-Z, sec. 608–11; W-VB, 37, 62; W-WCI, 81, 103–104; W-BB, 5–6, 15; W-PI, secs. 169, 176–77, 193–94, 466, 485, 631, pp. 193, 203; W-LC, 14–15, 18, 21; W-WCII, 4–5, 16, 38, 40, W-RPII, secs. 172, 175, 324; W-PG, 8, 10, 13, 16, 30, 60, 68, 70, 80, 97, 99, 101, 105, 110, 118, 168, 187; W-RFM, bk. I, sec. 128.

tiguity, or nearness in space (x must be proximal to y), and temporal priority (x must occur prior to y). He eventually concludes, however, that the most important feature of our belief in causality is necessary connection: "An object may be contiguous and prior to another, without being considered as its cause. There is a Necessary Connexion to be taken into consideration; and that relation is of much greater importance than any of the other two above mentioned" (H-THN, 77).

In order to conclude that my throwing the glass *caused* it to break against the wall, it is not sufficient to observe that the throwing was spatially proximal and temporally prior to the breaking; something must in addition be seen as relating the two events *necessarily*.

What is that necessity? For Hume, the answer is not to be found in the events themselves considered as such nor in the circumstances in which the events occurred; there is no impression to which the idea of necessary connection can be traced. Rather, necessity is a quality added on by a subjective source: "In all instances of the operation of bodies or minds there is nothing that produces any impression, nor consequently can suggest any idea of power or necessary connexion. Necessity, then . . . is nothing but an internal impression of the mind, or a determination to carry our thoughts from one object to another. . . . There is no internal impression, which has any relation to the present business, but that propensity, which custom produces, to pass from an object to the idea of its usual attendant. . . . necessity is something that exists in the mind, not in objects" (H-EHU, 78).

What are we to make of this account of causality as a subjective factor added on to the phenomena that are present? Consider the example "He threw the ball at the window and broke the glass." Was it the throwing that caused the glass to break or the darkness of the room at the time the ball was thrown? We say the former, but why? Hume's answer is that some extra element (necessary connection) must be added to the phenomenon, so that the throwing will be connected to the breaking in a way that the darkness is not. But in what way? The throwing and the darkness are both phenomena that accompanied the breaking of the glass. To invest one with logical force (which Hume does through his property of necessary connection), and not the other, seems arbitrary.

"What we decide the cause is depends on our point of view." For example, sociologically, we might say that the cause was overcrowding (which prompts people to throw things at windows). We usually conclude something could be a cause when things could have been otherwise—when the ball could have not been thrown, when overcrowding could have been prevented—when it is at least *imaginable* that such and such would not have happened. Viewing an event as a cause means distinguishing the event from the purely logical or contextual features of the situation in which the event occurs: it means imagining the situation *apart* from the event (that is why, for example, feet do not "cause" walking). Establishing one event as the cause, in opposition to another, then becomes—after such a distinction has been made—a matter of *experience*.

The plausibility of Hume's notion that there is a special property called necessary connection that is responsible for something being a cause is derived from a misunderstanding of examples that involve human agents ("I threw the ball"). Hume likens such examples to examples in which human agents are not present ("Flooding causes the soil to erode") by asking, "What makes *us* believe that such and such is the cause?" But that "I caused the window to break" is not something that *I*, as opposed to others, could establish empirically (rather, it is presupposed in our concepts of, for example, self and intention). Similarly, what necessarily relates flooding and eroding (necessary connection) does not stand in an external relation to flooding and eroding. That one phenomenon is a cause, and another not, is decided by observation; what allows us to make observations in the first place is the logic governing the situation in which we make the observations.

In viewing causality as a subjective factor added onto the phenomena, Hume separates the configuration, or arrangement, of objects and events, on one hand, and our attitude toward this configuration, on the other. He then goes on to ignore a crucial distinction—the distinction between the framework in which the phenomena occur (which has no empirical basis) and the causal relations that exist between the phenomena within that framework (which can only be established empirically). The problem underlying both of these mistakes is Hume's incapacity to see that meaning cannot be grounded empirically but is, on the contrary, the presupposition of all observation. Hume's starting point of analysis (the mind being struck by impressions) is, in fact, a point very far down the line. In order for the empirical object to be perceived at all, it must first take up a position in the logic of the situation. It is precisely in that logic, in the context in which all phenomena occur, that a basis for causality is laid; Hume's propensity to ignore all context (to analyze it away) is what drove him to conceive of causality as a kind of deus ex machina not so much lowered down as conjured up by the mental processes of the individual. What he failed to note is that these mental processes are themselves phenomena embedded in particular situations; they cannot therefore be "what causality consists in."

Hume was certainly right to believe that the causal relation is not grounded in an abstract process of pure reason or relation of ideas; where he went wrong was in concluding that it was therefore something nonrational. Rather, the causal relation is possessed of a reasonableness that obtains from the framework in which it is posited. Causality is not something either-or; there are indeed degrees of causality. The reason this is so is that when we say, "Such and such happened because . . ." we do not cite just one cause or observation. Although doing this may in some cases be sufficient, it is nonetheless true that waiting in the wings are a whole series of reasons and justifications that act as supports for the cause cited, none of which would necessarily be sufficient by itself but when taken together would be convincing. To make a judgment concerning cause, there must be, first, a background of belief. Consider the statement "Yesterday I destroyed that town." Compare the different contexts that we supply for this statement depending on whether it was uttered by a god in a myth; a pilot flying a bomber; a child; a construction worker in a demolition project; or a deranged person. In each case, the possibility of judgment concerning the truth of the statement is contingent on whether such a context can be supplied; there is no sense in talking about a relation of causality independent of context. At the same time, in order for us to come to a judgment concerning the truth of the statement, the logic or contextual framework must stand in the background and be readily distinguishable from the causal event. It is the same with phenomena observed in a scientific laboratory: we have to know and be convinced of what we are seeing before we will lend credence to it. Consider, for example, the failure of early scientists to "believe their own eyes" regarding the behavior of matter at super-cooled temperatures. And how is it that *we* so readily accept their reports now?

Thus, it should be clear that I am using the term *cause* in a modern, non-Aristotelian sense. Causality signifies (as it signifies for most social scientists and philosophers today) efficient causality; what Aristotle called "final causality" comes under the heading of what I have been calling meaning or logic (this modern terminology is not necessarily preferable; however, it is too well established to change). When I speak of the cause of a phenomenon, I am speaking of its empirical cause, that which can be verified by an agreed-upon system of measurement or description. To talk about the cause of a phenomenon is not to talk about reasons or, even less, grounds. Rather, any determination of causality assumes that the reasons are already given, that the meaning and logic in which the phenomena can be observed are established and accepted. Between meaning and cause there is a sharp distinction. Any conclusion concerning the causal determinants of a given phenomenon can only be the result of an empirical investigation, the result of, for example, making a hypothesis and observing what does or does not happen in an actual case. But the significance or nature of a phenomenon cannot be affected by such an empirical investigation (more precisely, it will be affected only to the extent that it may induce us to redefine the phenomenon). The reason for this is that we investigate causes only by assuming a given meaning; we agree to obey a certain set of rules for what does or does not constitute the phenomenon. Only in this way do we recognize or even see the phenomenon in the first place. The rules governing phenomena may, of course, change, just as the systems of measurement that science uses may change. But they will not and cannot change simply as a result of empirical observation. For all empirical observations are conditions; their limits are set by the framework in which they are made. Change does not occur outside this framework (all unexpected events take shape in the light of what is expected). In order for significant change to occur, the way we see such events must change; not just the objects, but also our vision itself, must be altered. The meaning must move, the logic must walk; but empirical observation has no feet.

2

The first example I would like to consider as a way of clarifying some of these difficulties around our concepts of meaning and cause is an example discussed at length by Wittgenstein, though my treatment will make no attempt to follow his. The example is the difference between what constitutes the definition of a color—say, yellow—and what constitutes a particular patch being identified as yellow. The former is conceptual; it consists in the assertion that such and such a color sample is yellow. The latter is empirical; it consists in the assertion that, given a color sample yellow, a particular patch is or is not yellow. This distinction seems straightforward; obviously, the definition of yellow is the basis for the determination that any particular patch is or is not yellow. Just as obviously, the definition is distinct from the empirical determination. Where then is the difficulty?

The difficulty comes when we try to understand what constitutes the distinction, for it may seem then that the definition of yellow is purely arbitrary or conventional. That is, we may think that the *sign* by which we designate the color yellow is arbitrary and that what we now call yellow could just as well be called "green," or "ant," or "xytz"—with no change in the underlying physical phenomenon that all these signs stand for. This underlying physical phenomenon will be, of course, the wavelength of electromagnetic radiation corresponding to what we now call yellow. Thus, the definition of yellow will be viewed as little more than the designation of this physical phenomenon by means of an arbitrary linguistic sign. Or, if this seems insufficient, we will think that what constitutes the concept of yellow is a mental image or idea or internalized picture of it—and that this mental image is the real sample or standard on the basis of which we determine any particular patch to be yellow or not. We will then say this internalized sample is the subjective counterpart to the wavelength of the color we call yellow.

The situation, thus, is now complicated—and confused. What we call yellow—which seemed so clear and unambiguous a moment ago—has now become hidden; it is constituted either by a certain wavelength (which can be determined only under conditions that are alien to the vast majority of situations in which we use the term *yellow*, that is, by means of a spectroscope), or it is constituted by a mental image that only the individual has access to. Before, what we meant by *yellow* was given by a simple action—that of pointing to a given sample and saying, "This is yellow." But now, it seems as though what yellow is must consist in something more than this action; it must have a basis that is behind or beneath the action and the accompanying phenomenon, something that, as it were, gives meaning to the mere action. "For," we would like to say, "if yellow does not consist in a certain wavelength, or a certain mental image corresponding to this wavelength, then what does it consist in? It must be *something*."

With this step, the supposedly "clear" distinction I made above between the definition and the empirical determination of yellow has been obscured. Both have the same basis—an underlying physical phenomenon. The difference is that the concept of yellow is thought of as a mental image corresponding to a physical phenomenon, whereas the yellow patch is still conceived of as something external. When we "define" a given sample to be yellow (when we link our mental image of yellow to the yellow sample), we are doing the same thing as when we empirically determine a given patch to be yellow; we are comparing an internal, or at least hidden, model with an external object or patch. The definition of yellow has been given an empirical basis; the *concept* of yellow has become a thing, whether we want to think of this thing as mental or material. We accordingly regard what yellow is as, in some hazy sense, being "caused" by a certain wavelength. Cause and concept have become confused.

In opposition to this line of thinking, my argument is as follows. Although it is true that "what yellow is" consists of something more than the mere act of pointing to a given sample and saying, "This is yellow," what this "something more" is, is not a mental image or even a wavelength measured by a spectroscope. It is the total range of uses of the term *yellow* that can be harmonized with the act of pointing to a given sample and saying, "This is yellow." These uses might include everything from pausing at traffic lights to the way an artist employs yellow in his paintings. Insofar as these uses will support and be consistent with the definition, the definition will be a "good" (not, strictly speaking, a "true") one. The finding that yellow corresponds to a certain wavelength might, of course, be included as one of these uses. But this finding cannot be equated *with* "what yellow is." For the finding is itself predicated on a prior understanding or recognition gained in the everyday activities and practices in which we use the word *yellow*. A Martian scientist who could determine the wavelength of what we call yellow but who had no experience or acquaintance with our everyday use of the word would not understand our concept of it. (As Wittgenstein said, "When we're asked 'What do "red", "blue", "black", "white", mean?' we can, of course, immediately point to things which have these colours,—but that's all we can do: our ability to explain their meaning goes no further" (W-RC, sec. 102).

I am, of course, perfectly willing to grant that if we wish to define yellow as a certain wavelength, we can do so, and in that case "what yellow is" will *be* that wavelength. But then the wavelength will not be, in any sense, the *cause* of what we call yellow. Rather, it will have acquired a conceptual status. A model dependent on certain everyday activities will have been replaced by one dependent on the spectroscope. Either we should identify yellow with what is logically presupposed in the range of uses and experiences in which we use the term *yellow* (of which the determination of wavelength is only one) or we should define color *as* wavelength. In neither case, however, will yellow be something hidden or mental. In conceiving of yellow as hidden—as beyond the practices and activities in which we use the word *yellow*—what we are doing is transforming a logical presupposition *of* our experience into a fact *in* our experience, even if the fact must be hidden or mental. It is as though we would like to reach out and take hold of yellow, but, failing this, are content to think of it as locked in a vault that can never be opened.

Consider the following: An artist points to a painting and says, "Yellow is good here." Can this be translated, "It is my subjective opinion that a certain wavelength of radiation should be here"— such that if another person disagreed and said, "No, green is better here," then the disagreement would have nothing to do with the phenomena of green and yellow as wavelengths, but simply with the attitudes adopted toward them?

But if the colors are defined by their uses, this could not be. For then, "Yellow is good here" must have something to do with the geometry of colors: the statement reflects the relationships that are perceived as existing between the colors. Whether or not yellow is good here (or whether it doesn't matter—in which case, there will be reasons offered) will be something that can be objectively shown by observing the ways in which the term *yellow* is used by painters; such an answer will be possible if there exists a tradition of painting. That two distinguished painters might disagree on the answer is due to the fact that there exist different traditions or that a particular tradition is changing. But it is, nonetheless, such traditions that establish what yellow "is" by establishing how it is used.

What we say the physical properties of the universe are is contingent on the sort of beings we are, which is, in turn, reflected in our practices and ways of life. The scientist in his laboratory or the commuter in his automobile, obeying traffic signals, may not have any use for such a truth—nor is there any reason he should. But the artist continually bumps his head against the limits of how colors are used; his exercise of judgment regarding colors will inevitably give him lumps. "Yellow is right here," he says, suggesting that the world *should* perceive it as such. And the world sees, or it does not.

3

As another example, consider the assertion "Such and such microorganism is the cause of disease x." This assertion sounds innocent enough, for after all, is it not a causal relation established by scientific methods? But in fact, there is a fallacy hidden in it. The fallacy, it is important to understand, has nothing to do with the fact that a given cause may often have more than one effect—that, for example, the causative agent of tuberculosis does not always produce the disease in a carrier (because the agent is, for some reason, rendered avirulent)—for all this does is make the relation of causality more complex. The real difficulty comes when the microorganism is not just posited as the cause of the disease, but is also used as a criterion of identity of the disease—as when a doctor identifies the disease by ordering a laboratory test to detect the micro-organism. For if the presence of this microorganism in the patient's body defines the disease, it cannot simultaneously be a cause; a causal relation can only be established empirically, by experiment. But if the microorganism is a necessary condition for the existence of the disease, then there is obviously no experiment that could be performed that could either affirm or deny the assertion that "the bacillus is the, or a, cause of disease x."

What is at work here is our tendency to invest an empirical fact (the fact that the bacillus causes disease x) with a logical status (in the same way in which we invest the fact that yellow corresponds to a certain wavelength with a logical status). We give the bacillus a sort of power to produce an effect, that is, the disease. In doing so, we etherealize disease x; we make it something mysterious and unknowable as our minds flutter back and forth giddily between "what disease x is" and "its cause." We fail to see that if the bacillus is a criterion of identity for disease x, then x cannot be defined with reference to its symptoms (they are only external manifestations) and that if the bacillus is the cause of disease x, it cannot be the same as x. Disease x is neither the symptoms nor the bacillus. So what is it? It seems to have disappeared.

At this point, we may be inclined to do something similar to what we did in the case of the color yellow: define disease x as a kind of mental idea or picture. Though such an alternative seems a good deal less plausible than in the case of color, it nonetheless satisfies the same urge, the urge to conceive of the disease as some sort of thing. It is as though we yearn so much for something fixed behind the phenomena we observe that we can never be content with what presents itself simply before us. We cannot be content to define the disease with reference to the family of symptoms (and the circumstances corresponding to those symptoms) in which it is exhibited. We do not want the line between those who have the disease and those who don't to fluctuate, though in fact it very often does. We yearn for an absolute (or to deny an absolute—the source of the impulse is the same). Out of this yearning, we fix on one factor in the disease process, the bacillus, and we invest it with contradictory powers.

Of course, just as in the case of the color yellow, we may *define* disease x as the presence of such and such bacillus. But then it makes little sense to say that the bacillus *causes* the disease. If we wish to allow for the possibility of a causal relation between the two, then they must *be* two—they must be capable of being defined independently.

The success of antibiotics in treating and curing infectious diseases makes it natural to devote a great deal of attention to microorganisms as "causes" of such diseases. But it is a metaphysical urge that then makes us go on to identify such causes *with* the diseases.

In the cases of both the color and the disease, then, when faced with a logical presupposition *of* our experience, we seek to make this a fact *in* our experience. We fail to recognize such logical presuppositions as rules or norms about practices and activities within a social and cultural context. This is also what we do with the self in general; we make it a sort of gaseous medium inside the head, a medium that can be treated as an object in temporal and empirical relation to external objects. Consider the statement "I intended to throw the ball . . ." The *I* here is not something that stands outside the action and causes it, any more than the wavelength and bacillus stand outside the color yellow and disease *x* and cause them. We have a tendency to regard the actions that the self performs (like the yellow patches and the symptoms of disease *x*) as public, while at the same time viewing the *I* itself (like the wavelength and bacillus, or their corresponding mental images) as hidden. In all cases, we give priority to what is hidden. The "experience" of the color, the constellation of the symptoms of the disease, become nebulous and ill defined; they become, in short, mental objects, just as the action performed by the *I* becomes an action only by virtue of a certain factor or force or moral quality that the *I* lends to it.

4

Let us now consider another example more closely related to the province of culture. The example consists in the effort to explain cultural beliefs and practices on the basis of the genetic or the physiological characteristics of the peoples involved, or both. This type of explanation, which was especially popular in the nineteenth century, is today widely regarded as racially motivated. The principal argument advanced against it—as, for example, by Franz Boas—is that there is insufficient evidence to support such a causal connection between genetic endowment and social behavior (*see*, for example B-MPM). According to Boas, both the "causes" and the "effects" are of such complexity that we cannot credibly and scientifically link the two, at least given the present state of knowledge. This is also, at bottom, the argument made by those opposing the idea that intelligence is inherited. In both cases, it is reasoned that the studies available, as well as the present state of knowledge on the subject in general, provide insufficient support for such conclusions.

Now, it is important to note that this method of argumentation leaves open the at least remote possibility that scientists may one day discover evidence that will make such a connection between genetic and physiological endowment, on one hand, and social and cultural behavior, on the other, scientifically plausible. It is, however, just this possibility that I am concerned with denying. My argument is accordingly directed not just against any account of culture in terms of racial characteristics, but also against the pervasive presumption that social practices and beliefs are of such a nature that they *can* be explained in terms of genetic or neurological processes. The argument does not deny, of course, that, for example, neurologists may one day be able to precisely correlate what we call happy or sad, rational or irrational behavior with certain areas or pathways of the brain. What it denies is that by such a correlation we have thereby given an account of the significance of such behavior. For the correlation itself depends on our prior understanding of such significance—and that has been gained in a nonscientific context.

The crucial fallacy is this: we think that there is something in the neurological structures of our brains that is somehow possessed of a capacity to reach out and cause social and cultural behavior (what, for example, it means to be happy or sad, and rational or irrational). Of course, it can be readily demonstrated that the stimulation of a certain area of the brain causes a certain type of reaction; this is an empirical assertion that can be demonstrated experimentally. But note that the assertion that, for example, behaviors x and y are controlled by the left and right sides of the brain goes far beyond the empirical assertion; the latter maintains (at least, implicitly) that there is a connection between physiology and behavior independent of any context, experimental or otherwise, in which it is demonstrated. Consider the following scenario: There exists a group of scientists with an enormously detailed and sophisticated understanding of the relationship between neurological processes and behavior. Only, as it turns out, these scientists are from a different planet, a planet inhabited by creatures with a form of life that has no counterpart to any on earth. Now, these scientists are brought down to earth and asked to predict, on the basis of neurological evidence alone, the behavior of earth people. Even if they had become thoroughly familiar with the structure and workings of human brains (they might be able to detect events and pathways that earth scientists had never observed), what would they be able to say? The answer, of course, is, little or nothing, for what characterizes the behavior of earth people does not have reference primarily to the workings of the brain.

The point is that there is nothing *in* the brain that can establish a necessary and universal connection between it and human behavior; although such a necessary and universal connection is stipulated, the stipulation is nonempirical and is a condition of experience, not a result gained from it. Because our culture places so much faith in science, it invests a particular result arrived at in the laboratory with a metaphysical status. That the stimulation of a certain area of the brain causes a certain type of reaction in the laboratory is, to repeat, not to be disputed. Moreover, this result could certainly be made use of outside the laboratory, as, for example, in the hypothesis that a person manifesting such behavior had a lesion in the designated area of his brain. Nonetheless, any result gained in the laboratory is gained with reference to a certain criterion or definition of behavior that does *not* have reference to brain activity. When the neurologist concludes that the stimulation of a particular part of the brain causes a person to laugh, feel pain, make a sudden movement, or feel hungry or sad, he is depending on certain public criteria of what constitutes such behavior, criteria that have little to do with what may or may not be going on in someone's brain. This doesn't mean that the causal relationship he establishes between a neurological and a behavioral process isn't valid; it does mean, however, that the causal relation is dependent on our acceptance of his criterion of identity for behavior (that what he calls laughing, for example, is distinct from being hungry) and that we cannot, therefore, suddenly turn the tables and say that such behavior is really defined with reference to a hidden neurological event. The scientist's conclusions gained from laboratory experiments ultimately have reference to a commonly accepted norm and standard of behavior. This standard can never be grounded in or justified by a procedure that is made on the basis of this standard. To think that it can is to confuse meaning and cause, the logical conditions of phenomena and the empirical relations established on the basis of those conditions.

Another way of putting all this is to say that the assertion that the functions of a certain area of the brain cause certain kinds of behavior can never be proven or disproven, because it is a definition, not a hypothesis. Or rather, it would only be a hypothesis if the behavior (emotional, irrational impulses) were taken as the particular reactions of individuals in a particular laboratory setting, the behavior at issue, therefore, being given a clear criterion of identity that would allow for a well-defined extrapolation from the laboratory to everyday behavior. But the sort of contention I am criticizing claims more than that; it claims that there is a general type of behavior manifested by humans in different situations that can be traced back to neurological processes occurring in the brain. What makes us generalize from the particular laboratory result to the more expanded claim is the implicit assumption that there must be some sort of brain activity that underlies all behavior. But that is not necessarily true and, in any case, can't be proven; it is a requirement that we impose on behavior, a way of defining its nature. (It would violate this a priori requirement—but not any scientific, empirical evidence—to discover a perfectly normal person with no brain. Science begins only when a framework of perception has been constructed.)

Once we assume that there is some sort of brain activity underlying all behavior, it makes little sense to hypothesize that a certain type of brain activity underlies a certain type of behavior in a situation in which we have no way of testing the hypothesis (that is, in a nonlaboratory situation). The hypothesis adds nothing to the assumption; all we really succeed in doing in making such a hypothesis (it really isn't a hypothesis, since it can't be tested) is to train our minds to see a sort of ghostly mechanism operating behind our behavior. We say to ourselves: "It is proven that in this particular way a certain sort of behavioral response can be traced to a neurological process. Therefore, all behavior must be capable of being traced back to such processes. It is only a matter of time before we discover them all." But no amount of experimentation will ever succeed in proving that which all such experiments are based on.

Even if everyone were to begin wearing electrodes, this would only succeed in making neurological activity more physically visible (the jump of the needle on the electrode would have the same status as the reddening of the face or the raising of the voice). It would establish neurological phenomena as one of the criteria of identity of behavior. If the criterion were universal, the statement "Such and such behavior is caused by neurological processes" would be without sense (the cause would be part of the behavior's definition). If the criterion were not universal, any relation of causality asserted would have to be made on the basis of experiment—and it could not therefore be assumed a priori that all behavior has some underlying neurological process associated with it.

5

The next type of example to be considered is one characteristic of a wide variety of students of culture, including both American cultural anthropologists in the tradition of Franz Boas and historians of religions. It consists of the effort to explain cultural beliefs and practices in terms of environmental and economic conditions. Earlier it was noted that Boas' concept of culture is a bifurcated one; it dictates that culture be viewed as a matrix of "subjectively conditioned relations" distinct from, but subject to, external forces. Nonetheless, it was further argued, such a concept is only superficially different from that of nineteenth-century evolutionists such as Tylor. For by positing the foundation of culture in hidden mental processes, Boas ultimately gives cultural phenomena an empirical status not essentially different from that of natural phenomena. Though the former are to some extent insulated from the material conditions of nature—Boas insists over and over that they cannot be reduced to external forces—they are still both defined in terms of, and subject causally to, such forces. This comes out clearly in such passages as the following: "Among the Eskimo, when the weather is propitious, the whole village has enough food, and every healthy person is happy. . . . The experiences of primitive man give no other basis for his imagination to work. Their occupations are the same, they hunt, eat and drink, play and dance" (B-RLC, 606–7).

It follows from this that when the weather is not propitious—as is often the case in northern climates—every healthy person is not so happy, and the character of the culture is accordingly affected. For Boas, as for so many other anthropologists and students of culture, the character of a given culture is determined—not wholly but to a very considerable extent—by its environmental conditions. Any account of a culture's beliefs and practices must take this fact into consideration and conform to it.

What is the basis of my objection to this quasi- (and somewhat disguised) naturalism on the part of Boas and many other students of culture? Certainly it is *not* that environmental forces are being used to characterize (as opposed to categorize) cultural phenomena. On the contrary, it is Boas' separation of culture from natural processes—his isolation of it within a privileged, nonnaturalistic and subjective sphere—that lands him in his difficulty. The difficulty hinges on what I have been calling a confusion of cause and meaning. That which is a universal and necessary condition of a culture (say, the harshness of its climate) cannot be given a causal role in explaining that culture's beliefs and practices. For in order for A to be a cause of B, it must have a status independent of B; and this is exactly what the harshness of the climate does not have. It does not have an independent status in relation to the cultural belief or practice being explained, precisely because it is a universal and necessary condition of that culture (in a manner comparable to that in which hunger does not have a status independent of eating; we cannot say that there is something in our bodies that *causes* us to be hungry and eat). The harshness of the climate may be the manner or mode—the "language"—in which a given cultural practice or belief is characterized and, ultimately, understood; but it will not be a cause.

Consider the contention that the Eskimo practice of leaving their elderly to die is the product of their harsh environmental and other conditions of life. What exactly is meant by such a contention? Why, that is, should it even occur to us that leaving one's elderly to die has anything to do with the harshness of a way of life? The answer is that such a practice is repugnant to us; it is an action that, if carried out in our own society, we would call murder. At the same time, however, we recognize in some dim sense that what the Eskimos are doing here is not murder. It is a result, rather, of the conditions in which they live. What conditions? Within our own culture, we would not, in many cases, label abandoning an elderly person "murder" when that action was performed under very extreme, abnormal conditions—as when a group of people were stranded in an isolated area without food, for example. We would see that action through the lenses of the very extreme conditions in which it was performed. Thus, when we explain the Eskimo practice of leaving their elderly to die in terms of their harsh conditions of life, we are really viewing it on the analogy of circumstances in our own way of life that are abnormal and bizarre—in much the same way some nineteenth-century anthropologists used to regard primitive peoples (and are now ridiculed for doing so) on the analogy of the inmates of our insane asylums. Explaining the Eskimo practice by their harsh conditions of life is a way of persisting in our own biased and (uncritically) normative view of their practice—a view that deems the practice undesirable at best and murder at worst—yet all the while pretending to ourselves that we are free from such normative concerns. The naturalistic explanation serves as a screening device to hide from us our own "human, all-too-human" perspective.

It is not that we should see the Eskimo practice of leaving their elderly to die from the standpoint of the Eskimo himself—what phenomenologists often recommend—but rather that only by cultivating a consciousness of our own normative concerns will the practice gain significance. For in explaining this practice causally, by reference to certain invariable conditions in the natural environment, we are missing its sense altogether. Meaning is given by a description of the rules governing practice—by a description of the choices made in any given action and the values implied by those choices. But to regard a practice under the aspect of material necessity is precisely not to regard it under the aspect of a rule. Or, more precisely, it is to posit necessity where none can exist; the necessity must consist in what is presupposed in the application of the rule (which may, of course, be intimately tied with any number of material conditions), not in the physical causes alone. To explain the Eskimo practice of leaving their elderly to die by their harsh conditions of life is, therefore, only to project our own logic and norms into an alien environment—and to do it in an unselfconscious, uncritical way.

These sorts of uncritical habits, however, can be avoided by always being careful to distinguish between the empirical and the logical features of the cultural phenomena being examined. For if this is done, when the suggestion is offered that the harsh conditions imposed by the environment account for the Eskimo practice of leaving their elderly to die, the question will be posed, Is this suggestion meant to be an empirical, causal explanation, or an effort to describe the sense and logic of the practice in question? If the latter, then we will simply accept the contention for the extremely limited amount of truth it contains—that conditions such as cold weather and scarcity of food form part of the way of life of the Eskimos, although they do not in themselves give us much of an idea of the significance of the cultural practice being considered. If the former, we will demand, What are the norms and values presupposed by such an explanation (for no causal explanation stands alone)? Then it will become clear to us that such norms and values are mainly our own—and with that recognition comes the first step of a critically normative account of the Eskimo practice.

As another example, consider the following passage from W. H. Ph. Römer's article "Religion of Ancient Mesopotamia." The perspective expressed here on the early Mesopotamians is quite typical of the views of many historians and students of culture:

> The heirs of the Sumerians were the Semitic-speaking Akkadians. Lack of food drove groups of inhabitants of the Syrian-Arabian steppe and desert regions into the Mesopotamian plain. . . . Because of their extraction and original living conditions, the relationship to the divine powers of these steppe dwellers differed from that of the sedentary inhabitants of the alluvial agrarian land with their efforts at order, regularity and security. Desert gods, such as those of Syria and Palestine where fertility depends on rainfall and not on inundation, are characterized more by power and arbitrariness than by a desire for order. True, rain and storm are limited to certain seasons, but they can less readily be forecast. The concept of god entertained by the aforesaid groups is therefore characterized by two features in particular: personal will-power and might. Related to this is also their endeavour to give a personalized representation of the divine, by which the feeling of dependence is given a personal aspect. One no longer feels caught up in an inexorable and unvarying cycle, but is as a servant before one's lord, a son before one's father. (HR-I, 123)

What is being contended here is that (at least in part) because of the unpredictable weather conditions in which they lived, the Akkadians attributed to their gods the aspects of "personal will-power and might" and viewed their own relationship to the gods as one of personal dependence. During the nineteenth-century, Max Müller, often called the Father of Comparative Religion, proposed in his theory of naturism that religion had its origin in the capacity of the mind to be impressed or "struck" by phenomena of the natural environment. Müller even argued that it was by gazing out upon the limitless horizon that man was first struck by the idea of the infinite, an idea that, according to Müller, served as the basis for many religious beliefs. Today Müller's naturism is ridiculed as naive and simplistic; but how different is it from the point of view that Römer is, in much milder form, assuming? For in both cases, what is a purely natural phenomenon is being invested with a conceptual status. Why should the fact that storms are difficult to predict lead the Akkadians to conceive of their gods as possessed of great will-power and might? Because one who is unpredictable is necessarily powerful and possessed of a strong will? But even if this were true, why should the Akkadians have even been struck by the fact that rain and storms are unpredictable? Why didn't they simply adjust themselves to this fact and organize their way of life around it? Why even should they have been inclined to associate a sudden storm with a manifestation of power that they then felt dependent on?

The point is not that there aren't answers to these questions, but that the answers can't be found by confining our attention alone to the natural phenomena as such. A fact or circumstance can be interpreted in any number of ways. We will insist, of course, that such facts or circumstances be consistent with the culture's way of life; but that doesn't mean their role will be especially important or noticeable—any more than, for example, the fact that the sky is blue and that most rocks aren't round will say anything significant about that culture's conceptions of the gods. That storms and lightning *are* significant in many peoples' conceptions of the gods is not because of any property of storms or lightning *as such*, but rather because of the significance and sense we attach to and associate with the words *personal will-power and might*. It is *natural* to us (and perhaps it also was for the Akkadians) to make such associations, but this fact only reveals (in part) what it is we wish to signify by *personal will-power and might*. When we explain the latter in terms of storms and lightning—implying that such phenomena are somehow causal—we ignore precisely what is at issue: what it means to say that the Akkadian gods were possessed of personal will-power (and the related contention that the believer sees his relationship to the gods as one of personal dependence).

I am not claiming that Römer's reference to weather conditions in the context of a discussion of the Akkadian gods' personal attributes is irrelevant. I am saying, rather, that he has given such conditions an improper, quasi-causal status and that having screened from view the cultural phenomena in this way, he has not felt it necessary to discuss what really would be of great importance and interest: those further characteristics and behaviors of the Akkadian gods that incline us to say they are possessed of personal will-power and might. A rule for the student of culture: if you must explain, then see that you first give an adequate description of *what* you are explaining.

Another example is provided by Antje Kelm in his article "The Religion of Ancient Peru":

> In order to understand the real characteristics of the ancient Peruvian religion, it is necessary to imagine both the geographical surroundings and the means of existence of the people. Not only in the coastal desert, but also in large parts of the Andes regions, considerable efforts were required on the part of the people to change dry lands into agricultural soil and to keep it as such. . . . The endeavor to obtain fertile soil and sufficient water, the nursing of the seedlings and the harvesting occupied the people of the pre-Columbian era for over two thousand years and it is in this light that their spiritual world, as well as the real content of their religion, can best be comprehended. . . . Like numerous other agricultural peoples of the world, the Peruvians closely connected the conception of the cycle of vegetable life with the course of human existence—birth, procreation and death. The idea of the necessary relationship between dying and resurrection as an expression of the anxiety for fertility, is one of the fundamental motives interlacing the myths and the religious practices of the ancient Peruvian; it determines the world-creating activities of the gods as well as the world-conserving acts of man. (HR-I, 680–1)

The idea expressed here (and it is one commonly found in accounts of agricultural peoples all over the world and throughout history) is that many of the rites of the ancient Peruvians, as well as their associated myths, are grounded in this people's "anxiety for fertility," an anxiety that, however complicated and esoteric its cultural manifestations, is ultimately rooted in biological needs and conditions.

According to this perspective, a given sacrificial rite, for example—
one that imitates the death and resurrection pattern found in nature—can be understood in terms of the Peruvians' belief that performing it will preserve the fertility of the crops. But here what we
conceive of as a belief can be misleading. On the one hand, to say that
the ancient Peruvians believed that performing the rite would ensure the fertility of the crops can mean simply that if queried on this
point, they would say yes. In this case, the "belief" has a purely empirical status, and it can easily be imagined that many of the Peruvians would say no. If enough of them said yes, however, it would be
reasonable to advance a causal relationship between the two. But
whether or not the hypothesis could be proven correct, this would
still say nothing about the meaning or significance of the rite itself.
To maintain that it would, would be like saying that modern man
has children because he believes that doing so will ensure the preservation of the species. If queried, modern man might admit to holding such a belief, in the same way that the ancient Peruvians would
admit to believing that the performance of the rite would ensure the
fertility of the crops. But it would still be terribly inadequate to say
that "what it means to modern man to have children is that it ensures
the preservation of the species." In fact, having children has reference in all sorts of complicated ways to a large range of aspects of
modern man's way of life, and the same is clearly true, to a greater or
lesser extent, of the ancient Peruvians and their sacrificial rites.

Of course, the term *belief* is not ordinarily meant in a purely empirical sense; rather, what the ancient Peruvians believed about the
rite is supposed to reveal its significance. In this case, the contention
that the ancient Peruvians believed that performing the rite would
ensure fertility is very misleading, for the significance of the rite is
not something that can be separated out from the performance of the
ritual (and the attitudes of the people engaged in the performance),
to be "believed" by the participants. It is, rather, what is presupposed
by the ritual and the attitudes toward it, in the same way that when
modern man has children, the meaning of this cannot be something
that he holds up to his mind's eye and then embraces. Rather, his
attitude toward having children is just one additional piece of information that reveals its significance.

In a similar fashion, the attitude of the Peruvians toward the rite—what they think or do not think will result from it—has a status too empirical to adequately characterize its significance. To think that it does adequately characterize its significance is like thinking that the ancient Peruvians *believed* that performing the rite ensured the fertility of the crops *in order that* such fertility would be ensured (*i.e.*, that they held up the meaning of the rite as a kind of mental object). But the "beliefs" of the ancient Peruvians regarding the fertility of their crops, like the "beliefs" of modern man regarding having children, are too deeply embedded in their actions to be separated out from them. They play a role in revealing the meaning of those actions, but they do not encompass such meaning.

6

In all these cases, then, the crucial fallacy is that we invest natural conditions, or the attitudes, beliefs, and mental states accompanying those conditions, with logical force. So far, however, I have not mentioned one of the chief impulses prompting us to commit this fallacy: our desire to compare different cultures according to certain very general characteristics and conditions. Thus, for example, it has long been noted by comparative religionists that the mythologies and religious practices of hunters and gatherers are, as a very general rule, of a consistently different kind than those of agriculturalists. The latter seem to have an abundance of mother goddesses, sacrificial rites, and sophisticated technologies, whereas the former seem to have an abundance of high gods, shamans, and primitive technologies. It is generally assumed, moreover, that these differences are, in some sense, the product of the different societies' economies and agricultural systems. Although this issue is much too complicated to fully address here, I would like to set up a hypothetical model that may throw some light on it.

Suppose there are two different groups of peoples, A and B, living in very different physical environments and possessed of very different economic structures and cultures. It should be noted at once that within each society, the economic structure is a universal condition and cannot explain any *particular* characteristics of the culture. On the other hand, we can legitimately associate the two so long as no relation of causality is postulated.

The relation of causality is possible only from a comparative standpoint. Why culture A rather than culture B? One answer might be, Culture A lives in a tropical climate, B lives in arctic conditions; or perhaps A has an agricultural economy, B a hunting and gathering one. A common basis of humanity is assumed here: we wouldn't make the comparison, for example, between Eskimos in the Arctic and animal life in the tropics. We assume that cultures A and B have some fundamental traits in common; the question is whether the differences between them are caused by their differing economic structures and environmental conditions.

If we're talking about a relation of causality, then it must be possible to imagine cultures A and B apart from the economic structures and environmental conditions (the former are products of the latter). But if this is the case, they are self-subsistent and can be characterized by some feature independent of the economy and environment. They become not just a particular form of observed behavior, but something mental. Yet, at the same time, they are in some sense defined by the conditions they are subject to.

The paradox is that if a given physical condition is a cause of culture A, then culture A must be defined as essentially different from its conditions. But the only characteristic of culture A that is self-subsistent is that which is common to all men. If we were to observe culture A under nontropical conditions, then the relation of causality would be disproved; it is because we don't observe this that it occurs to us to think of tropical conditions as producing culture A. Our proof (that culture A disappears under arctic conditions and is therefore dependent on the tropical conditions) assumes that there is something "behind" A that carries over and assures identity. Thus, there is an essential nature: under tropical conditions, this nature is modified to produce culture A; under arctic conditions, it is modified to produce culture B.

Suppose A and B are two different individuals rather than two different groups of peoples. To show that a particular condition caused a certain behavior of A and another condition caused a certain behavior of B, all else would have to be held constant (the surrounding environments of the two). But if this were the case, how would we establish the identity of the individuals, since the only difference between the two would be the behaviors of A and B, which are supposed to be causally subject to their conditions? We could indeed only identify the behaviors of A and B by means of the conditions that had produced them.

The observed behavior is dependent on the conditions, but the behavior is the criterion of identity (of a society, for example); if now the conditions are seen to produce the behavior, then the identity will reside in the conditions.

What we observe is no strict correlation between conditions and behavior, but only a kind of family of associations: we permit ourselves to draw a strict correlation because we have the picture of something behind the visible behavior, something that holds constant and is universal while the particular causes are being exerted. But as soon as the assertion of causal relation is put in rigorous form, we see how quickly this "thing" —*i.e.*, man as a cultural being— disappears. We realize that it exists only in a sort of perpetual darkness.

7

All of this brings us to the next type of example I would like to consider: the effort to explain cultural phenomena on the basis of universal needs and conditions. The principal case under this category is the contention that culture and religion act as psychological and conceptual shields against the knowledge of the universal fact of death. Kluckhohn writes: "In the face of want and death and destruction all humans have a fundamental insecurity. To some extent, all culture is a gigantic effort to mask this."[2] The idea here is that culture and society may be seen, in general, as a response to the fact of death; social and cultural phenomena shield man or make it easier for him to endure what he cannot help "knowing"—that he must someday die. Or it is claimed more specifically that particular beliefs and practices are prompted by man's consciousness of death. Thus, the discovery that Paleolithic man buried his dead and even took some steps to make the body appear "lifelike," dressing it with red ocher, is taken as indicating belief in an afterlife, which is in turn seen to have as its basis the consciousness of death. Or the rites of primitive tribes

2. Clyde Kluckhohn, "Myths and Rituals: A General Theory," in William A. Lessa and Evon Z. Vogt (eds.), *Reader in Comparative Religion: An Anthropological Approach* (New York, 1958), 152.

in which the dead are carried out of the back of the dwelling or even out of one of its windows, so as to "confuse" them and prevent them from coming back, are seen as motivated by a deep and consuming fear of the dead. Or the conception of the afterlife in general is viewed as the manifestation of an ineradicable need to deny or repress what in fact cannot be escaped—that we must all someday die.

The nature of my objection to this line of reasoning is as follows. A causal relation between two phenomena can only be demonstrated where the cause and effect are distinct. But this is clearly not the case in the examples above. We cannot assume that the burial of the dead implies a belief in the afterlife or even just the consciousness of death, and then turn around and claim that there is a causal relation between the two. Nor can we say that a given rite or practice (such as carrying out the dead the back way) has as its *raison d'être* the fear of death, and then simultaneously claim that such fear is its cause. Nor can we claim that the belief in the afterlife expresses a universal longing or need for the infinite, and then turn around and say that such a need is the cause of the belief in the afterlife.

If we wanted in any of these cases to demonstrate a causal relation, we would have first to separate the effect (say, the burial of the dead) from its hypothetical cause (the belief in the afterlife). If we could not make such a separation, we would simply have to admit that a causal relation could not be demonstrated; our task would be limited to description—revealing the logic of the practices and beliefs under consideration. If we could make the separation, we would have to examine a particular culture's practice of burial and belief in the afterlife. We would have to force ourselves to look at the actual phenomena—the specific practices around death—and not be continually looking through them to an underlying organic cause (the fact of death).

Thus, to give the consciousness of death a universal status is to make it a defining criterion of the phenomenon being considered and thereby deprive it of causal status. If the consciousness or fear of death is not regarded as universal, on the other hand, any causal status that it is given must be made on empirical grounds.

As a way of fleshing out some of these points, let us consider in some detail a contention advanced in Franz Boas' essay "The Idea of the Future Life." The contention is that "the objectification of the memory image" is one of the principal sources of primitive man's concept of the soul (Boas also discusses another source of primitive man's concept of the soul; however, the discussion is roughly parallel to the one being considered here). Boas' thesis is that the idea of the soul is formed out of the materials of memory images of the dead entertained by living relatives and friends. These images are then objectified and conceived of as "substances" or souls distinct from the body. To explain how this latter process takes place, Boas relies on the work of Tylor: "Tylor and others have discussed fully and adequately the effects of the products of imagination in dreams and trance experiences in which man finds his body in one place while his mind visits distant persons and sees distant scenes, or when he finds conversely distant scenes and persons appearing before his mental eye. These are based on memory images which attain at times unusual intensity" (B-RLC, 600).

There is, however, an important difference between Tylor's and Boas' explanations of how such memory images are turned into souls. For Tylor the process is rationalistically conceived; it derives from the nature of man's consciousness and reason. For Boas, on the other hand, it is nonrational: "Not by a logical process, but by the natural and involuntary process of classification of experience, man is led to the concept of the objective existence of the memory image. Its formation is due to the experiences of visual and auditory imagery" (B-RLC, 600).

In assessing the value of Boas' notion of the soul as memory image, two different approaches present themselves. The first is to regard Boas' contention as a hypothesis claiming an empirical relation between memory images and the notion of the soul. If this was Boas' intent, however, he offers no evidence to substantiate his hypothesis. He does not claim, for example, that the idea of the soul is strongest when the memory images of the dead person are strongest in the minds of the living—what might presumably provide support for the hypothesis. On the contrary, he presents evidence that militates against such a hypothesis: that the soul is often conceived of as an object or an animal—hardly what one would expect if the soul were derived from the memory image of a person (B-RLC, 600). Nor does he provide a plausible explanation of why, if the soul is derived from a memory, it does not grow less substantial with time, but is in fact conceived of as immortal (B-RLC, 603). It is peculiar, moreover, that if Boas conceived of his contention as an empirical one, he did not specify more precisely the particular cultures and conditions to which it applied, as he consistently urged his fellow anthropologists to do in formulating any hypothesis. Instead, within the space of just a few pages, "the Chinook Indians of Northwest America," an Eskimo tribe named the Chuckchee, and unspecified tribes "in Africa" are alluded to.

The other approach to understanding Boas' contention is that it was intended not as an empirical hypothesis, but as a way of characterizing the nature of the soul concept among primitive peoples. Unfortunately, if this was Boas' intention, he does little to make such a characterization concrete. Almost the only conceptual description Boas gives of the primitive idea of the soul is that it is conceived of as a "substance." Even here it is not at all clear how a memory image could be endowed with such substantiality. For the rest, Boas' descriptions of what he calls the "memory image soul" are all framed in the language of causal forces and say nothing about the soul as such, that is, what role it may play in people's lives. The following is a typical sample: "The concept of the memory image soul leads to different beliefs in regard to its localization. Its essential feature is that it is a fleeting image of the personality and that, for this reason, it is identical in form with the person. Shadows and reflections on water partake of these unsubstantial, fleeting characteristics of the image of the person. Probably for this reason they are often identified with the memory-image soul" (B-RLC, 605).

Whatever Boas' intentions, then, he succeeds neither in advancing a coherent hypothesis nor in providing an even rudimentary description of how primitive man conceives of the soul. But what is ironic about such a failure is that it was caused by Boas' effort to do both simultaneously. Throughout his essay, he seems to flit back and forth in his discussions between a phenomenon (the soul) and a cause of that phenomenon, without ever distinguishing clearly between the two. When Boas uses the term *memory image*, he is really formulating a certain concept of the soul; whereas when he uses the term *soul*, he is thinking of a psychological, associative process that somehow compels it to come into being. The phenomenon of the soul is made ethereal for the sake of advancing a causal hypothesis for which no evidence is advanced.

It is not, of course, that there is something intrinsically wrong with trying to formulate a hypothesis about the origin of the soul; if this could be done plausibly, then it would obviously be of great value, though its range of application would almost certainly be limited. Rather, what Boas is really to be faulted for in his notion of the memory image soul is that he has not taken the time to formulate how primitive man actually conceives of the soul. It is not a problem to Boas, for example, that primitive man speaks of the soul in concrete, physical terms. Like so many other anthropologists before and after him, he adopts the Western prejudice that the soul must be separate from the body, without even mentioning that in the sense (if any) this is true, "separate from the body" must mean something very different to primitive man than it does to modern man. The failure to discuss these difficult points is really just a way of applying our own categories of thought to circumstances in which they are highly inappropriate. By reading a universal and empirical cause behind cultural phenomena, we are saved the trouble of noticing the differences between ourselves and others.

"But," one might argue, "Boas' errors notwithstanding, certainly it is reasonable to assume that people's beliefs in the soul and the afterlife, as well as their attitudes toward death in general, derive in one way or another from the fact of death. For death is, after all, a fact—a universal condition." This statement means, presumably, that all living creatures are subject to certain processes of disintegration and decay that we call death. But do not these processes bear some resemblance to those undergone by creatures who yet continue to live? "Yes, but in the case of death, the processes are of such a nature that the organism can no longer go on. As a presence or thing, he ceases to exist." So death means not going on? "It means ceasing to exist—being nothing."

It is no more meaningful to say that death is a fact or a universal condition than it is to say that arms are a universal feature of human beings. In both cases, the statements are tautologies, true by definition. If we try to assert that they are true in any other sense, then they become at once very questionable. We want here to make what is a necessary and inescapable concomitant of all behavior a cause of a particular kind of behavior. The statement "Death is a fact, a universal condition," is nonsense in the same way that, as Wittgenstein maintained, the statement "There are objects" is nonsense.

"But all people surely have to deal with the fact of death, whatever status you give this fact?" Do we have to deal with the fact that we have arms? In both cases, the fact is one that, so to speak, embraces *us*, not vice versa.

If there were but one way of dying, then in answer to the question "What is death?" we could say, *this*. But that's just what we can't do. (If there were but one way of dying, then our concept of death would be very different from what it is now.)

One might perhaps still maintain that "even if we can't say 'what death is,' it is nonetheless true that people's behavior—individually and culturally—is to a large extent dictated by fear of it." But if the fear of death is universal (is equivalent to a general awareness among mankind of the fact of death), it cannot explain any particular kinds of behavior, social or otherwise. If the fear of death is not universal, on the other hand, it can have no *general* causal status. Our fear of death may indeed be not the cause but the product of a particular kind of behavior or custom or ritual. There may not even be any one definition of the fear of death that accounts for all the situations in which we see it. There is, rather, a family of resemblances, and although some members of the family are understood with reference to the inevitable degenerative biological process we call death, others may be judged as independent of it.

Consider, for example, what is often called the "disbelief in natural death." This refers to the widespread tendency found among primitive and archaic peoples to discount the necessity of death, to assume that the body, if left alone, is immortal and that all death is therefore the product of accident or witchcraft. Just how seriously (and at the same time, unseriously and ironically) this assumption of the immortality of the body is taken by many hunting and gathering peoples is brought out in the statement of an Apache shaman to a white observer: "My white brother, you will not believe it, but I am all powerful. I will never die. If you shoot me, the bullet will not enter my flesh, or if it enters it will not hurt me. . . . If you stick a knife in my throat, thrusting it upwards, it will come out through my skull at the top of my head. . . . I am all powerful. If I wish to kill any one, all I need to do is to thrust out my hand and touch him and he dies. My power is like that of a god" (E-S, 299).

Such an attitude is somehow not done full justice, I think, by referring to it, in the manner of many researchers, as a disbelief in natural death. By characterizing the primitive conception of death in purely negative terms—as a failure to perceive the reality of natural death—we emphasize its so-called delusory character. But exactly what is it about death that we are supposed to know that primitives do not? If I were to say, "I know I'm going to die eventually," it would mean something like "Rest assured, I'm not a lunatic."

"But certainly there is such a thing as natural life expectancy." What "natural life expectancy" is has not been established alone by certain facts (*e.g.*, that people live a given number of years); it has been established by our concept of death, which is in turn embedded in our concept of a human being. Both of these have grown out of a way of life. Thus, when a primitive people declares that they are naturally immortal (and that they die only by accident or witchcraft), or when the Old Testament refers to people who live five hundred years or more, they are not only contradicting certain facts: they are contradicting our own concept of death and the factual conclusions we draw on the basis of this concept. The questions of whether the people of the time of the Old Testament really believed that there were men who had lived five hundred years and whether primitive peoples really believe they are immortal can be understood only by becoming aware that we *have* a concept of death to begin with, and that this concept does not apply, or applies only partially, to other peoples' concepts. When the shaman says, "I will never die," we must try to grasp what it is he is saying (or alternatively, we can say, "That statement has no sense"—but that is different from saying it is factually incorrect). We must try to grasp what its criteria of truth are. Until we have done this, we have not even *heard* it.

If there were no cancer and no atomic bombs, then there would of course still be death. But what if all the various forms of death that we could possibly imagine were suddenly to disappear, like objects being removed from a picture, would we still know what death is? Would we still have a picture?

If death is nothingness, we still need to ask: what *counts* as nothing?

Freud said something to the effect that no one can imagine his own death. He had in mind here a certain picture of death—the physical disintegration of the body and the mind. By saying that no one can imagine his own death, he thought he had spotted a case in which the picture couldn't be applied. He didn't grasp that the statement "No one can imagine his own death" refers to a possible *event*, and if such an event can't happen, this just says something about the picture we are using. The defect is in the picture, not the person. Freud's reductionist picture is not at all in accord with common usage; a person can imagine his own death as little or as much as he can imagine the deaths of others.

An atheist, lecturing to a group of people, might say, "We all know that we will be annihilated and become nothing." A religious believer might then interject, "*I* do not know that I will be annihilated." This would be a protest—but *not* a protest against the fact of death.

When a child is first informed of death, he may be told that a particular person "has gone away on a long trip." But the child is given this information in such a way that he probably senses that the trip is of a very different nature than any other trip he has heard about or taken. The decisive point to take note of is that likening death to a long trip is part of the way we think about death, and not just an explanation invented for a child.

It is, therefore, never quite right to say that a child, or a primitive people, is unaware of the reality of death. It is better to say that they show signs of confusion when confronted with *our* awareness of death and the concept it presupposes.

There are many different ways in which people die. When we use the phrase *natural death*, we refer to *one* of these ways—but a way that is very special in our eyes. It seems to signify something closer to the real thing. But if there is natural death, then there is also "unnatural death." The edifice of meanings of the latter term seem to be built on the rock of the meaning of the former term. We want this rock to rest on grounds that are independent of our culture. My point is not to deny those grounds, but rather to get us to stop thinking that we have empirical justification for them, that they are in some way explanatory. When we conceive of death as a universal ground, we act as inhabitants of a particular culture—but a culture that wants, so to speak, to turn itself inside out.

What is the difference between two peoples, one disbelieving in natural death, the other obsessed with death? We get nowhere if we ask, How does any given individual from these two societies feel and think about death? On the other hand, if we view their differences as merely differences in external behavior—what is observed to happen—then we run again into a blank wall. Both attitudes toward death are shaped by the living process; they are a function of the total social life of the peoples.

"The peoples of certain societies throughout history have believed in a life after death. In such a way have they manifested the need to explain what happens when men die." But this misses the point. It is life that teaches us about death, not vice versa. Notions of a life after death affirm life. If there is such a thing as the immortal soul, we would not be able to perceive it any better after death than now.

In the statement, "I will live forever," it is the *I* that is troublesome, not the rest of the sentence. The notions of *I* as a body, on the one hand, and a soul or mind, on the other, are two different ways we have of clearing up the trouble.

The statement "I know that I am going to die" has a definite meaning when someone says, "I may as well enjoy life as much as I can now, since I know I am going to die," and then goes out and has a good time.

What we know about death cannot be a matter of certainty. But even here we try to get around this by saying, "Let us ignore what we do not know, so that at least we can know what we know." But why should what we do not know about something be less important than what we know? It's obvious that what we *know* in this case (the fact of physical death) may be inconsequential when compared with what we do not know.

As individuals we know as little about ourselves at two weeks after birth as we know about ourselves at two weeks after death. What we *know* is given to us through the culture and society in which we live. No culture or society can be its own foundation.

"But what if our culture is deceiving us?" And who *are* you to be so deceived? (If life is a dream, as Descartes conjectured, then this conjecture is itself part of the dream.)

Death is part of the face that man, as man, presents. Although the face may assume many different expressions, they should not be mistaken for masks. Man knows as much about death as his cultural beliefs and practices *show* he knows.

VI   The Subjectivistic Fallacy
History of Religions

The tendency of anthropologists to explain cultural beliefs and practices in terms of external causes leads them to confuse
the meaning of such beliefs and practices with their causes. Such
confusion is especially harmful in the case of religious beliefs and
practices, for here the accounts of events (historical or otherwise)
given by religious believers often stand in flagrant contradiction to
known scientific laws, and the propensity of the social scientist to
explain the belief or practice in terms of empirical causes external to
it is reinforced. Thus, a social scientist or historian, when confronted
with the report of a miracle, will commonly assume that the miracle
did not really occur, and then explain the report of it in terms of the
mental state of the person or persons making it. It is interesting to
compare the views of Hume, Kant, and Wittgenstein on the issue of
miracles. Hume asserted vehemently, and at length, that science had
proven, almost to a certainty, that miracles do not occur (H-EHU,
175); Wittgenstein just as vehemently denied this assertion;[1] and
Kant's position was somewhere in between.[2]

It should be clear that however *empirically* valid it may or may not
be to link the report of a miracle with the hyperactivated mental state
of the person making the report, such an explanation will tell us
nothing about what a miracle *is*.

What, then, it might be asked, *is* a miracle? According to Hume
and others, a miracle is basically an event of fantastic improbability,
an event such as a pond freezing in the middle of summer (which
physicists say is a theoretical possibility). It follows—by definition,
one might say—that we are pretty safe in assuming that miracles do
not occur. But to define a miracle as an event of fantastic improba-

---

1. See W-LE, 10–11; W-T.3.031; W-VB, 56.
2. This conclusion follows from Kant's philosophy as advanced in his first two *Critiques*. See also C. J. Clement Webb, *Kant's Philosophy of Religion* (Oxford, 1926), 44–45,
127–28.

bility is to misunderstand its significance. What is essential to the nature of a miracle is that it have the power to change the way we look at the world, that it throw our everyday lives into a different light and give them a different significance than we are ordinarily inclined to give them. It is not the fantastic improbability of the miracle per se that allows it to do this (a mere statistical rarity would not be in itself miraculous in any sense); at best, the fantastic improbability of the event serves a pointing function—it dramatizes the character of the miracle. But it is certainly not a sufficient argument against the claim that a miracle occurred to say that its occurrence was fantastically improbable. For nonempirical, nonpsychological reasons grounded in his religion or culture, a believer in a miracle grants the miracle its intrinsic power and significance; because and *only* because he does this, he believes that there could have occurred a situation and circumstance in which such fantastic improbability manifested itself. His attitude toward the miracle sets the context for him in such a way that the occurrence of fantastically improbable events becomes credible. He admits that under ordinary circumstances the event is improbable. But his point is that these circumstances are not ordinary.

Another way of putting this is: It is not just that science cannot establish with absolute certainty that a given miracle did not occur, for to admit this would be only to grant the miracle the status of being fantastically improbable. Rather, it is that science gives us no grounds for determining in what cases such fantastic improbability may or may not have manifested itself in the occurrence of a given event.

From this it follows *not* that the social scientist, in order to study and understand the phenomena of miracles, must *believe* in them, for the nonbeliever is just as qualified as the believer for such a task. The point rather is that the nonbeliever must be clear on what are proper grounds for his not believing. Such proper grounds do not include the physical impossibility of any such event as a miracle, for this makes it sound as though anyone who believes in miracles is irrational or even demented. The nonbeliever must grasp, on the contrary, that a belief in a miracle is a perfectly *reasonable* belief, given the religious grounds that the believer accepts. The nonbeliever, on the other hand, refuses to accept the miracle, because he refuses to accept those grounds, grounds that are in turn rooted in a culture, a history, and a way of life different from (not necessarily more or less reasonable than) those of the nonbeliever.

2

A miracle, therefore, cannot be defined simply with reference to physical events and processes. Any characterization of its significance in terms of physical events and processes will go astray. This same argument applies, *a fortiori*, to the myths and religious beliefs of foreign cultures. Such myths and beliefs must be understood in terms of their logic and norms and in terms of the criteria for truth and falsehood set within them. In a sense, our view of these myths and beliefs is much clearer than our view of miracles, since the former are (from our point of view) so completely fantastic as to not even tempt us to interpret them literally. But now we are on the verge of falling into another fallacy that, though quite different from the confusion of physical or natural cause with meaning, is just as great. It is the fallacy often committed by historians of religions who, unlike anthropologists, focus their studies on the specifically religious content of cultures. The nature of the fallacy can be seen if we briefly examine an essay, "The Truth of Myth," by Raffaele Pettazzoni, a leader in the field of history of religions and one who had a strong influence on Eliade in particular. As the title indicates, Pettazzoni's position on myth is diametrically opposed to that held (implicitly or explicitly) by anthropologists, who view myth as something illusory but nonetheless serving a useful function. Rather, for Pettazzoni, myth is first and foremost true: "The myth is true and cannot but be true."[3] It is evident here that Pettazzoni is using the word *true* in a different sense than that in which we often understand it. Pettazzoni makes this sense explicit when he speaks of the "life of myth, which is at the same time its truth."[4] Myths are true not by virtue of their correspondence with empirical reality, but by virtue of the fact they exist—an existence that is tied to the necessary role and function they serve for people: "It is thus evident that the myth is not pure fiction; it is not fable but history, a 'true story' and

3. Raffaele Pettazzoni, *Essays on the History of Religions* (2nd ed.; Leiden, 1967), 21.
4. *Ibid.*

not a 'false' one. It is a true story because of its contents which are an
account of events that really took place, starting from those im-
pressive happenings which belong to the beginnings of things, the
origin of the world and of mankind, that of life and death."[5]

In contrast to many anthropologists, who view myths as inherently illusory and nonrational, Pettazzoni accepts myths as inherently true and rational. He is able to do this, however, only because
he sees myth as dealing with a special realm, with a special kind of
truth. This of course is the realm of the sacred, or holy, and to accent
its special character Pettazzoni distinguishes between true myth,
whose domain is the sacred, and false stories, whose domain is the
profane: "In the true stories we have to deal with the holy and the
supernatural, while the false ones on the other hand are of profane
content."[6]

However well-intentioned such a view of myth, and however
much we may sympathize with its implicit critique of positivism, it
must be asked if it really does more justice to a myth to regard it as
inherently true rather than inherently false. Do we not in both cases
ignore the logic of the myth, a logic without which any judgment of
truth or falsity of the events occurring in the myth makes little
sense? Do we not in both cases fail to cultivate a critical consciousness of our own logic, that is, of the norms and values—even what
might be called the hidden mythology—of our own culture?

It is true that historians of religions, as compared with anthropologists, have attempted to preserve the autonomous and sui generis nature of cultural, or at least religious, phenomena, refusing to
allow natural processes a defining role. Yet, notwithstanding the
positive aspects of historians of religions' concept of religion, they
have made a mistake similar to that of the anthropologists. Meaning
is distinguished from external, empirical causes, and in this sense its
presuppositional, nonempirical features are heeded. But then a particular conceptual category is declared to be universal and is made
out to be a basic mental process built into the structure of consciousness. Instead of external, material processes being invested with a
logical status (so that they are able to carry their meaning in them-

5. *Ibid.*, 15–16.
6. *Ibid.*, 11–12.

selves), internal mental processes are invested with a logical status; meaning is seen as within—as apart from any external process or particular cultural belief or practice.

3

The tendency on the part of historians of religions to view religion as grounded in structural components of the consciousness has prompted them to seek (and find) similarities amid the vast assemblage and diversity of religious phenomena. Whereas Boasian anthropologists with their understanding of religion and culture as subjective have been content—at least in comparison with historians of religions—to record the diversity in rites and beliefs among cultures and, so to speak, leave it untouched, historians of religions have sought an underlying unity among such rites and beliefs.

The search by historians of religions for a unity of religious phenomena has generally taken two forms. On the one hand, it has caused scholars to speak of a universal *religion* underlying all particular religious forms. The idea of such a universal religion goes back to the beginning of modern comparative religion, when Max Müller proclaimed, "There is only one eternal and universal standing above, beneath, and beyond all religions to which they all belong or can belong" (E-K, 141). For Müller, "He who knows one knows none." Such a formula, for many early students of comparative religion, expressed the *raison d'être* and purpose of comparative religion itself. In recent times, however, such an approach has fallen out of favor with many historians of religions, and the emphasis tends to be less on the notion of a universal religion underlying all particular religions than on the notion of a universal religious *experience*, or category of experience, underlying all religious phenomena.

What the emphasis on a universal experience has allowed the scholar to do is to draw a sharper line between the *eidos*, or "essentials of religious phenomena" (BL-R, 6), and the phenomena themselves, thus elevating that element of universality to a higher, more abstract realm. Instead of formulating the essence of religion with reference to a theory based on the observation of particular religions and then generalizing beyond them, the scholar defines that essence or universal nature of religion in only the most general terms, as when Eliade says: "When a man becomes aware of his mode of being, he has something in common with the so-called primitive and the modern philosopher. We know from letters and publications of anthropologists that what the philosopher calls 'angst', anxiety and death, was experienced by the primitives. I mean that *la grande situation humaine* has probably been the same in every era. I consider this a kind of basic universal" (A, 211).

It is as a way of formulating the nature of religion as a universal but subjectively grounded experience that the definition of religion as a dialectic of the sacred and the profane is best viewed. Although Rudolf Otto in his book, *The Idea of the Holy*, popularized this opposition—which is actually just a refurbishing of the earlier opposition between the supernatural and the natural—Nathan Söderblom was actually the first historian of religions to give it a clear formulation: "Holiness is the great word in religion; it is even more essential than the notion of God. Real religion may exist without a definite conception of divinity but there is no real religion without a distinction between holy and profane. . . . An idea of God without the conception of the holy is not a religion. Not the mere existence of the divinity, but its mana, its power, its holiness is what religion involves."[7] Gerardus van der Leeuw expands on this formulation:

> In a quite classical way Söderblom has presented the contrast between holy and profane as the primal and governing antithesis in all religion, and has shown how the old viewpoint, that Wonder *Thaumazein*, is the beginning of Philosophy, can be applied with yet greater justice to Religion. For whoever is confronted with potency clearly realizes that he is in the presence of some quality with which in his previous experience he was never familiar, and which cannot be evoked from something else but which, *sui generis* and *sui juris*, can be designated only by religious terms such as "sacred" and "numinous." All these terms have a common relationship in that they indicate a firm conviction, but at the same time no definite conception, of the completely different, the absolutely distinct.[8]

To some extent, such a concept of religion depends on an etymology that derives the word *religion* (Latin, *religio*) from the verb

7. Quoted in Hans-Joachim Schoeps, *The Religions of Mankind* (New York, 1968), 12.

8. Gerardus van der Leeuw, *Religion in Essence and Manifestation*, trans. J. E. Turner (London, 1938) 47–48.

relegere, which means "to pay scrupulous attention to" and which would then give *religio* the connotation of a feeling of awe for higher powers (BL-S, 39). This etymology, however, is by no means universally agreed on, and other scholars give *religio* different connotations. Such disagreements aside, it is clear what Söderblom was trying to do in defining religion in terms of the holy and detaching it from any idea of the gods; he was broadening the concept of religion so that it could be applied to primitive and early cultures as well as advanced ones. Moreover, often this emphasis on the internalized nature of religion is buttressed by the claim that for the historian "only one evaluation is possible: the believers were completely right."[9] The idea here is that in order truly to understand a given religion, one must, in a sense, become the believer. Such a notion is grounded in a view of religion as a universal structure of the mind; one could not understand a given religion from within unless all religions were, in a sense, the *same* from within. Or, to put this in another way, although the sacred is identified with the apprehension and experience of Being—an ontological category—the stress is on the words *apprehension* and *experience*, quite as much as it is on Being. It is a category that can be applied most conveniently from the standpoint of an interiorized framework—that of the faith of the religious believers.

4

The crucial fallacy in the claim that religious phenomena must be understood from within is its identification of meaning with a mental state—with intention psychologically understood. For a psychological account of a practice no more gives significance to that practice than does a material or environmental one; the fallacy here is similar to that examined in the private language argument. When it is finally admitted that meaning cannot be explained in terms of external, empirical processes, there is a temptation to try to explain it in terms of internal, empirical processes. Consider the statement "Certainly I know why I do what I do." Such an assertion has validity not in an empirical sense, but a logical one; it presupposes a category of

9. W. Brede Kristensen, *The Meaning of Religion* (The Hague, 1960), 14. See also HR-II, 646; E-K, 31–58.

thinking and acting rooted in the social environment and in our concept of the self. A person does not know what he does and thinks and believes on the basis of an examination of his own mental processes. Rather, he "knows" (using the word in a logical sense) these things on the basis of his concept of the self, a concept that he himself did not invent, but that was *given* to him or that he was "born into." As noted earlier, the concept of the self is a social inheritance. Thus, when Otto says—in a discussion of the self that lies at the center of all religious experience—that "what the 'I' is cannot be defined,"[10] he, like Kant, has hold of a valid point. The problem is that he then goes on to try to define this I by positing it in a special, noumenal realm. Like Kant with his "transcendental unity of apperception," Otto does not grasp that to say the I cannot be defined is to say that it has a logical, not an empirical or subjective, status.

Historians of religions may declare, of course, that their efforts to explain cultural beliefs and practices in terms of the believer's stated intentions do not depend on psychology. This is, certainly, at least partially true. My point, however, is that only when all psychological elements are distinguished from the logical features of the phenomenon do we arrive at a clear account of it. By contrast, the methodological device of simply accepting as true or always right the believer's own explanations of his practices and beliefs—or even his explanations of his intentions—prevents us from making such a distinction. Thus, if a modern person were to claim that he or she has children in order to preserve the human species, or if a person from an early society were to claim that he or she practices sacrifice in order to preserve the fertility of the species, such claims would not alone give us an adequate account of what it is to have children or practice sacrifice. Such claims would be, of course, significant; but we would need to consider other, equally significant pieces of information. We must not think there is something in the *fact* of the believer's intentions that gives the practice meaning, that there is some basic mental process or attitude there that we must treat as inviolable. For in reality, any psychological process or mental state can at best be a proximate cause. There is nothing in the process itself (any more than there is in the facts of nature) that gives meaning, for

10. Rudolf Otto, *The Idea of the Holy* (New York, 1959), 315.

meaning is given by the rules governing action in particular contexts, whereas empirical processes must first be put into a context before they can gain significance.

5

In historians of religions' treatment of the concept of the soul, there is a marked absence of causal explanations such as Boas' notion of the memory image soul. It is true that historians of religions, like anthropologists, generally accept Tylor's assessment that "the conception of the human soul is, as to its most essential nature, continuous from the philosophy of the savage thinker to that of the modern professor of theology."[11] For example, Eliade is quick to conclude, on what seems to be the flimsiest of evidence, that the belief in the soul has existed since Paleolithic times (E-H, 24). Otto declares: "It is quite certain that all religion which is in any way complete, includes within itself a belief in the everlastingness of our spiritual, personal nature, and its independence of the becoming or passing away of external things."[12]

But unlike Tylor and other anthropologists, historians of religions such as Eliade and Otto have refrained from speculation on how the concept of the soul originated. Far from suggesting hypotheses of a causal nature, historians of religions have treated the notion of the soul as an a priori concept fundamental to the nature of man—a presupposition of man's experience in the world rather than a product of such experience. Such an understanding of the soul concept represents a great improvement over that of anthropologists. The notion of the soul, so intimately linked with that of the self, is such that any empirical explanation of it is nonsensical. Its foundation is logical in the Wittgensteinian sense—that is, it is grounded in a form of life.

The concept of the soul has a status similar to that of religious beliefs in that it is distinguished from empirical and factual beliefs not by being more subjective, but by being more directly and immediately related to the practices and life forms on which all belief is

11. Edward B. Tylor, "Animism," in William A. Lessa and Evon Z. Vogt (eds.), *Reader in Comparative Religion: An Anthropological Approach* (New York, 1958), 21.
12. Otto, *The Holy*, 281.

founded. Historians of religions are thus correct in viewing the notion of the soul as prior to any empirical influences or causes of it. Where they err is in seeing this priority as subjectively grounded, for it is precisely the belief in the soul that is not prior. As a belief, the soul has appeared in an almost unimaginable variety of forms. Most of these forms are no doubt related, but it does not follow that there exists some one criterion or set of criteria that all such forms partake of. Like the members of a family tree, the forms of the soul as they have appeared in different cultures throughout history are related in sometimes close, sometimes distant ways. In some cases, there may be no clear relationship, no common set of characteristics shared by two forms. Certainly, it is absurd to claim that the soul is, in all cases, a substance distinct from the body. On the contrary, for many primitive cultures, the soul is viewed as so organic and capable of the full range of human emotions that it would make just as much sense to say that the soul is a kind or type of body. To define the soul as a spiritual entity distinct from the body is to bypass what is, in the case of many cultures, the most critical problem of all—the nature of the distinction between soul and body. It is not just the belief in the soul that appears in a variety of forms, but also what might be called the belief in the body. Indeed, the two cannot be judged independently of each other. To define the soul as an entity distinct from the body is meaningful only if what one signifies by the *body* is reasonably constant. But this is manifestly not the case. Many primitive and ancient cultures do not conceive of the body as a physical entity subject to natural laws any more than they conceive of the soul as a detached Cartesian consciousness or mind. Moreover, such conceptual disparities exist not just between modern culture and ancient and primitive ones, but also between virtually all cultures throughout history. What is the link between the Ugaritic notion of the soul that has as one of its synonyms desire (HR-I, 218), and the twittering, enfeebled shades that inhabit the Greek Hades or the Hebrew Seoul? Or between the Paleolithic notion of the soul that was localized in a particular area of the body (E-H, 34) and the New Testament notion of the soul as *pneuma*, or breath? Or between the Hebrew *naphes* (soul) associated with *ruach* (the wind or spirit of the Lord) and the primitive concept of the soul as an entity that may be deceived and tricked and is often thought of as stupid?

The point is not that these notions may not all be significantly compared (likened and contrasted) with one another, but rather that such comparisons cannot take place on an a priori basis. There is not one defining characteristic that runs through or is behind all forms of the soul. Rather, we can define what the soul is only by examining how it and related notions such as the body are conceived of in particular cases, by describing the logic and form of life on which the concept of the soul is grounded. The fact that a given people distinguish between soul and body cannot in itself provide a basis for comparison; rather, what is important is the *way* in which these concepts are distinguished. When historians of religions try to give a definition of soul that applies to all cultures, they impose their own particular conception of the soul—or even of mind or consciousness—on those cultures. They objectify their own concept of the soul, thereby blinding themselves to the logic or meaning that informs the concepts of the soul in other cultures.

6

The widespread effort among historians of religions to define religion in terms of a dichotomy of the sacred and the profane presents a case similar, if more general, to that of the dichotomy of soul and body. As mentioned earlier, the notion of a dichotomy of the sacred and the profane, as conceived by historians of religions, was essentially a refurbishing of the more traditional concept of a dichotomy between the supernatural and the natural, as it was used by nineteenth-century anthropologists such as Tylor and Frazer. The advantages of the new distinction between the sacred and the profane were twofold. First, it allowed historians of religions to generalize their concept of religion to a point where it was no longer limited to the features of a particular religion—including the belief in gods or supernatural deities of any sort. In this way, historians of religions could feel that they had developed a general working definition of religion that was not based on the viewpoint of one religion. Second, it allowed historians of religions to internalize their notion of religion in such a way that its essence would be independent of any empirical—whether naturalistic or historical—influences on religion. This independence, it is important to emphasize, is implicit in the very notion of the sacred as the opposite or antithesis of the profane.

Since the sacred is what is characteristically religious, such a definition immediately consigns all "true" religious phenomena to a distinctively nonnatural status. To say that the sacred is produced through a negation of the profane is to say that the religious experience itself is produced through a negation of naturalistic experiences. Of course, one of the more important of the naturalistic experiences that needs to be negated is man's experience of himself as an isolated individual who is subject to the conditions of the natural (internal and external) environment. The religious experience enables man to transcend not only nature, but also himself as a natural being.

In understanding the fallacies involved in this view of religion as a dichotomy of the sacred and the profane, the first point that needs to be made is that, even granting that all religions can be defined with reference to the categories of the sacred and the profane, these categories are not seen by many cultures as opposed, much less opposite, to one another. Thus, W. W. Malandra, a student of religion sympathetic to the tradition of the history of religions, writes in his study of the shamanistic practices of the peoples of northern Eurasia: "When we look closely at the actual setting of a shamanistic performance we find it often difficult to separate the myth dimension from the profane ones."[13] Such a comment is, of course, directly at odds with Eliade's often-repeated assertion (in his *Shamanism* and many other works) that the practices of the shaman are performed in a sacred, mythological time and space that is the negation of man's profane, temporal existence. The point here, however, is not simply the point that anthropologists are fond of making against historians of religions—that there exists a great deal of evidence indicating that many peoples do *not* view their religious experience in terms of a dichotomy of the sacred and the profane—but also that the notion of the sacred and the profane, when taken as an absolute or fixed category, is little more than an a priori frame of reference that we impose on other cultures. Just as the contention that the belief in the soul is universal to man assumes a certain conception of the body alien to many non-Western cultures, so too the contention that all religions

13. W. W. Malandra, "The Concept of Movement in History of Religions," *Numen*, XIV (March, 1967), 67.

involve a dichotomy of the sacred and the profane assumes a certain conception of the profane alien to many non-Western peoples.

The definition of religion as a dichotomy of the sacred and the profane, though intended to overcome scientific naturalism, is really just an indirect way of capitulating to it, as Nadel makes clear in the following discussion:

> Any definition of the supernatural must introduce the contrast with the domain of empirical and scientific knowledge; more precisely, when judging any action or notion to be concerned with the supernatural we assert by implication that it is concerned with existences and influences (beings, "powers," "forces") the assumption of which conflicts with the principles of empirical inquiry and verification. And since those principles and their potentialities have been fully explored only in our own modern science, and can certainly not be assumed to govern the intellectual efforts of primitive peoples, the separation of the "natural" from the "supernatural" can have precise meaning only in our own system of thought. (SA, 150)

The fact that historians of religions usually speak of the sacred as being generated through a negation of the profane (rather than, for example, the profane being generated by the sacred) only points up the validity of Nadel's point more strongly. Similarly, the contention of so many historians of religions that primitive and ancient man must transcend his purely individual, natural existence in order to achieve a truly religious experience is based on the unwarranted assumption that primitive and ancient man conceives of himself as a purely individual, naturalistic being in the first place. This assumption is, in turn, based on the preconceived view that there exists in primitive and ancient societies an opposition between the individual and society similar to that found in modern cultures. In all cases, an a priori system of categories is applied to cultures for which such categories are not necessarily relevant. Instead of surveying the range of phenomena of a particular religion—a range that includes both empirical and conceptual elements, both conditions of the natural environment and religious beliefs and myths—and reading out of such phenomena the particular logic or meaning that characterizes that religion, the historians of religions impose an a priori conceptual system on the phenomena. The basic problem with such a priori theorizing is not, as anthropologists tend to suggest, that conceptual categories (such as that of the sacred and the profane) are employed, but that they are employed in the wrong way.

The notion of a dichotomy of the sacred and the profane may be very useful for understanding the religions of *some* cultures. With other cultures, on the other hand, the categories of the sacred and the profane may have to be reformulated; it may be, for example, that what we call the profane is not in any way opposite to what they imbue with sacredness. It may be possible, in other words, to characterize religions with reference to some sort of distinction between the sacred and the profane, but the kind of distinction made in different cultures (as that between body and soul) will vary enormously. In some cases, it may not be at all possible to characterize religious experience with reference to the sacred/profane dichotomy. The point is that such matters cannot be decided a priori. It is the effort to give a definition of religion in terms of a single feature or set of features common to all religions that is misconceived and must be abandoned.

To abandon the effort to formulate a definition of religion in these terms, is not—as anthropologists often give the impression of doing—to abandon the effort to understand and characterize the religious experience as it manifests itself in different cultures. For this latter purpose, the use of such categories as the sacred and the profane (as well as many others) is entirely appropriate. How the distinction between the sacred and the profane is formulated in a particular culture, however, must never be assumed, but rather must be the result of an investigation of the logic of that culture's religious beliefs. What the sacred and the profane are must emerge from, and be defined in terms of, the culture being examined.

The beliefs and practices of a given culture must be surveyed in such a way that we can make explicit the logical presuppositions of such beliefs and practices—that is, describe the nature of the distinction that that culture makes between the sacred and the profane. Once this is done, the logic of the culture's religious beliefs (which might be expressed as a kind of distinction between what we call the sacred and the profane) can be compared with the logic of other cultures. In this way, a sort of family tree of resemblances and differences can be constructed.

There is no one set of characteristics that appears in the religions of all cultures, but rather many overlapping sets that appear and disappear as one travels from culture to culture. The assumption that there is some religious essence or meaning that manifests itself (and is always constant) in the changing forms—the beliefs and practices—of particular religions must be abandoned. Rather, it should be recognized that these changing forms, these particular beliefs and practices, constitute what religion is. Applying categories like the sacred and the profane to them is only a way of making manifest their logic or meaning. There is nothing behind the forms of religious experience (whether these forms include, for example, the belief in gods, totemism, or nature worship), but only a way of describing those forms such that they can make sense to us.

The anthropologist, as we have seen, errs in posing a dichotomy between culture and nature, for culture is embedded in nature just as man's language games are embedded in a *Lebensform*. It is because of this false dichotomy of the empirical and the conceptual that the anthropologist thinks he can explain culture by reference to natural processes. He assumes man can adopt a standpoint outside his own conceptual and cultural framework.

The historian of religions, by contrast, does not conceive of natural forces as causal in the formation of culture and religion; he makes the defining criterion of religion and culture that which is non-naturalistic. In this way, he draws a line between nature and culture quite as sharp as that drawn by the anthropologist. Only now, instead of investing material conditions with a universal, logical status, the historian of religions invests subjective states of mind with a universal, logical status. Thus, by a different method the historian of religions repeats the mistakes of the anthropologist. He thinks that by separating the empirical and the subjective he has adopted an extracultural standpoint, when in fact all he has done is make absolute one particular cultural standpoint, one way of dividing up the empirical and subjective aspects of culture. Both the anthropologist and the historian of religions project their own logic or way of thinking onto cultures and circumstances in which it may not be appropriate. Anthropologists do this by adopting what they mistakenly think is a scientific point of view and then reading meaning into external, material causes. Historians of religions do this by reading a particular meaning or definition into the structure of human consciousness. In both cases, the conceptual eyeglasses of the researcher blind him to the logic or meaning of the beliefs and practices of the cultures he is studying.

The perspective I am advocating, on the other hand, is opposed to the Humean and Boasian approach in that it does not allow culture to be conceived of as a subjective, nonrational product of natural forces. But it is also opposed to the Kantian approach in that although it allows religion and culture to be characterized with reference to a given subjective category, it does not allow such a subjective category to be given an absolute, across-the-board status. What is subjective and what is material is contingent on the particular culture; the nature of such contingency is brought out in the logical presuppositions by which the line between the material and the mental or the profane and the sacred is drawn. A logical description is not the description of a static, once-and-for-all state of affairs (as Wittgenstein thought in the *Tractatus*). Rather, logic is dependent on *Lebensform* and therefore normative. To describe the logical features of a culture is to describe the rules according to which it functions. Thus, any logical description that makes explicit the values embedded in that culture, regardless of whether what we call ethical terms are used, is necessarily a normative description.

7

In terms of cause and meaning, the type of confusion seen in the natural sciences has a very different status than that seen in the social sciences. When a bacillus is regarded not only as a cause but also as a defining criterion of a disease, the confusion is one simply of our own concepts of cause and meaning. But when we treat the fear or consciousness of death as a cause of the beliefs and practices of another culture, there is a further complication, for we are not simply confusing cause and meaning, we are also confusing what we mean by a given phenomenon with what another culture means. In this way, we completely bypass and miss the phenomenon. When we see, for example, a given culture's notion of the afterlife as the result, ultimately, of the fear of death, we define that culture's notion of the afterlife in our own modern secularistic terms. We fail to see the significance that that culture itself gives to it. The reason for this is clear.

In trying to grasp the cause and meaning of phenomena, we have cultivated the habit of confusing the two. This habit has become second nature, so much so that when anyone draws attention to it he seems to be violating common sense.

In the natural sciences, we are often provided with convenient objects to sustain this confusion. The bacillus, for example, gives us a concrete object onto which to project our metaphysical fantasies. Such projection is, perhaps, not terribly harmful: even if the doctor regards the bacillus as both cause and criterion of identity, he may not let this view influence the way he actually treats the disease. His treatment may be based on a "total" knowledge of the disease, which encompasses, say, its manifold symptoms, the patient's history, the social and physical environment in which the patient lives. The presence of the bacillus will be one factor (sometimes decisive, sometimes not) in his construction of a therapeutic regimen.

In the case of the student of culture, however, the situation is different. There is often no object, no "bacillus," to be seen as both cause and criterion of identity. The mythology of ancient Egypt, for example, has no reference; it has nothing by which a hypothesis might be constructed to explain the causes of the ancient Egyptians' worldview. The only thing we have is the worldview itself—the mythology. To look for causes is often hopeless: all that may reasonably be accomplished is a description that reveals the meaning of the worldview. Nonetheless, the metaphysical habit is too strong to resist. We therefore make up our own causes and explain another culture's notion of the afterlife in the same way we explain our own religious views. Seeking a causal explanation, we invent a universal object— for example, the fear or consciousness of death—that denies us understanding of the meaning of the phenomenon we are studying. Historians of religions accomplish the same thing in a different way: by making rational and universal the subjective basis of man's practices and beliefs, they uncritically impose their own norms and ways of thinking on other cultures. What is thus merely a bad habit cultivated in the natural sciences has harmful effects when it is maintained in the study of culture.

The phenomena that the social scientist investigates are of a more normative, even moral nature than those that the natural scientist studies. But moral belief, as we saw earlier, is not distinguished from factual belief by its greater degree of subjectivity. On the contrary, moral belief lies closer to the heart of the forms of human action and behavior that sustain our way of life and on which all knowledge claims are based than does factual belief. For this reason, moral assertions are less empirical, less specific than factual assertions—but not necessarily less fundamental or less objective. Similarly, the subject matter of the social scientist, when compared with that of the natural sciences, is of a less empirical nature. This is shown above all by the fact that the possibilities of demonstrating causal relationships are, on the whole, fewer. This does not mean, however, that the subject matter of the social sciences is somehow less fundamental or less objective than that of the natural sciences. On the contrary, the social scientist is more directly concerned with that which grounds, or is the basis for, all knowledge claims. That the level on which he deals is more basic deprives him of doing what the natural scientist can do so elegantly, namely, demonstrate cause and effect. But as it does so, it increases the potential importance of his studies to human behavior as a whole. The point might be expressed in the following way. The world man lives in is like a three-dimensional sphere whose density approaches infinity as one moves toward the center. Science measures what lies at the perimeter of the sphere, what is least dense and clearest and can be resolved by simple, clear-cut empirical tests. As one travels inward, however, he is bombarded with new factors that can, potentially, change the status of the conclusions of science. By the time he gets to the center, to what is closest to him and to what he relies on all the time in his everyday life (*i.e.*, notions such as the self, the existence of the external world, and God), science is at a loss to say anything significant about them.

It is not that scientific knowledge is unreliable, but that such reliability is always contingent on an established way of life. It is society and culture that have made science possible by adopting certain assumptions about nature and the external world (for example, that both operate independent of our observation of them), assumptions that, in fact, neither science nor society is in a position to prove. Modern society grants the scientist the right to feel himself removed from natural processes (and thereby be in a better position to study them) in a way that, for example, the society of the Australian aborigine does not. The aborigine is consequently less capable of studying nature, because he is *not* permitted to feel himself *not* a part of it. This highly developed "cultural right," however, should not seduce us into thinking that scientific knowledge is capable of bursting free of the social context in which it is developed. Consider how we would regard scientific knowledge if it had no applications. Pure theoretical scientists claim, of course, that the validity of their results is independent of the technological applications of them. But if there were, in fact, no such applications, how would this claim be any different from that of the theologian, philosopher, or medieval alchemist? People are fond of saying that what distinguishes the claims of science from those of religion and philosophy is that those of science are testable. It is so often forgotten that what makes science testable, and religion not, is that certain conditions of culture obtain. In other ages, the reverse situation was often the case. For centuries, social scientists have been berating themselves for not achieving the sort of "hardness" and certainty of results achieved in the natural sciences, particularly physics. The philosophies of both Hume and Kant were formulated, in large part, as a response to this "lamentable" situation. But the reason for the difference between the natural sciences and the social sciences is simply that the subject matter of the latter is more fundamental than that of the former. Morals, religion, and culture in general—the study of these deal in a direct and immediate fashion with human behavior and action. They therefore throw into question the logic or meaning that governs such behavior and action.

The natural sciences, by contrast, gain their predictive power from the fact that they have designed methods to narrow the context with which they deal, to isolate and control experimentally the factors being tested. But precisely because scientific knowledge arises out of experience in relatively narrow, controlled contexts, great care must be taken in applying it to wider domains that lie at some remove. Indeed, many phenomena of a behavioral nature cannot be controlled for by a conventional experimental apparatus. The attempt to do so results only in the apparatus and the phenomena screening each other out, like two shadows passing through each other on a dimly lit street. Knowledge must have substance, must have the capacity to be used in particular contexts. Those who make sweeping claims for science's ability to understand and control social

behavior are like mental giants taking long strides over broad contextual domains. Although science has, of course, had a great deal of
success over the last century, this success is not to be explained (as
Kant and historians of religions are wont to do) by the fact that it
deals with an essentially different kind of knowledge than that of
history or even religion. Rather, it is to be explained in part by the
fact that it has developed such an effective social means, through
technological innovations, to broaden the context and therefore the
applicability of its knowledge. But this remarkable ability on the
part of science should be the object of a historical and sociological
inquiry; it should not necessarily be given an absolute status. Success
is not the only measure of truth.

VII   Culture and History

In the last two chapters, I argued that both anthropologists and historians of religions uncritically project their own "logic" or way of thinking into contexts in which it may not be appropriate. Anthropologists do so by adopting what they mistakenly think is a scientific point of view, reading meaning into external, material causes. Historians of religions do so by positing some one meaning or definition in the structure of human consciousness. In both cases, the cultural eyeglasses of the researcher blind him to the logic or meaning of the beliefs and practices of the cultures he is studying.

But this metaphor of cultural eyeglasses can be misleading. For it may lead us to suppose that the solution lies in simply taking the eyeglasses off or, if that is impossible, trying to design some method for seeing around them. Any such method, however, will succeed in increasing the thickness of the lenses, perhaps thereby changing our view, but not necessarily making it more accurate, and certainly not making it less culturally determined. Since meaning is intrinsically normative—grounded in what is familiar to us—there can be no normatively neutral grounds from which to grasp meaning. Any solution aimed at overcoming or denying the normative perspective of the researcher will thus be naive and uncritical, for there is no concept of fairness, impartiality, or objectivity that man is not capable of transforming into an instrument of his own limited concerns.

Earlier, it was noted briefly that the subjectivistic concept of culture adopted by comparative religionists necessarily dictates a non-normative stance on the part of the researcher. This can be seen in the case of Boasian anthropologists. For Boas, the internal, subjective elements of culture must be sharply separated from the more organic and universal ones. He writes: "It is . . . one of the fundamental aims of scientific anthropology to learn which traits of behavior, if any, are organically determined and are, therefore, the common property of mankind and which are due to the culture in which we live" (B-AML, 202). Since cultural phenomena are by nature subjective, nonrational, and individualized, the only neutral grounds the researcher can stand on are those conditions and needs universal to all cultures: "The freedom of judgment thus obtained is of great value. We may not hope to reach it with ease, because it depends upon a clear recognition of what is organically and what is culturally determined" (B-AML, 203–204).

The Boasian concept of culture thus makes a stance of neutrality possible by positing the characteristic features of culture as subjective and internal. Since those features are internal, all one needs to do in order to be objective is to adopt an external viewpoint. This external viewpoint will be external not just to the particular culture being studied, but to all cultures, including the anthropologist's. Such a viewpoint is made possible by the existence of a set of universal conditions and needs that all cultures are subject to and that do not characterize the nature of any particular culture. When the anthropologist adopts a neutral stance, he does *not* simply distinguish between the values of his own culture and those of the culture being studied. Rather, he makes an assertion about the nature of culture itself; he claims that all cultures have two aspects—one that is particular to the culture being studied and one that is common to all cultures. *If* it were impossible to make such a separation, if it were impossible to describe conditions and culture separately, *then* it would also be impossible to make a similar separation regarding his own cultural values and the necessary conditions on which his culture rests. In that case, he might still have the desire to be normatively neutral, but he would not know how to go about actually becoming so. He would not know what was external to culture and what was internal, what was common to all cultures and what particular to each one.

Boas, however, never entertained serious doubts about the ability of the researcher to separate the internal aspects of culture from the external. He did not entertain such doubts because he thoroughly accepted the notion of the mind as an "infinite source of ideas" that has the capacity to detach its purely logical operations from an admixture of traditional elements (B-JAF, 1). The picture of a dichotomy between the subjective and the empirical, by which Boas defined the nature of culture, thus structured his view of the proper methodological stance to be adopted by the researcher. In both cases, the mind was given an autonomy that allowed it to be the source of an infinite number of ideas. The interdependence of Boas' view of the nature of culture and his view of proper methodology is brought out clearly in the following passage, in which he starts by attributing to "the activities of the mind . . . infinite variety" (thereby characterizing the highly individualized nature of culture) and ends by attributing the same mental plasticity to the researcher:

> The activities of the mind . . . exhibit an infinite variety of form among the peoples of the world. In order to understand these clearly, the student must endeavor to divest himself entirely of opinions and emotions based upon the peculiar social environment into which he is born. He must adapt his own mind, so far as feasible, to that of the people whom he is studying. The more successful he is in freeing himself from the bias based on the group of ideas that constitute the civilization in which he lives, the more successful he will be in interpreting the beliefs and actions of man. (B-JAF, 1)

The subjectivistic and empiricist concept of culture adopted by Boasian anthropologists thus makes possible a stance of neutrality by providing the scholar a nonnormative position from which to view culture. So it is with historians of religions. By giving religion a subjective foundation, historians of religions have simultaneously given themselves a normatively neutral vantage point from which to view religion. That is why virtually all historians of religions, even those who openly express antipathy for the "reductionistic" methodologies of the natural sciences, maintain that the scholar must adopt an empirical method of study. He must acquaint himself with all relevant historical and ethnographic data before trying to find a meaning in that data, before trying to interpret it.

Although such a similarity exists between the ethical stances of the anthropologist and the historian of religions, there is also an important and visible difference. Whereas the historian of religions feels it necessary to acquaint himself with the empirical aspects of his subject matter, he by no means feels it sufficient; religion must be studied not just from the outside but, much more, also from within. Moreover, this difference in the methodologies used by the historian of religions and the anthropologist is directly related to their differing concepts of culture as rational and nonrational. For the Boasian anthropologist, culture is something that, in its interior dimensions, is fundamentally nonrational and therefore, by definition, not to be approached in a systematic manner; he must confine himself to external description.

For the historian of religions, however, the case is different. His understanding of religion as not merely subjective but also rational has allowed him to formulate a methodology to get at the interior dimensions of religion. This method is, of course, the phenomenology of religion. Moreover, phenomenology has given the historian of religions not only a means of penetrating to the internal core, or essence, of religion, but has enabled him to do this in a way that preserves the subjective character of religion. Religious phenomena are rational for the historian of religions in a way similar to that in which morality was rational for Kant—in a practical, "transhuman," or metaphysical sense, not in a scientific, theoretical one. The phenomenological method provides the historian of religions with a way of filling that "vacant place" that is left after all empirical and scientific description has been exhausted. It must be filled not with anything claiming to be knowledge in a scientific sense, for moral and religious phenomena do not have objects in the same, sensory sense that science does. Rather, the description of the internal aspects of religion provided by the historian of religions must be founded on an a priori acceptance that such aspects exist and can be approached; the validity of engaging in such description cannot be proved any more than the existence of God could be proved for Kant.

Precisely because there can be no proof, in an empirical sense, of the reality of the sacred realm, the historian of religions must rely heavily on a sense of empathy with the religions and cultures he studies. Otherwise, it would be perfectly possible for him to close himself off to the sacred (as he frequently regards the anthropologist as doing) and thus to the most important feature of his subject matter. That is why historians of religions so often defend themselves against the assaults of empiricists and reductionists by pointing up the "unscientific" character of the latter's methods—what Eric Sharpe calls their "a priori assumption of the non-existence of the supernatural" (SH, 105).

Historians of religions place a greater value and importance on the subjective characteristics of religion than do anthropologists by positing such characteristics in a domain that allows for no claims to scientific knowledge. They insist, quite as much as anthropologists, on the need to adopt a nonnormative stance. Such a stance ensures that whatever empathy or religious feeling they possess will be confined to a specific sphere and will not be applied to the domain of history and society in their external senses. In other words, historians of religions empathize phenomenologically with their subject matter only to the extent that they confine it to a specific domain of reality. In few cases do they make an effort to develop a consciousness of the way their normative concerns as a member of a particular culture may be influencing their perspective.[1] Rather, such concerns, if they are acknowledged at all, must be bracketed; they can only distort the investigator's view of the culture or religion he is studying. The empathy that the historian of religions feels he must cultivate is to be directed toward the universal religious experience. Moreover, that one can traverse the culturally specific and leap directly into the universal is not doubted or even raised seriously as a question. The historian of religions' conception of culture and religion as subjective necessitates that such questions not be asked—necessitates it, that is, if, in contrast to the anthropologist, he is to affirm the reality of the sacred. In certain ways, historians of religions have been even more strict than anthropologists in maintaining a stance of normative neutrality. For although the latter can feel secure in simply declaring a ban on the exercise of moral judgment in their studies, the former must simultaneously assert the appropriateness of cultivating a certain religious empathy and yet be careful to keep such feelings wholly general and not more applicable to one religion that to another. It is perhaps for this reason that the historian of religions, as Joachim Wach said, "has strong words only when he wants to convince us he has no convictions."[2]

2

The nonnormative stance adopted by comparative religionists, then, is dictated by their assumption that a proper understanding of other

1. There are, of course, exceptions, the most significant of which is probably W. Brede Kristensen, whose acute sensibility and self-consciousness of his own (Western) cultural bias allowed him to transcend, to some degree, the very phenomenological method he advocated.

2. Quoted in Ninian Smart, *The Science of Religion and the Sociology of Knowledge* (Princeton, 1973), 63.

cultures can be gained independent of the development of a critical consciousness of norms of one's own culture. It follows, conversely, that a normative concept of culture—whose crucial feature is that an understanding of other cultures is, in fact, dependent on such consciousness—dictates a normative stance on the part of the researcher. But what then of the fallacies associated with the propensity of social scientists and comparative religionists to interpret cultural phenomena empirically and thereby objectify their meaning? The root of such fallacies is not that we understand other cultures according to our own conceptual categories, but that we do so uncritically and unselfconsciously. The failure to develop a critical consciousness of our own presuppositions leads us to absolutize such presuppositions—and because modern man tends to place his faith in the facts, such absolutism leads inevitably to the adoption of an empirical account of meaning. We become, as it were, meaning-blind to the concepts of other cultures *by* our failure to recognize the normative—that is, finite, limited, and partial—character of our own concepts. To recognize the social scientist's task as normative is therefore not to *accept* our own prejudices, but to accept that we *have* prejudices, and to develop a heightened critical awareness of them.

This notion of cultivating a heightened critical awareness of one's own presuppositions, however, should not be understood as a conceptual *solution* to the problem of man's propensity to objectify meaning, for such a propensity takes too many forms, wears too many disguises, and is altogether too *primeval* an urge to yield before the flimsy defenses that any mere conceptual solution could provide. What is needed, rather, is a method or practice flexible enough to adapt itself to the possible difficulties. It is just such a method or practice I have in mind when I speak of cultivating a critical consciousness of one's own presuppositions. The value, if any, of such can be seen only in its application—in its ability to bring to light certain assumptions and methodological fallacies concerning culture, meaning, and morality that lie hidden in the practices and perspective of the comparative religionist.

But, one might ask, if the only basis for understanding other cultures is one's own partial perspective, then what is to prevent us from being intolerant and unfair in our assessments?

In answer to this, it needs to be pointed out, first, that the stance of normative neutrality itself serves a normative function. To the extent that comparative religionists maintain the essential similarity of all human cultures in terms of an underlying substratum of needs and conditions, they also put in a disguised bid for the superiority of their own culture. For historians and anthropologists would like to distinguish themselves from primitive and archaic man not with regard to their practices, customs, or even forms of social organization, but with regard to their ability to *understand* them; the greater the breadth of consciousness they exhibit, the more they are able satisfactorily to account for all the cultures of the world within their categories. It is by being theoretical that the comparative religionist constitutes for himself his sense of superiority. The neutral stance of the scholar thus masks a much deeper bias; it does not place him in a position outside the sphere that he is analyzing but is in fact an expression and affirmation of—even a boasting and taking pride in—his particular position.

The objection I am making to this position is not that it is taken, but that it is such a weak one to take. "A living thing," said Nietzsche, "can only be healthy, strong, and productive within a certain horizon."[3] Without this horizon, this common horizon of consciousness, spirituality is relegated to a private domain, and consciousness becomes isolated, either exploding itself beyond all boundaries or, what is the same thing, narrowing itself to invisibility. Comparative religionists have failed to grasp that the study of culture and religion is best constituted not by the elimination of prejudice, but by its rigorous refinement. We deceive ourselves if we think we can say anything meaningful about a culture without seeing ourselves in relation to that culture, without "participating" in it. What such participation means is giving up the effort to find a hidden, universal meaning or essence *behind* the forms of culture and religion (whether our own or anyone else's), investing instead with life and power that which lies *revealed* all around us. In the twenty-ninth chapter of Deuteronomy we read: "The secret things belong to the Lord our God; but the things that are revealed belong to us and to our children forever, that we may do all the words of the law." In

---

3. Friedrich Nietzsche, *The Use and Abuse of History*, trans. Adrian Collins (Indianapolis, 1957), 7.

their search for "the secret things," comparative religionists have missed the revelation.

Those who feel that adopting a normative stance in the study of culture will lead to judging foreign cultures unfairly and intolerantly forget that one can be fair only from a *particular* point of view. Fairness means not just refusing to judge others on the basis of criteria alien to them, but also—what is a necessary precondition for that—recognizing that one's perspective and judgments necessarily derive from the conditions of one's own culture. (For not even language is "neutral territory.") In a limited sense, adopting a normative stance in the study of culture is similar to cultivating what historians of religions often speak of as an attitude of "sympathetic understanding." The researcher must first try to "understand" a culture on its own terms, asking himself, To what extent are my own normative presuppositions being read into this culture? He asks this question, however, *not* in order to block such presuppositions, but to use them in a controlled way. By seeing the norms and values of culture in the light of his own, he provides himself with a tool for understanding more deeply what lies at the source of those norms and values, what human needs they satisfy, what problems they are designed to avoid. In other words, he adopts a posture of sympathetic understanding by injecting his own moral concerns into his studies, for only then can he see what motivates such values.

3

But if there exists neither an empirical substratum nor a set of universal concepts from which we might try to understand foreign cultures—that is, if there is neither an absolute nor a fixed basis common to all cultures—and we must instead try to grasp the norms and values of each culture on its own terms, are we not landed in the most sterile relativism? Are we not presented with a vast panorama of cultures each of which is possessed of its own separate values and logic, and none of which is necessarily related to the others?

The denial of any absolute basis from which to study culture does not imply that one must necessarily regard the norms and values of all cultures as being equal in status. Only when one regards norms and values as such does one commit oneself to a position of cultural relativism, properly defined. Another question, however, now presents itself: having taken the first step, how does one avoid going on to the second? For according to the normative concept of culture I am suggesting, although there may be nothing that all cultures have in *common*, it is nonetheless a necessary presupposition for the study of comparative culture that they be *related*. And why, in any given case, should there be such a relationship? Why, that is, should two cultures that have grown up on opposite sides of the "family tree" of culture have even a single characteristic in common? What, indeed, is the connection between a modern society and one existing in Paleolithic times, or even in the time of ancient Egypt? If there are no shared characteristics, how will it be possible to gain understanding? Where will we be able to gain a foothold in a culture that has no values in common with our own?

The answer to this query must be straightforward: We would *not* be able to gain a foothold in such an extreme (and hypothetical) case, for we could not gain a foothold on a surface that was perfectly smooth and frictionless. Or, to change metaphors, our cultural eyeglasses would not allow us to see the foreign culture, and there would be no objects on the horizon to which we could conceptually anchor ourselves. Indeed, we would be in a position similar to one in which we tried to understand the "society" of a school of fish. We could describe the behavior of the fish in human terms, but we would have no way of knowing whether such terms were in the remotest sense accurate (as, for example, when a child describes a fish as "mean-looking"). A culture with which we had absolutely nothing in common would not, in other words, be human in the sense in which we are accustomed to using this term. Indeed, it is because we have no means of understanding the way of life of a school of fish that we say they lack consciousness or intentionality; such contentions are ways of expressing our concepts of human and animal (they aren't empirical generalizations). Conversely, a culture that we did term human would necessarily have something in common with our own, something we could connect or link up with. Although there might be no common characteristic between ourselves and a given Paleolithic tribe, what would separate us from this tribe would not be a cultural abyss or nothingness (as in the case of a society of fish). There would be, rather, intermediate societies by means of which a connection could be established. But what exactly would the substance of this connection be? What allows us to see links where none at first sight appear? One might say that the connection between a species of fish and *homo sapiens* is given by the concept of biological evolution. The connection between any two given human cultures, then, is given by the concept of history. A closer look at the meaning of the term *history* is therefore in order.

Let us consider first the notion of history as it is reflected in the work of comparative religionists. For both Boasian anthropologists and historians of religions, historical process is not intrinsic to the nature of culture. What can be established to have occurred historically may have influenced and even determined the particular form a culture has taken, but it does not constitute the nature or essence of culture itself. The meaning of cultural practices and beliefs lies outside the domain of temporality. Thus, speaking of the historical description that he considered important to the task of the cultural anthropologist, Boas says:

> Even the fullest knowledge of the history of language does not help us to understand how we use language and what influence language has upon our thought. It is the same in other phases of life. The dynamic reactions to cultural environment are not determined by its history, although they are a result of historical development. Historical data do give us certain clues that may not be found in the experience of a single generation. Still, the psychological problem must be studied in living societies. . . . It would be an error to claim as some anthropologists do, that for this reason historical study is irrelevant. The two sides of our problem require equal attention. (B-RLC, 255)

Again and again, Boas emphasizes that a historical account of culture is not a *full* account (B-RLC, 296). Although Boas carefully notes that a historical perspective is necessary (B-AML, 208; B-MPM, 244), he also insists that the failure to keep separate the historical and psychological aspects of culture is the source of much conceptual confusion in anthropology (B-ANA, 313–314), as, for example, in his reply to criticism from Alfred Kroeber (B-RLC, 305–306).

In a similar fashion, historians of religions also posit a division between history and the meaning or essence of religious and cultural phenomena. In fact, for historians of religions this division is even more sharply maintained than it is by anthropologists; the meaning or sense of religious phenomena is placed wholly outside the domain of historical process, so that any causal relationship between the two is ruled out from the beginning. Religious phenomena are defined as both being radically subjective in character—having their source in the self and gaining objectivity only by being defined with reference to empirical processes—and having a universal, extracultural, and therefore extrahistorical status. Thus, Eliade emphasizes that "the sacred is an element in the structure of consciousness, not a stage in the history of consciousness" (E-Q, i); that "religious forms are non-temporal" (E-M, 137); and that "history cannot basically modify the structure of an archaic symbolism" (E-SP, 137). More generally, this dichotomy between meaning and history has given rise to what Philip Ashby calls a bifurcation in the discipline of the history of religions—between its historical and empirical aspects, on the one hand, and its religious and timeless, essential ones, on the other.[4] This account of a bifurcation in the history of religions is echoed by a large number of scholars, including not just Eliade,[5] but also Widengren (HR-I, 1; SH, 243), Bleeker,[6] Pettazzoni,[7] Werblowsky (HR-II, 2–3), Brandon,[8] Campbell,[9] and van der Leeuw (E-K, 65). The low esteem in which historians of religions hold historical evidence comes out strongly in the following passage by Eliade (he is speaking of the history of religions in its purely historical aspects):

> That is really all the material available to a historian of religions: a few fragments from a vast oral priestly learning . . . allusions found in traveller's notes, material gathered by foreign missionaries. . . . All the historical sciences are, of course, tied to this sort of scrappy and accidental evidence. But the religious historian faces a bolder task than the historian, whose job is

4. Philip Ashby, "The History of Religions," in Paul Ramsey (ed.), *Religion* (Englewood Cliffs, N.J., 1965), 25.
5. *Ibid.*, 232.
6. BL-R, 5, 32; BL-S, 3, 36; C. J. Bleeker, *Anthropologie Religieuse* (Leiden, 1955), 178.
7. Pettazzoni, *Essays on the History of Religions*, 215–19.
8. S. G. F. Brandon, *History, Time and Deity* (London, 1965), 2.
9. Joseph Campbell, *The Masks of God: Primitive Mythology* (4 vols.; New York, 1959), I, 37–38, 91, 108, 186, 215, 263–64, 350, 461–62.

merely to piece together an event or a series of events with the aid of the few bits of evidence that are preserved to him; the religious historian must trace not only the *history* of a given hierophany, but must first of all understand and explain the modality of the sacred that that hierophany discloses.[10]

The essential criticism I have of these accounts of the relation between culture and historical process is that the failure to distinguish clearly between the empirical (historical) aspects of culture and its purely logical and normative features (what grounds our concept of history, to begin with) is being made the basis for a false separation between the material and the mental elements of culture. Both anthropologists and historians of religions, in separating historical process and culture, fail to see that what gives significance to cultural phenomena (and therefore, in part, defines them) is closely bound up with historical process. Culture and history must be seen as weaves of the same cloth; the mental/material dichotomy must be dissolved. That just means, however, that the logical, normative structure embedded in both culture and history (in concept and fact) is to be distinguished from its empirical elements. To make explicit the logical, normative features of our concept of culture is at the same time to make explicit the deep connections that exist between all cultures, connections we term "historical."

4

One of the more difficult problems that must be confronted in order to gain a clear view of the nature of these deep connections is the relation between history and memory. Idealist philosophers of history such as R. G. Collingwood have argued that it is only when personal memory as such is transcended that history, properly speaking, begins.[11] Such philosophers maintain that unless history is seen as encompassing a sphere qualitatively different from that of individual experience—which is presumed to be the basis of individual memory—history will be reducible to a collection of facts or events

10. E-P, 5. See also E-P, 2, 426, 428, 431–32, 449, 450, 461, 462, 464; E-Q, ii, 36; E-H, 19, 44; E-SP, 16–17, 18, 62–63, 137, 232; E-S, xv, xix; Ivan Strenski, "Mircea Eliade, Some Theoretical Problems," in Adrian Cunningham (ed.), *The Theory of Myth* (London, 1973), 45, 49.

11. R. G. Collingwood, *The Idea of History* (Oxford, 1956), 86–204.

that can be, or at one time were, observed by some individual or individuals. But history, according to Collingwood, is not a mere stream of events that the individual remembers and turns into facts; rather, essential to what we call history is a subjective, interpretative component. That is why Collingwood calls history "a re-enactment of the past in the mind of the historian." But here again we see the same general type of error that is committed by phenomenologists of religions: in their efforts to deny that history has an empirical basis in the external, material world, idealist philosophers of history have given it an ultimately empirical basis in the inner, mental one.

The idealist position, therefore, must be rejected—and with it, the bifurcation between memory and history. This means not, however, that the positivistic view should be accepted, but rather that our concept of memory must be rethought.

Let us examine a claim that Wittgenstein countered in his private language argument. The claim is that when a person has a particular sensation, he assigns it a name. Later, when he has the same sensation, he is able to recognize it as that "thing" to which he had assigned the name and, in this way, construct a perfectly intelligible language. There is a fallacy, however, in that type of reasoning, one that centers on the use of the words *the same*. How is the inventor of the private language to know whether he has had "the same" sensation on two occasions? He could, after all, have made a mistake in identifying the sensation—something that all of us do regularly (our senses "deceive" us, as it is said). Under normal circumstances, the use and practice of language in public contexts allows us to correct such mistakes. But how could the inventor of the private language—who by definition does not use his language in a public context—make corrections? For he would have no way of discovering that he had committed a mistake. Indeed, in a private language, the words *correct* and *incorrect* have no sense, for whatever the person *says* was the sensation is the only criterion of identity *of* the sensation. He cannot be wrong. Without the ability to know whether there has been a mistake, the inventor of the private language is unable to give the term *the same* an intelligible meaning and, hence, construct a language.

That type of argument undermines the assumption—made by positivist and idealist philosophers of history alike—that memory has an empirical basis. It is not, that is, because certain events have occurred in the past and have left an impression on us (mental or otherwise) that we are able to remember them. Rather, we are able to do so because we have agreed to accept certain kinds of criteria as valid for determining whether or not an event has occurred. Consider, for example, someone who has a cyclical notion of time (as the people of many ancient civilizations did) and who recognizes as real only those events that recur. For such a person, the notions of the past and the future have a different sense than they do for us. To say, "Yesterday a given event will happen" might not be senseless to him, as it is to us; whereas he might have a difficult time understanding what we mean by calling something a unique historical event (Plato and Aristotle, for example, seemed to lack such understanding). It is not that what we call memory has no empirical correlates, but that the possibilities or range of such correlates is determined by the logical, not the empirical, features of our notion of time. A person might have the experience of having remembered going to the store yesterday and the experience of having remembered an event in his "past life." But we do not treat the report of these two experiences in the same way, because we do not allow that there are criteria that could establish the truth or falsity of the second memory. (Many cultures, however, have made just such an allowance.)

"So what you are saying is that our memories are not empirically grounded in any stream of events, but are, rather, imposed on the events by the observer?" No, the logical features of our notion of time govern not just the possibilities of succession in the external world, but also how the individual envisions and thinks about such succession. It is always with reference to public or social criteria that we judge the temporal frame of reference of a given event.

Consider the following three statements:

1. "I remember that yesterday I went to the store."
2. "I remember that twenty years ago I had an operation in which my hand was removed."
3. "I know that I have a bump on my nose."

In order for statement 2 or statement 3 not to be true, one would have to imagine oneself as deceived about a great deal; there are, in a sense, too many supports for these assertions. Statement 2 is like statement 3 in the sense that although it is the memory of a particular event, the event seems to have left a record—a physical record—of itself.

We allow that assertions like statement 1 could be untrue—but only under abnormal and carefully specified conditions (the person was in a state of confusion for one reason or another; he could therefore have made a mistake in a manner similar to the way a twenty-five-year-old college graduate could have multiplied 9×7 incorrectly). If we say, however, that under normal circumstances, statement 1 could be untrue, then it resembles more closely statements 2 and 3, for in that case one would have to be wrong about, say, what a store is.

Remembering that, for example, "Yesterday I went to the store" is basic to a way of life; only under relatively abnormal circumstances would it be called into question or asked to be proven. Constantly to have to prove or verify the truth of memories of this sort would make life inconvenient, if not impossible. It seems that the experience of or the empirical evidence for knowing that "Yesterday I went to the store" is like that of knowing "I have a hand"; it seems to be built into the form of the assertion—which is to say, is part of a large number of practices intrinsic to a way of life—that they are not doubted. But to give several impressions or memory images as support for the truth of the assertion "Yesterday I went to the store" is insufficient; for it would be extremely easy to invent a strange set of circumstances alien to our way of life in which those impressions would be interpreted differently or would make no sense at all.

Compare the notions of expecting and remembering. One expects *something* (in the future); one remembers *something* (in the past). In the first case, we have the shadow of an anticipated fact; in the second case, the shadow or image of a prior fact. The fallacy in both cases is the implicit idea that the fact can somehow reach backward or forward to cause its meaning (intention or memory).

In "I intend to go to the store" and in "I remember that yesterday I went to the store," the fact is equally present—that is, in both cases it constitutes an element of the meaning, not the meaning itself. Consider "I remember that yesterday I went to the store" versus "I remember that I have two feet." It only makes sense to talk about remembering when one can also talk about forgetting.

A memory must be *of* something—something that may or may not have happened, but could have *possibly* happened. *I remember, I intended*—these are grammatically defined. One remembers the seconds before and during a serious accident as if they had occurred in slow motion. The memory is intense, vivid, for years afterward. But if the accident had not occurred, one would certainly not remember those seconds so vividly.

If I said, "I remember that yesterday I went to Mars," then everyone would agree that this was just an imaginary idea and that the event did not really occur—which shows that the objectivity of the memory must be established. Moreover, that some memories ("I remember that yesterday I went to the beach") will under many conditions be automatically accepted as true does not show that their truth does not need to be established, too: they must fit the criteria we give for a true statement. Thus, when I say, "I went to the beach" or "I went to Mars," the objective or illusory status of these statements can not be shown to depend, exclusive of any context, on what I really did, for that is just an abstraction until it is judged and established in a social setting exactly what I did or did not do. (The past act is objectively established, but only as a layer of the present.)

The past, therefore, does not "cause" the present. There is no necessary relation between the two, just as there is no necessary relation between the present and the future. (In other words, the necessity is stipulated by *us*—though not, of course, us as individuals.) The future can have an objective reference to the same degree that the past can, as cyclical notions of time imply. But we can no more say that the events of the past, by occurring, determined the makeup of the present than we can say that the events of the future will determine what is happening now.

5

What all this means is that our concept of the past presupposes not just a stream of disconnected events, but the capacity for one event to transform others in accordance with their sequence; one moment carries the history of other moments along with it. It is important to our concept of such a capacity for change that the transformation effected be not only complex, but also qualitatively different. This is best understood by an analogy with the learning process. When someone acquires a skill or capacity to perform a specialized activity, he acquires something that he often cannot get rid of. Consider someone who has learned to ride a bike and is then ordered to forget this knowledge. Is he capable of doing this? He might, perhaps, get on the bike, pedal a couple of times, and then fall to the ground—the way he did when he was first learning to ride. But any similarity between the two moments is superficial, for in the former, he tried and failed, whereas in the latter he "let himself" fail, and thus did not really fail in the sense we have in mind. What a person learns in riding a bike (or swimming or driving a car, not to mention more basic activities, such as walking or being toilet-trained) becomes a part of who that person is. Of course, it is possible to imagine a person forgetting how to ride a bike, but it is important to our concept of riding a bike that this could occur only after a long period of time or in unusual circumstances. We would not, in general, be inclined to give credence to the claim "Yesterday I could ride perfectly," were it made by someone whom we had just witnessed to be unable to ride.

This characteristic of the learning process is not limited to physical activities. The permanence of acquired knowledge is even more pronounced in cultural activities. Our habit of grounding man's capacity for culture in remarkable mental processes makes us overlook what is truly remarkable about such a capacity: that man acquires abilities and learns behavior that, though fully cultural (and clearly lacking a strictly organic basis), becomes wholly involuntary. People learn to read books, listen to music, see what is represented in paintings—and could no more forget such knowledge than they could lose the abilities to ride a bike, swim, or ski. Similarly, one does not say of a normal adult that he cannot be held responsible for his behavior because he did not know, or temporarily forgot, how to will and intend. It is by means of such capacities that we understand other cultures—and we do this even when the peoples being studied may, as frequently happens, have very different concepts of willing and intending than we have. Imagine listening to a conversation between two people, both of whom are speaking your native tongue. Now imagine trying to listen attentively to the conversation and not understand what they are saying. Considering how difficult it is to learn language, it is remarkable that it should be so hard to forget language. Try staring at a green patch and saying, "That is red," or, to use one of Wittgenstein's examples, try behaving toward everyone you meet as if they were machines or computers. What is being violated in these cases is not an empirical fact about colors or human beings (the difference between a person and a computer is conceptually, not empirically, grounded), but something intrinsic to the nature of color or human being as we have learned these concepts. We have acquired a knowledge of these things that is so bound up with what they are that the knowledge cannot be properly spoken of as "about" them. Moreover, we have incorporated such knowledge into our own way of acting and behaving to such a degree that we would have to undergo a self-transformation of sorts to unlearn such knowledge. It is not, in other words, knowledge that is being acquired here, but rather a certain logical category in which we act and think.

My point in bringing this out is that these categories, once acquired, become not only a part of our thinking and acting, but also the basis for the development of other ways of thinking and acting. Such categories are not simply discarded and replaced by others over the course of time, but become, as it were, buried within us, giving depth—depth in meaning—to our present activities. A new system of measurement, a new laboratory procedure, a new way of defining disease may all be introduced on the basis of empirical observations. Once these new procedures are introduced, however, they become, potentially, the basis for making new *kinds* of observations (which may in turn generate other kinds of procedures). The logical system of reference is built up, enlarged, and transformed—but not discarded. No matter how many predictions and explanations made on the basis of the old theory can be shown to be wrong by the new theory, the new theory will still owe a great debt to the old one. That debt is the capacity to judge certain explanations and predictions as true or false, explanations and predictions that were not possible before the introduction of the old theory. The development of modern physics is inconceivable without the prior development of Newtonian physics.

Similar points can be made regarding nonscientific cultural traditions. A good art or literary critic, for example, will examine a piece of work in the light of past works of its kind. He will do so not just to provide a setting or historical background against which to view the work, but because he knows that its significance can be understood only in terms of its tradition. One might have a difficult time identifying clearly points that *Waiting for Godot* and *Hamlet* have in common, but it is nonetheless true that a critic who had never read Shakespeare would be limited in his understanding of Beckett's works. Similarly, an American is necessarily going to miss a great deal when viewing a Japanese Noh play or a Chinese opera. It is for related reasons that filmmaking today cannot be placed on an equal footing with poetry, drama, or even the novel. Film does not have the tradition behind it that these other art forms do; it lacks the "possibilities of meaning" that are built up over a period of time. It is not that film, or even television, is inherently inferior to other art forms (in limited ways, they may be superior); it is that both lack the depth and "felt life" that is the product of tradition.

6

All of this brings us to the central issue at hand: that it is not just the different activities *of* a culture that are linked to one another by the historically cumulative process of tradition, but different practices and beliefs *between* cultures. It is, indeed, such links that make it possible for the comparative religionist to understand the cultures he studies. When we read of Paleolithic hunting practices or the human sacrifices of the Neolithic era, we are gazing into ourselves—into a deeper, more basic level of ourselves that is normally concealed. Indeed, many everyday human gestures, as Marcel Mauss has pointed out, are, in essence, remnants of ancient sacred rituals.[12] Our gaze into the past is a gaze into what might be called our origins—the materials out of which we have been formed. That is why twentieth-century comparative religionists, in rightly rejecting the search for historical origins in an empirical sense (as it was conducted by nineteenth-century evolutionists), were wrong to abandon the quest altogether. To seek our origins in the past is to seek ourselves and, hence, what we will be in the future.

But such a quest is by no means unique to modern, historical man. Eliade, for example, has emphasized that many peoples express a

---

12. Daniel Lawrence O'Keefe, *Stolen Lightning: The Social Theory of Magic* (New York, 1982), 67.

longing to return to their primordial, "sacred" beginnings and abolish by means of myth and ritual the merely historical, "profane" world of everyday experience. They seek to live in a perpetual, ahistorical "now," valuing only what is permanent and unalterable. A different way of positing value by means of a temporal framework is that of the modern evolutionist, who proposes that there is a certain factor or quality—the need to survive—against which the panorama of development is enacted.[13] Distinct from either of these is the Hebrew concept of sacred history, in which the new is given value, but is set within an enduring, sacred context. The cosmos is conceived of as a sort of evolving eternity. Still another way is that of the "Trickster" origin myths (found among American Indians and other peoples), in which creation is portrayed as a careless, whimsical act. One detects here that boundless self-confidence, so alien to all "civilized" peoples, that refuses altogether to give the present the "prop" of the past. In all cases, the positing of origins is a way of affirming and enacting what is important, what one values. Upon these values, a way of life arises.

Modern man's way of positing what I am calling origins is by viewing the phenomena of other cultures through a historical frame of reference. That frame of reference is given by what is presupposed in our causal explanations of historical events—what permits us to advance hypotheses regarding connections between events and cultures while assuming that a connection of a more general, fundamental type exists. It is the process of comparing ourselves to past cultures and seeking our origins that reveals our historical frame of reference and shows our concept of history. Thus, it belongs to what we call a linear conception of time to disallow such questions as,

---

13. Even at the level of animal development, a mechanistic understanding of evolution is not fully adequate to account for the difference between, say, a school of fish and a herd of buffalo. On one hand, the constancy and generality of the so-called struggle for survival reduce its importance—in giving a causal explanation of the manifold forms of life—to an extremely low level. On the other hand, environmental forces acting in conjunction with mutations (produced via the DNA self-replicating process) provide a plausible mechanism for *how* evolution takes place, but tell us nothing about the capacity of the DNA molecule to so direct the course of evolution by bringing about a succession of qualitatively different changes. That capacity was not acquired as the result of a mutational process.

Could a future event have already occurred? Could a future event have occurred before a past one? We would not reply to the question "Did the Russian Revolution of 1917 determine the outcome of the French Revolution of 1789?" with "Perhaps. We would have to know more about history to give a definite answer." Our conception of time determines the kinds of phenomena that we recognize as *possibly* occurring, though not, of course, what actually happened (the possible being here logically, not empirically, prior).

It is due to a failure to adequately grasp the presuppositional character of our concept of history that such statements, commonly seen in history texts, as "The invention of writing helped bring about the development of civilization," are misleading. They give us a picture of a certain event (the invention of writing) and the occurrence of that event somehow causing the development of civilization. But what we call writing is not an event or an occurrence that causes civilization; it is what, in part, *constitutes* it. Even if we insisted on translating "the invention of writing" into an event—which might be imagined as an individual in Sumeria making scratches in the sand, then one day suddenly realizing that the scratches could be used as symbols of spoken words, telling others about this, etc.— such a recital would not inform us much about the development of civilization and the importance of writing in this development. An event, *as* an event, does not carry its historical meaning in itself; rather, it gains such meaning from being embedded in a social and cultural context.

Our concept of history is thus closely tied to our concept of culture. There is no stream of events that forms the substratum of culture and is independent of it. Rather, that we perceive events in a linear flow belongs to our concept of cultural processes. Only on the basis of our concept of history do we recognize or see at all certain events in the past as being linked with present-day cultural phenomena (only on the basis of our concept of writing as a historical phenomenon do we refer to what the ancient Sumerians achieved as "the invention of writing"). Of course, once we see events in such a light, it is an empirical matter to decide whether a given event was the cause of a given cultural phenomenon. It is, however, never the occurrence of the event as such that allows it to be seen as a cause; rather, what allows that is that the possibility of historical development is written into the concept of the cultural phenomenon from the beginning. Through history, culture gains depth.

Wittgenstein examines these points in the following passage from his essay on Frazer's *Golden Bough*. He is commenting on Frazer's discussion of the Beltane custom of drawing lots as a means of selecting victims for human sacrifice:

> But in a case like this we often say: "this practice is obviously age-old." How do we know that? Is it only because we have historical evidence regarding ancient practices of this sort? . . . whence the certainty that practices of this kind must be age-old (what are the data, what is the verification)? But have we any certainty, may we not have been led into a mistake because we were over-impressed by historical considerations? Certainly, but that still leaves something of which we are sure. We would then say: "Very well, the origin in this case may be different, but as a general rule certainly it is age-old." It is our *evidence* for it, that holds what is deep in this assumption. And this evidence is again non-hypothetical, psychological. . . .
>
> What I want to say is: What is sinister, deep, does not lie in the fact that that is how the history of this practice went, for perhaps it did not go that way; nor in the fact that perhaps or probably it was that, but in what it is that gives me reason to assume it.
>
> What makes human sacrifice something deep and sinister anyway? Is it only the suffering of the victim that impresses us in this way? All manner of diseases bring just as much suffering and do *not* make this impression. No, this deep and sinister aspect is not obvious just from learning the history of the external action, but *we* impute it from an experience in ourselves. (W-BUF, 15, 16)

The connection we feel between ourselves and other ancient or primitive cultures is simultaneously logical and historical. Our historical frame of reference imposes on us the necessity of seeing ourselves as products of the past, a necessity that is built into the way we look at the past and that could never be justified empirically. The relations that bind cultures are thus internal; they depend on the nature of those cultures themselves.

To view a culture *in* history is to view it in a certain relation to ourselves; it is the historical frame of reference that gives us the capacity to see other cultures as both like us and unlike us. It is the historical frame of reference that gives meaning to the characteristics that we, on the basis of empirical observation, attribute to it. A culture that fell completely outside history would also fall outside the limits of our vision; no matter how much data we had on it, we would be meaning-blind to the import of that data. Thus, although we possess a not inconsiderable amount of empirical data on the culture of ancient Egypt, no historian has managed to dispel the strangeness and sense of alienation we feel when confronting that culture. Over and over, historians have expressed this sense of alienation by referring to the culture of ancient Egypt as outside time, or a world unto itself, or as being "static" during the fifteen hundred years of its heyday. What is not culturally meaningful to us is not historically meaningful to us. For similar reasons, the many modern primitive cultures that anthropologists have studied so extensively have not lost their air of strangeness and mystery; as representatives of an era (the Paleolithic) that stretches back a seemingly immeasurable amount of time and seems, in a way, to make the whole idea of historical development odd and almost laughable, such cultures must, by definition, be strange to us.

The historical frame of reference, however, allows us to do more than see through the falsity of the notion of a set of separate, discrete cultures and recognize that in a very significant sense a culture *is* a culture only insofar as it falls within history; it allows us to see that there exists no single, ultimate ground of being outside history. That we are constantly positing such a ground is the product of our propensity to project, as Nietzsche said, "the conditions of our existence as predicates of being in general." We seek to absolutize our own origins and make them extracultural. But to the extent what we call our conditions of existence are fixed and unchangeable, they constitute part of the structure or framework of history, not something that lies outside history. It is as if we had laid a ground of needs and conditions for ourselves, then called the life that grew out of them human nature, further declaring it to be the *only* one. What is really happening, however, is that we are slowly and painfully transforming ourselves through social and historical processes, taking on what might called elements of a second nature. This second nature cannot be gained except by positing the values that would sustain it; this we do by drawing on elements of the past. We continually choose from the past that which we sense is most life-giving and nourishing to our future growth. We gain a past a posteriori, by evaluating it from the perspective of the future that awaits us. To say that there are no absolute grounds is not to say, therefore, that the investigation of the grounds of our existence is unimportant; it is rather to say that we must be continually cultivating such grounds, providing them with nutrients so that when we rise, they will rise with us.

Our concept of history linking different cultures shows that the past neither disappears like a series of individual, unique events nor exists as a subjective entity that has meaning only as part of the present; instead, the past shows its objective nature by its being continually carried along with the present. The past, in a sense, is part of the meaning of our present experiences; it is what gives them depth and, *as* meaning, has anything but a subjective status. The grounds established in history recur as elements of our past revealed within the present. They recur eternally.[14]

It is true that the perspective we adopt is but one particular cultural perspective in history. It is also true, however, that it is the product of a large part of what history has become. In the same way that meaning is bound to what we see of phenomena and is not enlarged by consciousness, so too the eternal is already in the historical event and does not have to be separated from the merely historical. Our ontological foundation is not static, but is in the process of continually adding new elements to itself, changing its shape in such a way that the patterns of the past eternally recur. Thus, historical objectivity is linked necessarily to the ability to posit a future. Since objectivity is given by process, not by reference to a static, nonhistorical moment, to give ourselves grounds is not only to see our relationship to the past—to trace our "origins"—but to see the historical process or tradition in which we exist as a continuing process or tradition. To know the past is to know, in a logical sense, the future. The past, present, and future are a whole cloth that is continuously woven;

14. Our historical concept of time has itself developed *out of* other, more cyclical concepts. This comes out in the role we give to dreams in foreshadowing the future or in the credence we give to statements like "Martin Luther King Jr. knew he was going to die." Positing psychological explanations here misses the point; what is clearly needed is an examination of the temporal "I-He" relationship parallel to the one Wittgenstein conducted for sensations. My point, however, is simply that our historical concept of time is *built on* a cyclical one that is not "the same" as those of past cultures but is rather genealogically related to them.

what is eternal are the weaves, the forms and patterns of temporality. Those forms are like rules read out of the data of experience, the logic of our expressions that permeates the constant flux of its applications. Eternity is carried along *through* history; we must *submit* to it.

Thus, history gives us grounds on which to place ourselves, but only so long as we seek eternity within history and action, not outside it, in a static substance. To say that eternity is the form of temporality is to say that we construct the eternal out of the temporal. Time is not, as Plato said, a "moving image of eternity,"[15] but rather an eternity that moves.

7

Our cultural eyeglasses, in sum, are at the same time historical eyeglasses; that our perspective is culturally bound and limited is the ground on which we may be placed in historical relation to the cultures we study. To maintain the relativistic position that all cultures may be regarded as equal in status is to deny that historical relation by placing ourselves outside history in a normatively neutral stance. History is an arena of values; we may not be neutral spectators in it. We can, of course, acknowledge that opposing or incompatible knowledge claims are equally valid. But what we cannot do (without relying on the illusion of an extracultural, extrahistorical perspective) is to pronounce the logic, norms, and ways of life in which those knowledge claims are grounded as equally valid. Fairness in the study of culture is to be gained by recognizing the historical finiteness of our own position. Moreover, it is precisely because our position is historically finite that our meaning-blindness, though at times severe, will never be total. As creatures who are part of a continuing process that we do not control, we can no more be totally blind than we can be totally illuminated. Although our initial view of a strange culture may be distorted, the way to correct this distortion is by adjusting our lenses, not by shutting our eyes and trying to be neutral. It is by imposing a certain meaning on a given cultural practice or belief that we gain a basis for understanding *its* meaning. Con-

15. Plato, *Timaeus*, in Edith Hamilton and Huntington Cairns (eds.), *The Collected Dialogues of Plato* (Princeton, 1961), 1167.

fronted by a strange practice or belief, we may initially be at a loss; but if we apply a given concept, we will be able to judge its accuracy on the basis of our own experience. In other words, openly and self-consciously applying our prejudices will put us in a position to see where they are valid and where they are not. Precisely because we are exercising our own values, we will be sensitive to values that are not compatible with our own. By such a process, laboriously applied, we may work our way to some approximation of the meaning of the given cultural practice.

Understanding a foreign culture can be likened to following a path through unfamiliar territory. At times, the direction that the path takes is clear, as when we stumble upon the footprints of artifacts and manuscripts. At other times, we are confronted with an empty expanse in which the path seems to lead everywhere and nowhere; we must then supply a "woods"—a backdrop of possibilities drawn from our own culture—that the path can go through. This backdrop provides a context by which the features of the culture we are studying gain significance. But it also does something else; it gives us a new perspective on the territory of our own culture, both acquainting us with the forgotten pathways of our past and directing us to the unmade pathways of our culture's future. To get to know another culture is to understand better the possibilities of one's own. The foreign territory the student of culture travels through is always close to home.

Index

Aborigines. *See* Primitive people
Abortion, 123, 127–28
Absolutism, 57, 65–67, 80, 81, 216, 231–32
African cultures, 2, 182
Afterlife. *See* Immortality
Aged. *See* Elderly
Agricultural societies, 175, 177–78
Alderman, Harold, 12 *n*2
Analytic propositions, 43–47, 43–44 *n*10, 80
Animals: distinctions with humans, 15, 30–31, 85–88, 91, 96, 119–20; and emotion, 82, 85–88; and moral precepts, 113; souls conceived as, 181; human understanding of, 217–18; evolution, 86, 228, 228 *n*13
Animism, 17. *See also* Soul
Anthropology. *See* Cultural anthropology; Social anthropology
Aristotelian logic, 45–48
Aristotle, 11, 12 *n*2, 151, 160, 222
Art, 63, 163–64, 226–27
Ashby, Philip, 219
Augustine, St., 65
Australian tribes, 11, 18–19, 206–207

Beck, Lewis White, 45 *n*11
Beliefs, 125–29, 176–77
Bias. *See* Prejudices
Bible: New Testament, 11, 198; Old Testament, 11, 152, 185, 198, 215
Bidney, David, 22 *n*22
Bleeker, C. J., 219
Boas, Franz, 6, 15, 21–24, 75–77, 166, 170, 171, 180–81, 209–11, 218
Boasian anthropology. *See* Cultural anthropology
Brandon, S. G. F., 219

Campbell, Joseph, 219
Capital punishment, 83–84

Causal fallacy: Wittgenstein, 156 *n*1, 161–64; Hume, 156–60; culture and physiology, 166–70; culture and environment, 170–77; reasons for, 177–79; universal needs, 179–88; past and present, 224; history, 229
Civilization, 14, 82. *See also* Society
Climate. *See* Weather
Collingwood, R. G., 220–21
Colors, 56, 120, 161–64, 166, 225, 226
Comparative religion, 5 *n*3, 14, 16–21. *See also* Historians of religions
Compassion, 82–86
Computers, 89–90, 226
Comte, Auguste, 16
Consciousness, 75, 79, 110, 192, 204, 209, 215. *See also* Mental processes; Self
Conventionalism, 49, 66–68, 133
Criminal activities, 135–36. *See also* Murder
Critique of Practical Reason (Kant), 45, 51, 53, 116–18, 117 *n*5, 118 *n*7, 122, 149
Critique of Pure Reason (Kant), 43, 45, 51, 53, 79, 116–17, 117 *n*5, 149
Cruelty, 82–86
Cultural anthropology: and Hume, 5; subjectivistic nature, 15, 21–24, 27–28, 193, 203–204, 209–11; definition, 22 *n*22; and religion, 26; causal fallacy, 170; myths, 191–92; neutrality, 210–11
Cultural evolution, 16, 19, 20, 77
Cultural relativism, 129–33, 216–17
Culture: compared with study of foreign languages, 1–2, 6–8, 10–16, 20, 24, 26, 28, 29–30; definition, 14–15, 22 *n*22, 81, 82; first use of term, 14 *n*3; and nature, 30–34, 76, 81–85, 95–98; universal conditions, 75–78, 80, 95–96
—causal fallacy: and physiology, 166–70; and environment, 170–77; reasons for, 177–79; universal needs, 179–88,

205, 210; history, 229–33
—normative basis: definition, 1–4, 1 n1, 34; meaning and, 2, 4–5, 71–72, 81; perspective of social scientists, 6–9, 84–85; Wittgenstein's contributions, 74, 81, 95–96; logical features, 204; consciousness of bias, 213–16; relationship between cultures, 216–18, 233–34
—subjectivistic approach, 5, 14–15; Boas, 15, 21–24, 27–28, 75–77, 170, 171, 209–11; cultural anthropology, 15, 21–24, 27–28, 193, 203–204, 209–11; historians of religions, 15, 25–29, 74–75, 78–80, 82, 96–97, 203–204, 209, 211–16; Hume, 74–75; Kant, 74, 78–80
—subjectivistic fallacy: myths, 191–93; universal religious experience, 193–95; religion grounded in psychology, 195–97; soul, 197–99; sacred/profane dichotomy, 199–204; sciences and social sciences, 204–208

Darwin, Charles, 16, 19. See also Evolution
Death, 2, 27, 29, 95, 179–88, 204, 205. See also Immortality
Death penalty, 83–84
Descartes, René, 12 n2, 88, 188
Description versus explanation, 59, 64, 204
Dilthey, Wilhelm, 5 n5
Disease, 164–66, 204–205
Dostoyevsky, Fyodor, 144
Drama, 227
Dreams, 181, 188, 232 n14
Durkheim, Emile, 16, 22 n22, 55, 97–99, 102, 109

Economic systems, 24, 28, 107–108, 130–33, 170, 177–78
Egyptian culture, 205, 231
Einstein, Albert, 125
Elderly: Eskimo practices, 84–85, 171–73
Eliade, Mircea: nature of culture, 25; nature of religion, 26, 78–79, 197, 200, 219–20, 227–28; value-free nature of work, 28 n29; influence of Pettazzoni,

191; universal experiences, 193–94, 197
Emerson, Ralph Waldo, 109
Emotions: compassion, vengeance, cruelty, 82–86; and animals, 85–88; purposeful behavior, 86–87; hypocrisy, 88; neurological basis, 167; Hume, 74; and moral judgment, 113–15, 133–34, 136, 140, 146, 154
Emotivism, 112 n1
Empirical/logical distinction: opposed to separation, 29–30; opposed to material/mental distinction, 31–34, 76; Wittgenstein, 36, 50–53, 55–57, 62; Hume, 37–43, 43–44 n10; Kant, 43–47; Boas, 76, 170, 210–11; concept of self, 104–106; fact/value dichotomy, 120–22; causality, 160–61, 165; history, 220, 226, 299–30; memory, 221–22
Enquiry Concerning Human Understanding (Hume), 40
Enquiry Concerning the Principles of Morals (Hume), 122
Environment, 170–78
Epistemology: Hume, 39–43; Kant, 43–47, 43–44 n10; Wittgenstein, 50–51, 62; Boas, 76–77; historians of religions, 78–79; basis of, 129
Eskimos: and elderly, 84–85, 171–73; and weather, 170; nature of soul, 182
Eternity, 228, 232, 233. See also Immortality
Ethics, 53, 129, 149, 211. See also Neutrality, Ethical
Evans-Pritchard, E. E., 22 n22
Evolution: cultural, 16, 19, 20, 77; biological, 86, 228, 228 n13
Evolutionists (nineteenth-century), 5 n3, 16–21, 77, 170, 227

Fact/value dichotomy, 112–25, 128–29, 205–206
Faith, 116, 152–55, 195
Fallacies. See Causal fallacy; Naturalistic fallacy; Subjectivistic fallacy
Family resemblances: language, 65; culture, 96, 100–101, 179, 217; concept of death, 184

Feelings. *See* Emotions
Fertility rites, 173, 175–76, 196
Finch, Henry LeRoy, 58, 61
Foreign languages: compared with study of culture, 1–2, 6–8, 10–16, 20, 24, 26, 28, 29–30; and nineteenth-century evolutionists, 20; judgments about, 63–64
Forms of life, 57–73, 87, 94, 203–204
Frazer, James, 16–19, 199, 230
Free will, 116, 119, 122, 144–45
Frege, Gottlob, 48, 62
Freud, Sigmund, 125, 186

Galileo, 123, 124
Gandhi, Mahatma, 135
Geometry, 46, 47
Gestures, 94–95, 227
Gift-giving, 108, 150
God(s), 116, 153, 173–77
Goethe, Johann Wolfgang von, 154
Goldenweiser, Alexander, 21
Grammar, 67, 70, 71
Greek culture, 198

Harris, Marvin, 21
Hebrew beliefs. *See* Judaism
Historians of religions: and Kant, 5; subjectivistic concept of culture, 15, 25–29, 74–75, 78–80, 82, 95–96, 205, 209, 211–13; nature versus culture, 30–34, 82, 203–204; causal fallacy, 170; myths, 191–93; subjectivistic fallacy, 191–208; universal religious experience, 193–95; soul, 197–99; sacred/profane dichotomy, 199–204; neutrality, 211, 213; historical evidence, 218–20
Hobbes, Thomas, 102
Holiness. *See* Sacred/profane dichotomy
Human capacities: distinguished from animals, 15, 30–31, 82, 83, 85–88, 91, 119–20; mental processes, 30–34, 83, 87, 119–20; emotions, 82–88, 154, 167; as animal traits, 60; distinguished from machines, 89–90; language, 91–95; moral judgments, 119, 149–51; caused by brain, 167–70
Human sacrifice. *See* Sacrificial rites

Hume, David: and cultural anthropology, 5; concept of meaning, 12 n2, 37–43, 43–44 n10, 68, 115; ideas versus facts, 37 n6, 38–43, 43–44 n10, 44, 46; concept of self, 46, 74–75; morality, 74 n1, 112–16, 123, 128, 133–34, 136, 140, 144, 145, 149–51; subjectivism, 74–75; ethics, 149; causality, 156–60; miracles, 189
—works: *Enquiry Concerning Human Understanding*, 40; *A Treatise of Human Nature*, 40, 149; *Enquiry Concerning the Principles of Morals*, 122
Hunting and gathering societies, 177–78
Husserl, Edmund, 78
Hypocrisy, 88

Ideas: Hume, 37 n6, 38–43, 43–44 n10, 44, 46, 74; Kant, 74, 75. *See also* Mental processes
Immortality: afterlife, 27, 29, 179–80, 187, 204–205; of body, 184–85
Inanimate objects, 88–90, 113
Indians. *See* North American Indians
Individuality, 101–11, 141–55. *See also* Self
Insects, 22 n22, 86–87. *See also* Animals
Intention, 31–33, 86–87, 90, 119, 137–41, 145, 153, 225
Interpretation and explanation, 64

Judaism, 96, 126, 198, 228
Justice, 83–84

Kafka, Franz, 87
Kant, Immanuel: and historians of religions, 5; concept of meaning, 12 n2, 43–47, 43–44 n10, 68; noumenal/phenomenal dichotomy, 44–47, 54, 78, 80, 116–18, 196; concept of self, 46–47, 54, 74, 78; Wittgenstein similar to, 51–57; morality, 52, 74, 116–19, 126, 128, 134, 135, 140, 144, 145, 149–51, 212; nature of knowledge, 52; concept of ideas, 74, 75; subjectivism, 74, 78–80; miracles, 189
—works: *Critique of Practical Reason*, 43, 51, 53, 116–18, 117 n5, 118 n7, 122,

149; *Critique of Pure Reason*, 43, 45, 51, 53, 79, 116–17, 117 *n*5, 149
Kelm, Antje, 175–77
Kerford, G. B., 10–11
Killing. *See* Murder
Kluckhohn, Clyde, 14, 179
Kristensen, W. Brede, 213 *n*1
Kroeber, Alfred, 14, 22 *n*22, 218

Lang, Andrew, 20
Language: meaning as use, 3 *n*2, 4, 35–36, 57, 62–64, 74; meaning as referring to internal/external objects, 10–13, 20, 24, 26, 28, 29–30; normative nature of, 35–37, 54–57, 61–78, 81, 101–102; language versus reality, 48–49, 52–56, 57; logic and, 48–57, 93; common elements of, 49, 65; picture theory, 52–53; family resemblance between words, 65; conceptual absolutism, 65–73; arbitrary nature, 67–68, 71; invented language, 68; private language, 73, 101–102, 109, 195, 221; Boas, 76, 218; human capabilities, 91–95; gestures, 94–95; sign language, 53, 94. *See also* Foreign languages
Language games, 36, 55–56, 57–73, 81, 96, 100
Learning process, 224–26
Levi-Strauss, Claude, 22 *n*22
Literature, 226–27
Logic, nature of: Wittgenstein, 31–34, 36, 47–65; Hume, 37–43, 43–44 *n*10, 115, 118; Kant, 43–47, 43–44 *n*10, 118; Aristotelian logic, 45–48; transcendental logic, 45, 47 *n*14; language and, 48–57, 93; Russell and Frege, 62; Boas, 76, 77; concept of self, 105; and morality, 115–19; fact/value dichotomy, 120–22; and moral beliefs, 133–37; mental processes, 192–93; soul, 197, nature of culture, 204. *See also* Norms; Rules
Logical space, 3, 81

Machines, 89–90, 226
Magic, 18–19, 82, 130, 184–85
Malandra, W. W., 200

Malinowski, Bronislaw, 21
Material/mental distinction, 31–34, 76, 77
Mathematics, 41, 43, 45, 46, 63, 115. *See also* Geometry.
Mauss, Marcel, 227
Meaning: of words, 3 *n*2, 4, 10–13, 29–30, 101–102; Wittgenstein, 3 *n*2, 4, 35–36, 57, 61–74, 81; and culture, 4–5, 20, 24, 26, 28; Hume, 37–43, 43–44 *n*10, 68, 115; Kant, 43–47, 43–44 *n*10, 68; grounded in the familiar, 72–73; Boas, 76; causality, 158, 160; historians of religions, 192–93; normative nature, 209; and history, 219
Meaning as use, 3 *n*2, 4, 35–36, 57, 62–64, 74
Memory, 220–24
Memory images, 6, 181–82, 197
Mental processes: versus material, 31–34, 76, 77; Hume's concept of ideas, 38–43, 77; Wittgenstein's concept of thought, 60–61, 60 *n*29; Boas, 75–77, 170; and culture, 82, 170; distinction with animals, 87; and individuality, 106, 110; moral judgments, 119–20, 138–41, 145; causality, 159, 161–62, 165–66; basis of religion, 195–97, 203–204
Mesopotamia, 173–75
Metaphysics, 45, 46, 47 *n*14, 52, 53–54, 116–19, 151, 154
Miracles, 189–91
Money. *See* Economic systems
Moore, G. E., 57, 134
Morality; Kant, 52, 74, 116–19, 126, 128, 134, 135, 140, 144, 145, 149–51, 212; Hume, 74 *n*1, 76, 112–16, 123, 128, 133–34, 136, 140, 144, 145, 146, 149–51; standards, 83–84; fact/value dichotomy, 112–25, 205–206; based in self, 118, 141–55; arguments about, 123–24; action-oriented, 125–29; and reason, 133–37, 145; normative nature, 135; intentionality, 137–41, 145; universal nature, 145–48; judgment of, 142–48. *See also* Neutrality, Ethical; Relativism

Morawetz, Thomas, 60
Mortality. *See* Death; Immortality
Müller, Max, 16 *n* 7, 174, 193
Murder, 123, 146–47, 171–73
Myths: Boas, 75–76; creation, 126, 228;
   primitive people, 126, 175–76, 228;
   subjectivistic fallacy, 191–93

Nadel, Siegfried Frederick, 201
Natural versus social sciences, 204–208
Naturalism, 16, 17, 20, 145, 171
Naturalistic fallacy, 134
Nature: and culture, 30–34, 76, 81–85,
   95–98; and society, 100
Naturism, 174
Negation, 70–71
Neutrality, Ethical: description of, 28–
   29; 209–16; Boas, 210–11; historians
   of religions, 211–13; history, 230–34.
   See also Relativism
New Testament. *See* Bible
Nietzsche, Friedrich Wilhelm, 57, 108,
   153, 215, 231
Norms: definition, 1, 1 *n* 1, 35; and cul-
   ture, 1–5, 6–9, 34, 74, 80–81, 204, 209;
   and language, 4, 35–36, 61–74, 81;
   fact/value dichotomy, 120–21; moral
   beliefs, 124–25, 135
North American Indians, 107–108, 150,
   182, 184–85, 228
Noumenal/phenomenal dichotomy,
   44–47, 54, 78, 80, 116–18, 196

Objectivity, 8, 9, 28–29, 74, 78, 118,
   118 *n* 7, 210–11, 213
Old age. *See* Elderly
Old Testament. *See* Bible
On Certainty (Wittgenstein), 61 *n* 30, 65
Origin, 227–28, 230–32
Otto, Rudolf, 25, 79, 194, 196, 197

Personality, 106–11, 155. *See also* Self
Peru, 175–77
Pettazzoni, Raffaele, 191–92, 219
Phenomenology, 5, 25–26, 78, 212,
   213 *n* 1, 221
Philosophical Investigations (Wittgen-
   stein), 35, 57, 69

Philosophische Grammatik (Wittgenstein),
   35
Physics, 46, 47, 57
Pierce, Albert, 100 *n* 10
Plato, 12 *n* 2, 64, 108, 154, 222, 233
Positivism, 192
Potlatches, 107–108, 150
Power, 107–108
Prejudices, 1–2, 7–8, 203–204, 214–16,
   233–34
Primitive people: aborigines, 11, 206–
   207; belief in souls, 11, 17, 181–
   84, 197–98; condescension toward,
   18–21, 172; symbolism, 91, 92, 130;
   myths, 126, 175–76, 228; causal fallacy, 170–77; religions, 173–77, 200–
   201; shamanism, 177, 184–85, 200;
   death, 179–80, 184–85; commonality
   with, 217–18, 227–28; strangeness
   of, 231
Private language, 73, 101–102, 109, 195,
   221
Private sphere, 106–11, 138, 215
Profane. *See* Sacred/profane dichotomy
Psychology, 195–97

Radcliffe-Brown, A. R., 22 *n* 22
Rationalism, 40, 45 *n* 11
Reason, 31–32, 43, 54, 77, 117, 118,
   133–37
Redfield, Robert, 28 *n* 29
Relativism, 66–68, 216–17, 218, 227–33
Religion: Durkheim, 16, 99; Tylor, 17–
   18; nineteenth-century evolutionists,
   19–20; definition, 26; symbolism,
   78–79; and science, 121–26, 152–53,
   207; nature of, 151–52; primitive
   people, 173–77, 200–201; subjectivistic fallacy, 191–208; universal
   experience, 193–95, 213; based on psychology, 195–97. *See also* Comparative
   religion; Historians of religions; Miracles; Myths; Sacred/profane dichotomy; Soul
Rhees, Rush, 57
Rilke, Rainer Maria, 92
Rituals, 126–27, 176–77, 227. *See also*
   Fertility rites; Sacrificial rites
Römer, W. H. Ph., 173–75

Rules: and nature of culture, 3, 5, 80–81; and language, 4, 35–36, 54, 67–69, 71, 74; definition, 35; and logic, 60; fact/value dichotomy, 120–21. *See also* Norms

Russell, Bertrand, 48, 62, 69

Sacred/profane dichotomy, 26, 79, 192, 194–95, 199–204, 212–13, 227–28

Sacrificial rites, 73, 82, 176, 177, 196, 227, 230

Schopenhauer, Arthur, 56

Science: and mathematics, 41; Hume and Kant, 46–47, 52, 116–19, 149; and religion 121–26, 152–53, 207; measurement, 123–24, 205–206; causality, 156, 159–60, 164–66; culture based on physiology, 167–70; and miracles, 190; and social sciences, 204–208

Self: Hume, 46, 74–75; Kant, 46–47, 54, 74, 78, 118; Wittgenstein, 53–54, 73, 103–106; and society, 106–11; private versus personal, 106–11; basis of morals, 118, 141–55; as object, 166; religious experience, 196

Self-interest, 107–108, 149–51

Sentiments. *See* Emotions

Shamanism, 177, 184–85, 200

Sharpe, Eric, 18, 212

Showing versus saying, 34, 48–51, 53, 59, 60, 62, 94, 95, 188. *See also* Sign languages

Sign languages, 53, 94

Smith, Norman Kemp, 38 n7

Social anthropology, 21–22, 22 n22

Social sciences: bias in, 1–2, 7–8, 203–204, 214–16, 233–34; need for normative approach, 2, 6–9, 71–72, 84–85, 209, 213–16, 233–34; subjectivistic concept of culture, 3, 5, 15; objectivity, 8, 9, 28–29, 74, 78, 210–11, 213; Wittgenstein's contributions, 71–72, 81; fact/value dichotomy, 122; and miracles, 190–91; and natural science, 204–208

Society: different perspectives, 16–17, 22 n22; definition, 97–99; and nature, 98; and individuals, 101–11; and moral action, 141–48

Sociology, 22 n22

Söderblom, Nathan, 25, 194–95

Solipsism, 104–106

Sorcery. *See* Magic

Soul: Boas, 6, 180–81, 197; primitive people, 11, 17, 181–84, 197–98; Wharton, 15, 120; distinctiveness of humans, 88; nature, 126; historians of religions, 197–99

Spencer, Herbert, 16, 19, 20

Spirit. *See* Soul

Spirituality. *See* Religion

Stroud, Barry, 40

Subjectivism: and culture, 5, 14–15; definition, 12 n2; meanings of words, 12–13; cultural anthropology, 15, 21–24, 27–28, 193, 203–204; Boas, 23–24, 27–28, 75–77; historians of religions, 25–29, 74–75, 78–80, 82, 203–205; Hume, 74–75, 115–16; Kant, 74, 78–80; origin in self, 101–102; values, 112; morality, 115–16

Subjectivistic fallacy: miracles, 189–91; myths, 191–93; universal religious experience, 193–95; religion grounded in psychology, 195–97; soul, 197–99; sacred/profane dichotomy, 199–204; in science and social science, 204–208

Sumerians, 229

Supernatural. *See* God(s); Religion; Sacred/profane dichotomy; Soul

Symbolism, 78–79, 91–93, 94

Synthetic propositions, 43–47, 43–44 n10, 80

Thoreau, Henry David, 109

Thought. *See* Mental processes

Time, 229, 232 n14, 233

Totemism, 91, 92

Tractatus Logico-Philosophicus (Wittgenstein), 35, 43, 47–48, 51–57, 59, 61, 64, 72, 93, 95, 119, 204

Treatise of Human Nature, A (Hume), 40, 149

Trust, 65. *See also* Faith

Truth, 58, 61–64, 69–71, 80, 188

Tylor, Edward Burnett: nature of culture, 14 n3, 77, 81–82, 170; nature of religion, 16–18; primitive peoples,

19–21; nature of the soul, 181, 197; dichotomy between supernatural and natural, 199

Utilitarianism, 140, 140 *n* 11, 145, 146

Values: and nature of culture, 3, 5, 80; of individual, 107, 108; versus facts, 112–25, 128–29; and history, 228. *See also* Morality
Van der Leeuw, Gerardus, 25, 78, 194, 219
Vengeance, 82–84, 86
Virtue, 113, 148–55. *See also* Morality

Wach, Joachim, 213
Waismann, Friedrich, 55
War, 91–92, 134
Wealth, 107–108, 132. *See also* Economic systems
Weather, 170–71, 173–75, 178
Werblowsky, R. J. Zwi, 219
Wharton, Edith, 15, 120
White, E. B., 109
Widengren, Geo., 219

Wiener, Norbert, 89–90
Will, 31–32, 90, 153, 225
Witchcraft. *See* Magic
Wittgenstein, Ludwig: meaning as use, 3 *n* 2, 4, 35–36, 57, 62–64, 74; normative view of language, 4, 5, 35–37, 57–74, 81; concept of logic, 47–65; similarities to Kant, 51–57; concept of self, 53–54, 73; otherworldly sphere, 53–54; and linguistic philosophy, 57–58; forms of life, 57–73; language games, 57–73, 81, 100; fictional natural history, 66, 81; private language, 73, 101–102, 109, 195, 221; causality, 156 *n* 1, 161–64; miracles, 189; sacrificial rites, 230
—works: *Notebooks, 1914–16*, 35; *Philosophische Grammatik*, 35; *Philosophical Investigations*, 35, 57, 69; *Tractatus Logico-Philosophicus*, 35, 43, 47–48, 51–57, 59, 61, 64, 72, 93, 95, 119, 204; *On Certainty*, 61 *n* 30, 65
Words. *See* Language
Writing, 229

DATE DUE